Awaken Your Grail Wisdom

Coming Back to Wholeness and Divine Connection

Saira Salmon

© Saira Salmon 2018. All rights reserved

This edition: 2024

ISBN: 9798322956068
Imprint: Independently published

Other Books by the Author:

The Divine Human – *Starseeds, Soul Frequencies and Humanity's Hidden Origins*
Complete Chakras
Your Inner Goddesses – *A Guide to Archetypal Feminine Energies*

Pathways to Consciousness Series:
The Wheel of Life
The Universal Laws
The Tree of Life
The Elements and Elemental Energy

Cover image: My thanks to Jeremy Rye www.jeremyrye.com

Dedication

To David Leesley
Words do not convey the depth of gratitude I feel for the insight and guidance you have given me over the years. Thank you!

'Our deepest fear is not that we are inadequate.
Our deepest fear is that we are powerful beyond measure.
It is our light, not our darkness that most frightens us.
We ask ourselves, 'Who am I to be brilliant, gorgeous, talented, fabulous?'
Actually, who are you NOT to be? You are a child of God.
Your playing small does not serve the world.
There is nothing enlightened about shrinking so that other people won't feel insecure around you.
We are all meant to shine, as children do.
We were born to make manifest the glory of God that is within us.

Marianne Williamson

Contents

PART 1 13

INTRODUCTION TO THE GRAIL COSMOLOGY AND MYTHOLOGY 13

   INTRODUCTION TO GRAIL WISDOM 15
      What is the Grail? 16
   THE SYMBOLOGY OF THE GRAIL 19
   THE IMAGINAL WORLD 23
   THE GRAIL AND SOVEREIGNTY OF THE LAND 27
      Hieros Gamos 29
   THE GRAIL AND THE SACRED FEMININE 31
   WHAT IS THE GRAIL QUEST? 35
   THE GRAIL STORY 37
      The Original Grail Story 38
      The Later Version 41
   THE RAPE OF THE WELL MAIDENS 45
      Comment 48
   THE GRAIL HALLOWS 49
   THE GRAIL QUESTIONS 51

PART 2 53

THE GRAIL AND EARTH WISDOM 53

   THE GRAIL AND EARTH WISDOM 55
   COSMIC VISION 57
   GAIA CONSCIOUSNESS 67
   THE SUBTLE ART OF GEOMANCY 69
   EARTH ENERGIES 73
   PHYSICAL LINES 75
   NON-PHYSICAL LINES 79
      Ley Lines 79
      Telluric Currents 80
      Dragon Lines 80
      Vortex 81
   CONSCIOUSNESS GRIDS 83
      Crystalline Grid 83
      The Gaia or Earth Grid 86
   GEOPATHIC STRESS (OR SAD DRAGONS) 89
   SACRED SITES 93
   PILGRIMAGE 95

- ELEMENTALS, ... 97
  - *Air Elementals* *98*
  - *Water Elementals* *98*
  - *Earth Elementals* *98*
  - *Fire Elementals* *99*
  - *The Fifth Element* *99*
- DEVAS, NATURE SPIRITS AND FAERIES 101
  - *Nature Spirits* *101*
  - *Devas* *101*
  - *Faeries* *103*
  - *The Fae* *104*
- GWION BACH & THE CERIDWEN MYSTERIES 107
- CYCLES AND RHYTHMS 111
  - *Solar Festivals* *111*
  - *Lunar Cycles* *112*

PART 3 115

THE GRAIL AND THE HOME DOMAIN 115

- THE GRAIL OF THE HOME DOMAIN 117
- SICK BUILDING SYNDROME 119
- GEOPATHIC STRESS 123
- EMFS & TECHNOPATHIC STRESS 127
  - *Exposure - Outside the Home* *130*
  - *Measuring EMF and Microwave Exposure* *132*
  - *Solutions* *132*
- TOXICITY IN THE HOME 135
  - *VOCs* *136*
  - *Household Cleaning* *137*
  - *Personal Care Products* *137*
  - *Food* *137*
  - *Mould* *138*
  - *Plastics* *138*
  - *Heavy Metals* *138*
  - *Gardens* *139*
- THE ART OF FENG SHUI 145
  - *Yin/Yang* *146*
  - *Five Elements* *147*
  - *The Bagua* *148*
- SPACE CLEARING 151
  - *Clearing Clutter* *153*
  - *Predecessor Chi* *155*
  - *Presences* *155*

Symbolism	159
The Language of Colour	163
Orgone Energy	171
The Ancestors	175
Benefits of Ancestral Healing	*178*
Your Garden	181

PART 4 185

THE GRAIL OF THE PHYSICAL BODY 185

The Grail of the Physical Body	187
The Morphogenetic Field	191
Diamond Sun DNA	195
Chakras	199
The Subtle Bodies	203
The Meridian System	207
The Electrical Being	209
The Light Being	213
The Placebo Effect	215
The Energy of Water	217
Sound & Vibration	223
Earthing	227
Dowsing for Health	231
The Holistic Model of Health	235
Pasteur v. Beauchamp & Terrain Theory	*235*
The Disease Tree	239
The Iceberg	241
Healthy Helpers	243
Herbs	*244*
Nutritional Supplements	*245*
Essential Oils	*246*
Flower Essences	*248*
Phytobiophysics	*249*
Homeopathy	*250*
Shamanic Healing	253
Pottenger's Cats	257

PART 5 259

THE GRAIL ESSENCE 259

The Grail Essence	261
Becoming You – The Importance of Authenticity	265
Befriending the Shadow	269

YOUR SOUL BLUEPRINT 275
ASTROLOGY 279
HUMAN DESIGN 281
THE GENE KEYS 283
ARCHETYPES 285

PART 6 289

BECOMING THE GUARDIAN 289

THE ALCHEMY OF BECOMING A GRAIL BEARER 291
QUALITIES OF THE GRAIL INITIATE..297
THE ROLE OF FAITHKEEPER...301
RISE UP, SPIRITUAL   WARRIOR!..303

PART 7 - APPENDICES 307

Appendix 1- Ritual to Open Sacred Space...*307*
Appendix 2 - Solutions for High EMF Readings..*311*
Appendix 3 - A Space Clearing Ceremony *314*
Appendix 4 - Closing Down A Portal *318*
Appendix 5 – Big Pharma – Deliberate Manipulation *321*
Appendix 6 - The Nine Metaphysical /Occult Laws....................................*324*
FURTHER READING 327
RESOURCES...335

Part 1
Introduction to the Grail Cosmology and Mythology

Introduction to Grail Wisdom

Grail Wisdom speaks to a philosophy, a way of viewing and understanding the world and our place within in it that is designed to bring us back into a sense of wholeness and connection not just with ourselves, but with the whole Creation within which we live.

The Grail Wisdom, or Grail Mysteries, relate to an understanding of our place in the world, our connection to the many layers and level of consciousness that permeate everything and the flows and architectures of energies that surround us.

Much of it is an invisible world – until you learn how to 'see' through the veil. Much of it is hinted at in our stories and mythologies and all of it is our birthright.

Most of us live very disconnected from both our true potential, our True Self, if you will, as well as from our environment and the many other levels of being we should have access to.

Within us we have the ability to penetrate through into other dimensional levels, other worlds and frequencies, but it has been badly damaged and disconnected and there is a need to heal the damage that has been done to our own energetic templating before we can reclaim these skills.

To be human is to be part of a long lineage of what are called Angelic or Christos races who inhabit all dimensional levels of the universe within which we live.

The story of how we came to be separated from them is long and complicated and not for this book, but suffice it to say that we have suffered a fall from the heightened levels of consciousness that are our birthright and our memory has been wiped clean of our history and our origins.

We are just beginning to 'wake' back up, come back into a remembering of who we really are and what we are truly capable of. We have been living in the proverbial wasteland for many thousands of years and finally it is time for us reclaim the Grail – a very real essence which lies within us – and bring the wasteland of our planet, of our disconnected societies and our unhealthy, unhappy bodies back into the place of abundance and energetic connection from which they fell.

Through the Grail Cosmology and the mysteries to which it relates we begin to understand more fully the Creation within which we live and the part we have to play, the challenges that have to be overcome and how we can begin to reconnect back into the Divine potential that lies dormant within us.

We are living at a time of immense change. Vast cosmic energies are sweeping through this sector of the galaxy, our solar system is aligned with the Galactic Centre and great waves of evolutionary energy are bathing us with ever growing intensity. And the opportunity presents itself to free this planet from the chains of unconsciousness that have bound it through its Dark Ages.

As a consequence, the focus of cosmic attention is on this planet at this time, to ensure that humanity can come back to the fold and once more become the Guardians of the Earth and the Diamond Sun consciousness which is our legacy.

What is the Grail?

In short, you are! We embody the Grail essence and all it stands for, if only we knew how to access it.

It is a concept, an ideal, a way of being, energetic connection with our surroundings and.....a cosmic bloodline. It lies dormant within us, waiting to be healed, re-activated. It has been abused, corrupted, denied, constrained, lost and, indeed, forgotten by most during the long period of amnesiac sleep to which humanity has been subjected.

But the seeds still lie within, waiting to be nurtured back to life once more.

And that time is now.

We catch the merest glimpse of what the Grail encompasses in the Grail mythos of stories told and re-told to help in the remembering, when the time was right (and safe) for our true understanding to return.

During the long slumber the telling and retelling of the body of Grail stories and King Arthur and his Round Table have kept intact a kernel of truth, heavily disguised, and held within our planetary lightbody awaiting the time we would once more be able to 'tune in' and begin to access our legacy once more.

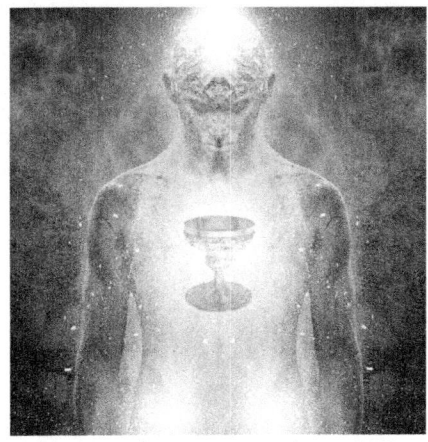

Here, in this book, we will begin to take the first steps into that remembering. It will act as an introduction to the many energies that surround us and that we are able to interact with - the unseen world of elementals, earth energies, your own energetic anatomy, and much more.

We will be learning about many different techniques and ways of connecting into the unseen worlds, techniques shamans and spiritual initiates alike have been aware of and using down through the centuries. We will also be looking at ways we can support ourselves to clear the blockages and boulders that stop us moving forwards or trip us up.

You will be asked, again and again, throughout this book, to look at things from a different perspective, a different point of view and understanding to that you have been taught within mainstream education. An open mind, an open heart and a willingness to follow particular threads and check things out for yourself is integral to the quest.

Part of the new understanding is to take time to look more carefully at the miracle that is our body – a superb receiver and transmitter of energy, a beautifully designed vehicle for your consciousness, delicately balanced, and often overlooked.

To live in tune with ourselves, our environment and the cosmos is a vast undertaking, one we are born to, and once was as innate to us as drawing breath. We are, once more, like a toddler taking its first steps, but the memory of who we really are and how to do these things is still encoded into our DNA, our cellular and race memory, and within the energy grids of this planet.

It is just a matter of unlocking that knowledge once more and tuning back into your own gnosis to reveal what has always been there, waiting for us to wake up and once more take up our heritage.

Every journey begins with the first step – there is a long way to go and many wonders to unfold. Here you can begin to Awaken Your Grail Wisdom, a place of beginning to give some foundations. I hope you will then become my companion on the journey ahead as we dive deeper into all the mysteries and miracles that await us as we reclaim ourselves, our loved ones and our beautiful planet from the Wastelands.

Are you ready to begin the journey back to Grail consciousness?

The Symbology of the Grail

The quest for the Holy Grail ranks amongst Western Civilizations more important and enduring mythologies.

The body of the Grail stories was written at a time when corruption in the Church was rife, and it ruled with an iron grip which squashed individuality, demanded unquestioning obedience and cracked down hard on any new ideas or thought.

This spanned the time of the Albigensian Crusades which saw the Cathars exterminated, the rise and fall of the Knights Templar and the birth of the Inquisition which wrought such savagery across the continent and killed millions.

It was also a time when the Church was rampantly corrupt and people were beginning to question Catholic doctrine and awareness of themes such as the Self, the inner landscape, the natural laws of the cosmos and intellectual thought. The seeds of the Renaissance started to grow from this time, and many of our contemporary ideas around individuality, self-identity and realisation have grown out of the thought fields of this time.

The renowned Jungian psychologist Robert A Johnson says:

> 'The Twelfth century began so many of the issues that we struggle with today. It has been said that the winds of the twelfth century have become the whirlwinds of the twentieth century'.

Today we are reaping the harvest of what was sown back then – the final, devastating banishment of the Divine feminine from everyday life. This had been underway for many thousands of years but the full demonization and suppression reached its apogee during this time, carried out to such effect by the witch burnings of the Inquisition when millions of innocent women were terrorised and murdered.

This was a deep wounding to what Robert A Johnson calls the 'feeling function', leading to the primacy of the rational, the intellectual and the literal, and the separation of the individual from the natural laws of life and the triumph of dogma over vision.

It has inexorably led us to where we find ourselves today, in a wasteland of the spirit and disconnection from the source of life, our beautiful planet desecrated and our societies driven to the brink of destruction by those lacking both soul and vision.

The image of the Grail is a vital symbol for all that has been lost in the West – we can no longer turn our back on the aridity of the world we have created – what Henry Corby calls the 'catastrophe of the modern world' - the soullessness and spiritual vacuum of modern western materialism.

To bring the Wasteland back to fertility, to lush abundance, we must return to the Source that nourishes it. We have to seek the balance we have lost at every level in our lives, that ancient harmony and wisdom which will allow our land – and ourselves – to flourish.

The metaphor of the Grail can be read at several levels.

So many today are living lives of quiet desperation. High levels of disconnection from the physical body, rising levels of disease, lack of well-being and confusion alongside a disharmony with natural rhythms and understandings have left many adrift, depressed, demotivated, lacking vitality, sick, disconnected, lost, confused, off balance and off course.

So much wasted potential.
So much wasted passion.

The tools our culture gives us are inadequate for our requirements, and give us little understanding of the underlying reasons for the malaise. Instead we are medicated with mind-numbing medicines that fail to heal, dumbed down with booze and recreational drugs, box sets and soap operas. We are crammed together in environments that fail to nourish our senses or our soul and all around us Mother Nature is brutalised, poisoned and dishonoured.

Why? What is it about our culture, our society, which means that at a time when we have never been so connected by technology at one level, we are SO disconnected from what brings us joy, grounds us in this world and connects us to our uniqueness?

This is the modern Wasteland, the home of the Fisher King of the Grail legends.

It speaks to the soullessness and spiritual vacuity of our modern western materialism. This ever-deepening spiritual vacuum, combined with the nihilistic approach of much of modern science has left us staring into the Abyss.

Estranged not only from our own inner world, we are also estranged from the soul of Nature, and our psychic and imaginal reality denied and trashed. There is a poisonous duality between spirit and matter that creates this Wasteland. Functions that should be balanced and harmonised with each other are divided in opposition instead:

> Thought v feeling
> Sensation v intuition
> Masculine v feminine
> Reason v ecstasy
> Science v ancient knowledge
> Religion v imagination
> Religious dogma v inner knowing
> Myth v history
> Human technology v the cycles of Nature

The symbolic is denied its place as the fulfilment of the Real, and there is no place for the Imaginal World which holds the tensions between spirit and matter.

Mankind is made up of opposites, full of contradictions, but also blessed with unique gifts to enable him to balance and harmonise these opposites. Strip this away and you are left staring into the Abyss and this leads towards destruction, it is the way of madness – as Nietzsche[1] discovered when he stared in the Abyss and saw only darkness.

We experience the world as we have made it, in our own image, and the inner despair stares back at us from the Society we have created. It is not a pretty sight.

---

[1] German philosopher Freidrich Nietzsche declared in the 19th century 'God is Dead'. He saw no place for god, or spirit, in the modern world. He had a complete mental breakdown and lost his faculties, dying in this state.

The Imaginal World

This is the term coined for the place where matter and spirit meet.

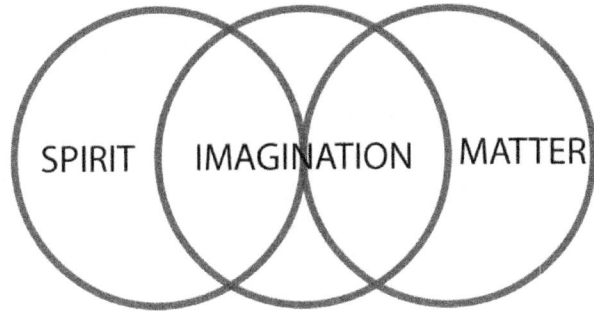

It is the place where we can begin to find a middle path through the contradictions of trying to balance opposites, acting as a bridge between two seemingly intractable dualities. It is a middle realm where opposites can be united, where vision and imagination helps us find an equilibrium, a way of balancing within us the material and the spiritual.

This really harks back to the way our forebears had of *being* in the world. They had a different way of perceiving the world to our modern approach. They believed that when we knew something we were *conjoined* with it, we were not separate to it. It is what I call 'knowing something in your cell tissue'. By contrast today we experience the world as 'out there' or what is called *disjunctive* knowledge. For our ancestors inner knowing and outer being were one seamless whole.

This split, or 'divided self' is deemed to have come in sometime during the twelfth century, the time when the Grail myths were being formed as an attempt to salvage something from this loss, and since this time life's dualities have been thrown into ever sharper contrast until not only do we have the seeming tension of opposites, but there is a disempowering of the imagination, a lack of comprehension or even appreciation of the symbolic and the role it has to play in human well-being and its ability to transform consciousness.

And yet, it is probably just this ability – the ability of the imaginal world to literally transform consciousness, to show us how to understand both the literal and metaphysical held within the same form, to balance and have a place for both faith and gnosis - that has been deemed to be so dangerous to the tight control so beloved of our institutions from the Church to Government.

By denying both the sacredness of Nature and the naturalness of the sacred both our body and our soul suffers. Each denies the importance of the other. This division impacts every level of our culture. No matter where it is found – societal or religious – faith, in this context has to be blind faith, there is no room for shades of grey. Think of religious extremists or even scientists who dogmatically refer to 'The Science' when any scientist worthy of the title knows there is only 'science' and its ongoing investigations.

Knowledge lacking vision, insight and imagination becomes little more than a piling up of facts. The insistence now found in the so-called 'scientific' ideology that denies anything which can't be seen or observed, measured and duplicated in an experiment seems to reject much of our lived experience and inner gnosis.

Where does that leave those who plainly see the short comings of this approach, or who 'feel' deep inside that something important is missing or that a vital aspect of being human is being denied?

Adrift, mocked, ridiculed and dismissed, struggling to find their roots and susceptible to any spiritual snake-oil salesman who happens past, promising a solution to fill the void, that's where.

Because a void does open up, leaving a lack, an emptiness at the heart of being. And in to this Void we today have much of the New Age nonsense which has grown up, which leads us further down dead ends and spiritual cul-de-sacs.

As this abyss began to open up in the Middle Ages, the image of the Grail began to rise up. The Grail speaks to wholeness, to a harmonious blending of both the esoteric and the exoteric, of Nature and the Sacred. It was something to cling to in the darkness, a beacon of light that hinted at what we instinctively felt was missing as the gloom began to descend.

And today we still cling to these stories as a light in the murk that is modern day spirituality and spiritual seeking.

The Grail myths demonstrate the need for an actively developed imagination in order to reveal the spiritual in the material world, the Divine in everyday life, and the need for a sense of purpose in being.

The Grail and Sovereignty of the Land

The land has always been seen as being sacred – it is the body of Mother Earth, or Gaia, and is an aspect of the Great Goddess or Cosmic Mother as the Great Creatrix.

Through all the cultures of mankind, century after century, millennia after millennia, she has been called various names – the Great Mother, Isis, Inanna, Demeter, Gaia, Mary – and try as they might the great patriarchal religions have not been able to see her off entirely even if her worship had to become covert.

For most of history mankind has lived in close contact with the land. His very survival depended upon the land remaining fertile and the weather being clement, and upon his ability to connect to and 'read' the currents of information and energy that flowed.

Going back to beyond the threshold of modern recorded time, (our history is far older than you have been led to believe) the land was seen to be in the gift of the Great Goddess. Whilst today we see the land as something to be owned, fought over, possessed, lost and recaptured, our forebears, deeply connected into her rhythms and ways, saw things differently.

The land was the domain of the Goddess, and when it comes to its sovereignty it is not the God who rules, but the Goddess. The land is in her gift, and no-one could become King unless they had her blessing. The gift of kingship was only given to one who was seen as being worthy of taking on rulership of the land – who had the best interests of both the land and the people in his purview. It was not about power, but about service, about nurturing and cherishing what he was gifted.

The Goddess is Earth-Spirit
The King is Guardian of the Earth.

During the King's coronation he would be ritually initiated and ceremonially married to the Goddess in a contract of sovereignty. The Goddess would be represented by a 'heirodule', a sacred sexual priestess, who embodied the Great Goddess and the spirit of the land. She acted as a conduit for the transmission of the sovereignty of the land and the sacred sexual rites were an integral part of it. The rite would seal the contract between political rulership and responsibility for the land's well-being which was invested in the King.

We know that as far back as ancient Mesopotamia the King and the Goddess, represented by a priestess, would perform yearly rites to both cement this relationship and to bless the fertility of the land for the coming year.

Sacred sexuality is more than just sex. It is a means of spiritual initiation. Sometimes called sex magic, or earth magic, we catch a glimpse of what these rites used to be in Tantric yoga from India, which is one of the only surviving remnants of this tradition.

In some ancient traditions inheritance of the rulership of the land was through the female line. The Queen was representative of the feminine principle of the land, whilst her chosen King became the protector of the realm.

Within the Grail mysteries this speaks to the lineages of the Maji Grail Kings and Queens, who ruled in heirogamic union over specific areas of the planet to protect, nurture and balance the land and its peoples in their benevolent care.

Hieros Gamos

Hieros gamos literally means 'sacred marriage' and is a spiritual act through which the male and female come together in order to experience god (or Goddess!). This was a deeply sacrosanct ceremony, and tapped into metaphysical principles and anatomy whose aim is to awaken the higher brain centres or levels of consciousness.

Resonating from this higher vibration, the King who has been awakened and initiated in this way quite naturally comes into service as the higher vibrationary levels preclude the baser instincts such as selfishness and lust for power. It is a form of inner alchemy, transforming the baser self into a higher, more evolved state.

On another level entirely Hieros Gamos relates to the sacred union within both ourselves and also at the planetary level of the coming together in perfect balance of the masculine and feminine energetic principles as we ascend toward full unity or Christos consciousness.

Part of this process is to evolve at the *biological* level ie. within the body, the energetic balance between the masculine and feminine energies and bring them into unity.

It is a highly sacred process and one we must all master as we ascend towards full embodiment of the Grail.

The Grail and the Sacred Feminine

The Grail can be interpreted at a variety of levels, but one that consistently comes from common Grail symbology of both the sacred vessel of the Celtic Goddess to the Cup of Christ is that of the Sacred or Divine Feminine.

The Grail can be traced to its Celtic roots as both a cauldron – the cauldron of Plenty that never runs dry, and the Cauldron of Rebirth that brings the dead to life – as well as Otherworld cups of myth and legend that hold the water from the Well of Wisdom, and the Emerald Cup of Virtues, a faery vessel with life-giving, protective properties.

There are also stories that the goddess, who personified the land, selected the next king by offering him a chalice of red ale.

So the cauldron or cup has been associated, both within our culture and others, with the feminine for millennia. As both a symbol of the female body, and the receptive qualities of the feminine energies it speaks within the psyche and is part of a family of symbols which are all images of the divine feminine – cup, cauldron, bowl, vat, crucible etc.

The Grail is also a symbol of the Soul, which itself is also seen as being feminine, and the Mother Goddess, from whose womb pours the waters of life.

The feminine principle is one of the two great archetypal foundations of life – the masculine being the other. The feminine energy is associated with the Great Mother or Cosmic Mother, the womb of the Universe, from which all creation flows, and was considered by many ancient cultures to be the founding energy of the Cosmos.

It was the stranglehold which Christianity took on the Western World which finally replaced the great Creatrix with the Great Creator – a male god who ruled alone. And our culture has been suffering ever since.

The feminine softens the hard-edged rational, logical, action-orientated energy in our society. It is nurturing, life-giving, receptive, intuitive, open, creative and about community. For centuries these very qualities have been suppressed and much of the unique wisdom and insight that women can bring has been ignored, eradicated, cast out and shamed. It has been driven underground where aspects of it have been kept alive, although its totality and a true understanding of it in all its glory is currently lost to us.

The Western philosophical tradition from Plato onwards has valued the intellect, the rational and logical. It argues that this is what makes us humans stand apart from the animal kingdom, makes us superior to nature which is wild and untamed, instinctual and –whisper this quietly – chaotic.

Reason and intellect are male attributes, and it therefore follows that men are superior to women as women are emotional, instinctive and have a wild creative energy – or so the logic goes. The wild, the instinctive, the emotional is to be overcome, controlled.

Matters just got worse when French philosopher Descartes declared 'I think therefore I am' in the seventeenth century, and mind became everything. Wild creation was reduced to a mechanistic universe and nature was just something that was at the service of mankind. The Industrial Revolution followed and continues today to lay waste to the planet as resources are squandered, whole species are eradicated and anything that does not serve Man has no value.

What a sorry place we have come to.

We have alienated ourselves from Mother Nature.

The archetype of the Great Mother is bountiful, abundant, nourishing, sustaining, a vast cornucopia of beauty and Life. When honoured she is generous in her blessings, but when she is dishonoured and withdraws those blessing the world becomes a wasteland – plants and bushes die, trees drop their leaves, fruits die on the vine, the wells dry up and the land turns brown and withered

The Great Mother has positive characteristics – to nourish and protect, give warmth and security and growth and transformation (the essence of Mother Nature). Of course, there is a flip side – devouring, wild, untamed and destroying – a dark powerful energy which gives life and takes it away, as part of the vast cycle of death and rebirth. Maybe man is right to fear this energy, but as anyone who has done 'shadow work' knows, you do not dismiss what you fear, you do not hide from your demons, you confront them and face them and integrate them. Only then do you master them and take that power back into yourself.

Archaeologists and ancient wisdom seekers alike tell us that there was a time when the masculine did not fear the feminine and feel the need to denigrate and dominate it. There was a time when its creative and life-giving aspects were honoured and worshipped and had an equal place in the world.

Even in the time of the Celts it would seem that, unlike women in Greece and Rome, in 'the Blessed Isles' as these lands were known women had a social standing that they lack even today. They could rule, were active in politics and religious life and no aspect of their society was closed to them. The owned property, decided who they married, could divorce and if they were attacked and raped could demand – and receive – recompense. They also trained with weapons and could not just participate but also lead men into battle. They were sovereign unto themselves – and it has been a long, dark and woe-filled time before this level of acceptance has once more started to emerge.

Many young women today take for granted the freedoms they have, which have been hard won, and are still very fragile. As the need for the feminine to re-emerge into every aspect of our lives – political, business, financial, industrial, technical, social, cultural – we are having to think very hard about what a landscape where both masculine and feminine energies sit in balance looks like.

It is certainly not what we have now, even with the gains made. The destruction of nature and the planet, along with human health and well-being carries on apace.

The return of the Grail, with its feminine, nurturing, mystical and life-giving properties is desperately needed….

This is the work that lie ahead for many who are drawn to work with the Grail mysteries…the re-imaging and vision of a New Earth.

What is the Grail Quest?

So what might the grail quest look like in the twenty-first century?

Because, make no mistake, if you undertaking any sort of spiritual development work, making the choice to evolve and expand your consciousness and begin to work in service to both your own Divine Nature and the world, you are on a Grail Quest.

The Grail Quest will take you into territory uncharted by the educational authorities, and avoided or blanked by much of the population which fears 'woo-woo' stuff. It will bring you face-to-face with who you *really* are - not who you want to be/think you are/have been told you are. It will strip away the illusions and delusions we have all be fed by the culture's within which we live, our education and the general propaganda fed to us by those organisations and governments bodies who do not want the individual to thrive.

You will learn about the miracle of being in a human body, and how to use it to become aware of the many worlds and denizens who live alongside our own at different energetic frequencies, you will learn how powerful you *really* are, the limitations and restrictions put on you will be shown for the shackles they are. You will begin to see and read the signs and symbols which have been left as a bread crumb trail for us by those who have gone before.....and so much more.

Staggeringly more, in fact.

The colour, texture, taste, smell and sound of the world around you will change as your horizons expand.....and expand.

In the Grail Quest as the Grail Knight or Maiden comes to understand who they are, they are empowered by what they learn as they step forward in service to both the Divine within and to life in general. They stand between worlds as the mediator and guardian and help to hold the balance. They nourish and bring back to greening the Wasteland, both within and without.

To take the Grail Quest through to completion is not for the faint-hearted. But it is a quest filled with wonder and marvels and brings great joy as you learn to connect to all Life around you, and to come back to your True Self. It is not the work of a moment. It requires commitment and stamina, but the goal – wholeness of Self and oneness with Life – is a pearl beyond price!

The Grail Story

Before we go any further let us just remind ourselves of the Grail mythos, as we can find important clues and prompts to our remembering within them.

The Grail myths developed over a period of years during the Middle Ages with the first version of the Grail story being written down towards the end of the twelfth century, but large elements of it can be traced back to the oral Celtic tradition from which it has borrowed heavily.

Later versions of the grail story became more and more Christianised but still contain many pagan undertones. We find within the original version themes which almost seem closer to paganism, Gnosticism, Hermeticism and the beliefs of the Cathars than to those of mainstream Christianity at the time.

The first version of the Grail was written by Chrétien de Troyes in the court of Champagne in the second half of the twelfth century, thought to be between 1180 – 90. Chrétien wrote four Arthurian Romance tales, culminating in *Perceval* or *Le Conte du Graal* (*The Story of the Grail*). It was left unfinished and it is thought that Chrétien died before he could complete it.

Further writers went on to 'finish' this poem in what are known as the *Continuations* between 1190 -1210, and also another French poet Robert de Boron writes a 'prequel' to Chrétien 's story. One of these also has the knight Gawain, rather than Perceval, partially completing the Quest.

Then in 1210 the German poet Wolfram von Eschenbach writes *Parzival* which draws quite heavily on the Chrétien version.

In 1215 we see the beginning of the Vulgate Cycle, a vast sequence of French prose romances which reworks the whole tale, including the 'prequel' , making Galahad, not Perceval, the hero of the story and denigrating Gawain's character. This is where the heavy hand of Christian dogma starts to be felt in the reworking of the stories. Gawain, as a hero, is clearly felt to be too worldly, too 'real', and the saintly Galahad takes centre stage.

In 1230-40 parts of this are re-fashioned to form a new sequence called *La Haute Escriture del Saint Graal (The High History of the Holy Grail)* with Galahad once again being the hero of the story.

That is a brief outline of the sequence of the Grail writings, but it is clear that they originally drew on more ancient tales, probably heard in the Courts of Europe from the wandering minstrel storytellers, who would have been familiar with both Celtic tales of the old Gods and the Otherworld and various Gnostic themes. By the time we get to the final writing it has become highly Christianised (indeed Benedictine monks are thought to be the authors), but, despite this, still retains many of the underlying Celtic/Gnostic themes and symbols.

There are three different heroes – Perceval, Gawain and Galahad. Galahad is the most Christianised of the heroes, whose only wish is to see the Grail and die.

The Original Grail Story

The original tale tells of Perceval, a Welsh boy, who is brought up by his widowed mother in the Waste Forest – a metaphor for our World. His mother will not talk of his father or elder brothers, but one day Perceval hears a clanking in the forest, which turns out to be knights riding through. Perceval initially mistakes them for angels, so shining are they in their armour! They tell him of the Court of King Arthur and he conceives a passion to become a Knight.

He returns to his mother who weeping, tells him that his father and brothers were all knights, who have been slain in battle, and she does not want her youngest son to share their fate. Perceval, full of visions of chivalry and knighthood, does not listen to her and sets off for King Arthurs Court, looking back as he departs his home to see his mother falling to the ground. In his eagerness he ignores her collapse, taking it to be just a faint, and carries on. But she had dropped down dead, her heart broken.

He goes to the Court of King Arthur where, after training, he is made a knight. During his period of training he asks question after question, until he is shamed into silence, being told this is not the seemly thing to do. (How many of us does this happen to as we grow up?)

After various adventures he is made a knight. He rescues a lady, Blanchefleur, who sleeps with him and offers him sovereignty of her land, but he rather belatedly remembers his widowed mother and says he must first find her again.

As he tries to find his way back home he comes upon countryside that is laid waste and barren. When he finally comes to a river he sees a boat floating on it and man sitting in the boat fishing. Perceval asks where he may stay the night nearby, and the Fisher King –for it is he – offers him shelter in his Castle nearby.

Perceval enters the Grail Castle to find the Fisher King lying on a couch, unable to walk, due to having sustained a severe wound in the groin which will not heal. Whilst they sit talking the King's niece comes out and gives Perceval a sword, which she says is destined for him only. Then there comes a strange procession of a boy carrying a white spear, from the tip of which flows drops of blood. He is followed by two more youths bearing gold candlesticks, blazing with light. Then comes a beautiful maiden holding a beautiful vessel, the Grail, in her hands, which shines with a light that makes the candlesticks look dim. She is followed by a further maiden carrying a beautiful platter. They pass before the couch on which the King lies, and Perceval marvels at what he sees but doesn't say a word, in the mistaken belief that he should not talk or ask questions too much in company. Instead he decides to ask one of the lads at Court about what he has seen before he departs.

There follows a great feast, and then the company retires for the night.

When Perceval wakes the next day, the Castle is deserted. In the courtyard his horse awaits him, already saddled, and as he crosses over the drawbridge it slams shut behind him on his horse's heels.

As he is puzzling over this he comes across a maiden weeping in the forest over the body of her lover who has been slain by an evil knight.

The maiden explains to Perceval that he has spent the night at the Castle of the Fisher King. She questions him about his stay there, wanting to hear if he saw the procession and if he asked about it. When he says he kept silent she is full of woe for, had he asked about it all, she informs him, the Fisher King's wound would have been healed and the land would have been restored to its fertility.

The maiden tells Perceval that his failure to ask the right questions is a moral failure due to allowing his mother to die from sorrow when he left her. She also reveals that she is Perceval's first cousin.

Perceval asks her to go with him, but she refuses to abandon her lover until she has buried him. Perceval reacts with a lack of compassion – let the dead bury the dead – which underlines his indifference to the plight of others.

Perceval has failed the test and returns to King Arthur's Court, where a hag on a mule arrives and upbraids Perceval for failing to ask the vital questions. As a consequence, she tells him, the king cannot rule, his land will lie barren, people will die and all because he failed to ask the questions.

In shame Perceval sets off again, determined this time to find the Grail and ask the questions. Many years and adventures later he encounters a hermit who turns out to be his uncle. He gives him spiritual guidance and counsel and it is here the narrative breaks off.

The versions that follow begin to draw more clearly the parallel between the Grail story and the Crucifixion and as each version seeks to root the story more concretely as a literal interpretation of the Christian mysteries then its symbolic, visionary aspects are lost and the liminal understanding it offers to the soul becomes mired in Christian dogma.

The Later Version

So let's take a look at this more christianised Grail myth that we know today.

It begins with the crucifixion where Joseph of Arimathea, said to be Jesus' uncle has both obtained the cup used by Christ at the Last Supper, and Jesus' body to bury in a tomb. Whilst preparing the body for burial blood flowing from the wounds is caught in the cup.

After the Resurrection, Joseph is accused of stealing the body, and is thrown into prison, where he is left without sustenance for many years. He is kept alive, however, by the miraculous appearance of a holy wafer in the cup daily.

He is finally released from prison in 70 CE and goes into exile overseas with a small group of followers.

He sails to Europe, and from there to Britain where it is said he establishes the first Christian church at Glastonbury – dedicated to the Virgin Mary – where the Grail cup is housed, and used to celebrate Mass.

An alternative version has him only going so far as Europe, where the guardianship of the Grail passes to Bron, his brother-in-law, who becomes known as the Rich Fisherman, and settles at a place called Avaron.

From here the Grail is taken to Muntsalvache (The Mountain of Salvation) where it is housed in a temple and an Order of Grail Knights founded to guard it. The priest-king for this is the Grail-keeper. He is wounded by a fiery spear in the groin or generative organs and becomes known as the Maimed or Wounded Fisher King. The countryside around the Grail Castle becomes barren and is known as the Waste Land. There is a direct connection between the state of the countryside and the Fisher King's wound to the groin.

As the story develops the spear becomes identified with the lance of Longinus, the Roman centurion who pierced the side of Christ whilst he was on the cross. The Grail Castle contains 4 objects associated with the Grail which become known as the Grail Hallows – the spear, the cup, a sword that is said to be broken, or break at a crucial moment, and a serving platter or stone. These are the four sacred treasures that must be sought.

This is the time of the legendary King Arthur and his Knights of the Round Table and one Pentecost the Grail cup makes an appearance as they sit feasting. It floats through the hall, and on every plate appears the food the individual most likes to eat. It then disappears.

The Knights then pledge themselves to the Grail quest – the Quest to find this holy object.

All sorts of adventures ensue – many of them clearly initiatory. There are five main knights who participate in the Quest – Gawain, Lancelot, Perceval, Bors and Galahad.

Three find the Grail – Perceval, Galahad and Bors.

Galahad, the perfect knight, fully achieves the Quest and looks into the Grail and then dies – for his desire to have direct knowledge of God means he cannot live in the world - and is taken up to heaven. The Grail is said to be withdrawn to heaven at the same time.

Perceval gets to see the Grail and becomes the new guardian of the Grail Castle, taking up residence to await the return of the Grail and Bors returns to Camelot and King Arthur.

This is the essence of the final story which comes down to us, although there are a variety of variations on this theme, and many stories about the encounters the Knights have on the Quest. The highly Christianised version turns it into a spiritual quest leading to transfiguration, rather than an inner quest for the individual. It is only the perfect knight, Galahad, who can achieve it and having seen it he departs this world. Like so much of Christian dogma, it is not something the 'man in the street' can aspire to.

The Rape of the Well Maidens

This is really a 'prequel' to the main Grail story, but goes to the heart of the significance of the Grail myth in the psyche of the Western World. It comes from a story called 'The Elucidation' written in the early 13th century by an unknown author and preserves a far earlier story of the Grail.

It alludes to the kingdom of the Fisher King, which was rich and abundant.

Long ago in the lush and far-reaching forests of Britain there were many sacred springs spread across the land where travellers within this kingdom could take their rest and refreshment.

The guardians of these sacred springs were the Well Maidens, who tendered to the weary traveller and ensured the springs ran sweet and pure. They had golden cups from which they served travellers with the pure, clear water, and golden platters from which they served food.

There was a faery, or fae, element to them

> *No one who wandered the highways,*
> *Whether at night or in the morning,*
> *Ever needed to alter his route*
> *In order to find food or drink;*
> *He had only go to one of the wells.*
> *He could ask for nothing*
> *In the way of fine and pleasing food*
> *That he would not have forthwith,*
> *Provided he asked reasonably.*
> *At once a damsel would come forth*
> *From the well,*

This alludes to the fact that it was believed that the waters rose up from the Otherlands, deep beneath the earth, and these waters were what gave life to the earth.

The Well Maidens were chaste, and beautiful and their wells were seen as gateways to the Otherworld. They were also known as the Voices of the Wells, for there was also an oracular quality to them.

One day, an evil king, King Amangons, lusted after one of the well maidens, and stealing her golden cup from her, he raped her. His men, following their King's example, also stole and raped and dishonoured the other Well Maidens.

As a result the Well Maidens withdrew back into the Otherworld, closing down what was once a channel for numinous power from the Otherworld to this. With the life-giving properties of the water being withdrawn the wells dried up, the land became barren, and the people suffered.

> *The land was so wasted*
> *That no tree ever bloomed there again,*
> *The grasses and flowers withered,*
> *And the streams dried up.*

The Voices of the Wells fell silent and the reciprocal link between this world and the Otherworld was broken.

As a result of this desecration the Fisher King, who alludes to the connection between the King and the Sovereignty of the Land, was wounded in his groin and became impotent, and his Court was withdrawn from the world.

The Land has become a Wasteland, and until what has been lost is once more restored it will remain in this state.

The only relief the Fisher King can find from the pain of his wound is fishing on the lake. This is a clear metaphor for what has been lost – water represents the feminine, and her intuitive, emotional aspects. He is fishing for the return of this dishonoured and banished aspect of the psyche to be returned. He is also fishing for the Salmon of Knowledge, which in Celtic lore represented deep inner wisdom.

It is clear what needs to happen to make the Wasteland fertile once more:

> The Well maidens need to be honoured
> Their golden chalices must be returned
> The links to the Otherworld and the numinous in life need to be restored to bring the life-giving waters back.
> The Fisher King must be healed.

Only then can the land green again and harmony return.

Comment

When we look at this narrative as a whole – the Rape of the Well Maidens, the wounding of the Fisher King, the Perceval quest, the Court of King Arthur and the Arthur mythos – we come to see within Celtic tradition the Well Maidens would be recognised as either priestesses or as otherworldly women whose task was to keep the ways open between worlds and to keep alive the ancient mysteries which nourish the spirit and ensure the sacredness of the land.

The link between the Otherworld or 'Faery' was very strong and very real to the Celts. This link nourished and sustained this world and was a vital part of its fertility.

The Well Maidens can also be seen as the feminine aspect of the land – and this relates directly to the soverignty of the land, which was gifted to a worthy man, through the Goddess , or her representative, by the offering of a Grail cup of red ale. The Grail here refers to the essence of sovereignty, the gift of the land over which the man may rule. Once this gift is seized, not given, the power in the land shifts from that of service to the land to domination over the land, and the land suffers as a result.

The Grail Hallows

The four Grail Hallows are interesting as the cup, the sword, the lance and the Stone or platter come straight out of Irish folklore about the Tuatha de Danann who are of the faery or fae lineage, also called Sidhe (pronounced Shee).

When they came to Eire, they brought with them four sacred objects:

> - The Sword of Light from the city of Gorias in the East
> - The Spear of Victory from the city of Finias in the South
> - The Cauldron of Plenty from the city of Murias in the West
> - The Stone of Destiny from the city of Falias in the North

These were known as the Faery Hallows, which passed through the Celtic stream into that of the Grail stories, becoming the Grail Hallows.

Furthermore they are living reminders and representative of the four elements of the physical plane:

The sword – Air
The spear or lance - Fire
The cup or cauldron – Water
The Stone or Platter - Earth

What we come to see is that these have become keystones of the Western magical tradition and also correspond to the four suits of the Tarot - Swords, Cups, Wands and Pentacles

In addition, they are also found within the four suits of a standard pack of playing cards

– Spades (Sword), Hearts (Cup), Clubs (Wand) and Diamonds (Pentacle or Stone).

The Grail Hallows also form a double male-female pair

> Grail cup and platter or stone – feminine
> Sword and lance – masculine

In some version drops of blood flow from the tip of the spear and fall into the Grail itself – an image of the life force pouring from the male to the female.

This same image is found in the Irish tales of a magical spear, belonging to Lugh, god of Light, plunged into a cauldron of water, and the theme of a divine force flowing into a sacred vessel is also found in Hermetic teachings.

So within the symbology of the Grail Hallows we have captured some ancient knowledge and magical wisdom which hints back to the ancient origins of the Grail stories we know today, rooted in a much older stream of knowledge than is suggested at first glance. It also gives us direct connections back into the fae lineages, which are hinted at again and again in the early Arthurian/Grail stories.

The Grail Questions

It is also worth taking a few moments to consider the questions that Perceval should have asked. They differ from version to version, but a summary is:

> What purpose does the Grail serve?
> Whom does the Grail serve?
> What is the Grail?
> Why does the lance bleed?
> Where is the procession going?

And to the Fisher King, the most basic of enquiries: What ails You?

Perceval's failure is seen as a failure of compassion and also an adherence to the *status quo*. He has been told, as part of his knightly training, not to question or speak too much and, even when faced with marvels, he subsumes his natural curiosity and does as he is told.

This tells us clearly that Perceval has lost touch with himself and become inauthentic.

To ask the Grail questions is to commit to being a Grail Bearer, an instrument of healing – one who is not afraid to challenge what is wrong in this world, and not afraid to be who they truly are. Indeed, it is vital to be authentic to be able to embody the Grail essence. You are a warrior for the Light, seeking to redress the balance at all levels – not least to question a world where the masculine has become aggressive and dominant, dishonouring the sacred feminine in our Mother Earth, within our Society, within women and the soul within the body.

The Quest for the Grail symbolically is ultimately a quest to right what is wrong, to seek the path of self-sovereignty, and the return of the Divine Feminine in sacred marriage to her Divine partner, and to develop a higher level of consciousness in order to redeem both ourselves and make the Waste Land bloom again. It is to seek the Divine within all things and honour this principle above all else.

Part 2
The Grail and Earth Wisdom

The Grail and Earth Wisdom

We are living at an extraordinary time in both the evolution of mankind, and the evolution of this planet.

Earth is evolving, and as creatures living on her surface, and in close connection to her – indeed we are totally reliant on her resources – we too are having to evolve and adapt. You may not be aware of this, most of us are now so disconnected from the Earth and her rhythms that we are not tuned in at this level, but it is inevitable that changes to the various earth energy and electromagnetic grids are being felt by us in some form or other, even if we are not consciously aware of it.

In this section we are going to start by looking at our beautiful Mother Earth, and the many aspects, seen and unseen, that make up this great Being.

At one time in mankind's history this understanding of Mother Earth and her creatures and energies was totally integrated into our world view – indeed many indigenous peoples still cling to the remnants of this understanding and, in recent times, it has been the indigenous cultures who have kept this understanding alive whilst the so-called 'civilized' Western world went through a very dark phase.

Slowly, more and more people are waking up out of this dark dream (or nightmare!) and remembering the legacy of our forebears and looking to help others become aware once more of the consciousness inherent in ALL things.

And it is not a moment too soon – the damage our thoughtless, greedy and ignorant ways have caused in HUGE – and whilst Mother Earth is suffering as a consequence, be under no illusions as to who it is in the long term who will suffer the consequences.

Mankind!

Indeed, we are already suffering unparalleled levels of suffering at so many levels as a result of our thoughtless and careless ways.

According to scientist we are in the middle of a mass extinction process. Whilst these have happened in the past cycles of the Earth, this one differs in that it is being caused not by natural phenomena such as a meteor strike, but by mankind himself.

Indeed, through poisoning our environment and our bodies in numerous ways most are too asleep or dumbed down to recognise we are shortening our already much truncated life expectancy even more, as well as impacting every other living thing on the planet.

As we increasingly sees species after species heading toward extinction there is a peculiar blindness to the fact that the apex of this process will be the destruction of Man himself!

Mother Earth WILL survive – damaged and hurting, toxic and weary maybe, but she works in great cycles of time that over the millennia will see all traces of this iteration of Man and his destructive ways healed and erased.

Time is running out for Man, not Mother Earth!

We must mend our ways and come back to who we TRULY are and were designed to be before the Long Sleep we have fallen into – the Guardians and Keepers of Mother Earth.

Cosmic Vision

Let's take a moment to see the bigger picture of what is currently going on at the moment.

Many of you will be aware that we are at an extraordinary time in the evolution of both Mankind and the Earth.

We live in a multidimensional universe, which has a long and interesting history, and humankind here on 3rd dimensional Earth is part of a great galactic family whose lineage stretches from the Founder fields of consciousness at the very apex of our universe.

This is not the time or place for our full galactic history, but know that it is one that until relatively recent times we all knew. A series of invasions and devastating incidents have served to make humankind a shadow of who we really are, subject to mass enslavement, mind-wiping and abject dumbing down.

We have lost access to so much knowledge, and been fed either corrupted or entirely wrong information regarding much of what we think we know. Take almost any topic and I can point to where, at best, we are missing vital concepts or understanding (or even worse, being called weird and ridiculed when we do find this information) and where deliberate misinformation, corrupted information or downright lies are being fed to us.

One of the things which has characterised the last few years for so many people is that they have realised the reality of what is going on around us is almost diametrically the opposite of the many media, government and corporate stories we are fed.

It is like we have been looking in a mirror where a very particular narrative has played across the surface, and now we are finally able to turn around 180° we are seeing that the reality bears little relationship to what the mirror has been portraying.

Many are finding this quite devastating, and are rightfully angry at the betrayal and deceit. Many others are finding it extremely difficult to get their heads around the wickedness of it. All of which is justified, but it is important we don't get caught up in this and fail to move forward in retuning and re-educating ourselves into correct understandings and knowledge as we have so much to gain by moving forwards rather than just wallowing in existing wounds.

Awakening your Grail Wisdom is very much about beginning to reclaim, and learn once again how to utilise this knowledge and information, and is as much about coming back into alignment with yourself and all around you as it is about a whole body of knowledge and understanding that, to date, has been denied you.

Our universe was birthed out of vast source fields of consciousness, one of many universes to have been birthed in this way. All structure within this universe is based on energetic templating and architecture upon which eventually the matter constructs of the world we know have been formed.

It was originally structured as a 15-dimensional architecture – I say originally because there are indications that this is changing as part of the necessity of correcting the immense damage that this last Dark Aeon has seen deliberately inflicted by certain beings, but that is something to be explored in more depth by those who wish to continue to dive deeper with this particular wisdom stream.

For now, it is enough for us to understand the basic structure we have dwelt within and has been our home for vast ages.

You may hear me referring to our universe as our Universal Time Matrix, God World or even the Milky Way Galaxy at various times. Know that they are all ways of referring to the same construct.

So, we have 15 frequencies, or dimensions, of energies, which further divide down into 5 planes of density, with the uppermost density being 3 great consciousness fields of sound and light which entered this construct to act as the founding energies for the whole Time Matrix. They are generally referred to as the Trifold Flame, or Eieyani Council, made up of the Blue Flame (or Emerald Order), the Gold Flame (or Gold Order) and the Violet Flame (or Amethyst Order).

This top density is referred to as Harmonic Universe (HU) 5 and contains dimension 13, 14 and 15.

The next one down, HU4, dimensions 10, 11 and 12 is deemed to be the entry point into densification of matter and is made up of great fields of hydroplasmic liquid light. All beings here are made of this, and therefore at best appear to us as great light beings with only the vaguest of forms, which are a stepped down forms of consciousness from HU5. The Blue Flame races are known as the Elohei Elohim, the Gold Flame as the Seraphei Seraphim and the Violet Flame as the BraHaRama races. They encompass a wide variety of 'forms' within each of these.

The next density, HU3, is made up of etheric matter and encompasses dimensions 7, 8 and 9. Here live many races which are a further stepped down or fragmented level of consciousness, with races such as the Oraphim and the Azurites who have immensely complex and high frequency DNA templating.

In HU2 we have dimensions 4, 5 and 6 and beings here are semi-etheric in form. Here we have the direct precursors to Earth humans in the Turaneusiam of 5D Tara, and the Maharaji grail lineages amongst many others.

Finally we come to HU1 and dimensions 1, 2 and 3, the home of full densification of matter or full physicality where we humans, along with the Maji grail lines and various other beings reside on 3D planet Earth.

Getting your head around our multidimensional universe, planet and selves can take some doing. We are used to thinking in very linear terms of reference, rather than multi-dimensionally and quite frankly, it can make your head hurt!

Primary Sound Fields of Source Energy/Consciousness Matrix

HU	D	Matrix	Description
HU 5	D.15	Trifold Flame Matrix	3 Primary rays of sound and light
	D.14	Blue Flame Gold Flame	No matter, no time
	D.13	Violet Flame	Home of Eieyani Council or Founders
HU4	D.12		Entry point into densification of matter
	D.11	Avatar Level Matrix	Non-physical pre-matter template Hydroplasmic Christos liquid light field
	D.10		Solar Logos & Solar Dragon fields
HU3	D.9		Etheric
	D.8	Oversoul (monadic) level Matrix	Home of Planetary Logos or Mind (D7), Galactic Core (D8), Causal Body (D9)
	D.7		HU 3 home of 7D planet Gaia
HU2	D.6		Semi-Etheric
	D.5	Soul level Matrix	Home of Astral and Emotional Body (D4), Archetypal Body 9D5), Celestial Body (D6)
	D.4		HU 2 home of 5D planet Tara
HU1	D.3		Full physicality
	D.2	Personality level Matrix	Home of Subconscious Intelligence (D1), Instinctual Intelligence (D2) and Conscious Mind Intelligence (D3)
	D.1		HU 1 home of 3D planet Earth

HU = Harmonic Universe or density

The illustration on the opposite page is a linear presentation which I have found is the easiest way to begin to work with it. What you will find as you dive deeper into getting your head around all this though is that in reality each density and dimension is nested within the next, rather like a series of Russian dolls.

But we are just beginning to take first steps here, so let's stick with what is easiest to work with. Once you have grasped this basic structure and that it runs through every level from ourselves to planets, solar systems and the whole galaxy and what this means in terms of a vertical axis of reference to where you are in the galaxy, as well as a horizontal one you can begin to play with how you might want to depict it further.

***

We live in a dynamic multidimensional universe filled at all densities or frequencies with living beings. These beings and their elemental helpers moulded and birthed the physical substance of our planet. And countless non-physical beings continue to nurture and care for her – and us!

The various holy and sacred texts of Earth give abundant reference to the existence of Creator Beings. No matter the tradition (or myth) they all point to an order of Creator Beings, also called the Founders, the Builders or the Architects, who are responsible for bringing the many wonders of our natural world into existence down through the densities.

Scientists can clearly see within the evolutionary history of our planet, (as far as we are aware of it) that there have been quantum leaps in evolution in regular waves in our planet's history. That we are approaching (or rather within) another one of these waves of evolutionary leaps is attested too not just by the teachings of ancient wisdom prophecies, but also by scientific data.

These waves of evolutionary energy, which have been likened to universal consciousness, are pulsing out from the galactic core and bathing everything in its path with these impulses.

And our solar system is currently within its path – everything within our system is being influenced – planets, creator beings, plants, animals....and of course, humans!

The Eagle and the Condor

The Eagle and the Condor is an ancient Amazonian prophecy that speaks of human society's splitting into two paths – that of the Eagle and that of the Condor.

The path of the Condor is the path of the heart, of intuition and of the feminine.

The path of the Eagle is the path of the mind, of the industrial, and of the masculine.

The prophecy says that the 1490s would begin a 500-year period during which the Eagle people would become so powerful that they would virtually drive the Condor people out of existence.

This can be seen in the conquering of the Americas and the oppressing and killing of the indigenous peoples in the last 500 years.

The prophecy says that during the next 500-year period, beginning in 1990 the potential would arise for the Eagle and Condor to come together and fly in the same sky, and to create a new level of consciousness for humanity.

The prophecy only speaks of the potential, so it is up to us to activate this potential and ensure the new consciousness is allowed to rise.

We all embody both birds.

Which choice are you going to make?

We are also in the process of what is called a Stellar Activation Cycle, which comes around approximately every 26,000 years. We shall look at what this is a little further on.

For now, just understand that when we talk about this being an important moment in our planet's evolution, it is. There are plenty of people talking about planetary and personal ascension and ascension energies. Everything is being asked to expand and refine its consciousness to a higher vibration, to lift itself above the very dense vibrationary fields of deep matter and move to a higher and finer frequency.

Ultimately, if you chose to dive deeper into the Grail Wisdom you will come to understand both the mechanisms and processes behind this and the many problems there have been in the past around it.

This time round there is everything to play for, and we are being given an unprecedented chance to make a huge leap, both planetary and personal.

Not everyone will chose to do so, but for all those who want to participate it is a time of both enormous change and opportunity.

So What Does This Mean For Humans?

It is said that man came into matter from the finer, higher vibrations of Creation, stage by stage. Mystics such as Rudolf Steiner attest to this, as do myths such as that of Sophia and the Demi-urge.

When you come to understand in its entirety the origin of Earth's human races, how long we have been here, and the original reasons for us being placed here you will come to understand that the stories, myths, commentaries and narratives are all hinting at what really happened, whilst our so-called official 'history' denies this and points us towards a chance encounter of amoeba and ape cousins[2].

Over recent millennia, in the process of coming ever deeper into matter we not only lost sight of our more spiritual origins, but also access to many of the innate skills and senses that were once at our disposal, leaving us with only the 5 we are all familiar with, and stories that hint at the greater powers we once had which we are told by our Overlords are fairy tales.

They are not.

Somehow, despite all that has been done to us every age has had a few enlightened seers and initiates, who have managed to navigate their way through the cosmic energies and denser levels of the material world to a deeper understanding of 'reality' and have kept alive the path for others to follow the clues.

It has been a dangerous path to follow for many millennia, being hunted down and eliminated if discovered, but the rewards always outweighed the fear for the true initiate.

They came to a spiritual understanding of what the modern day scientist is struggling to get his head around – the world of quantum physics where

---

[2] There is a reason it is called the Theory of Evolution, as it is just that, a theory. It still remains unproven despite over 150 of trying to do so. Draw your own conclusions.

the rules of the physical world, of Newtonian (3D) physics are turned on their head. In this world you CAN walk on water, levitate, heal instantly and so on. You just have to understand how to move from the world of matter to the world of energy which underpins matter!

This information was only ever shared within strictly controlled spheres – not only is it subversive but dangerous in the wrong hands! The ancient mystery schools would only take each initiate as deep into the mysteries as the individual's spiritual evolution dictated. As one mastered the higher realms of finer vibration the lower emotions of greed, anger, lust for power and material gain etc naturally fell away as these denser emotions have no part of this vibration, and service to humanity was the guiding ethos.

The individuals who mastered this science were powerful, but due to the careful training and selection process used these powers in service to humanity.

There came a time though that these ancient spiritual schools were infiltrated and taken over by those whose motives were not for the betterment of humanity, and the true teaching became deliberately corrupted, eviscerated or otherwise damaged.

The old mystery schools were eventually either driven underground or disappeared entirely by the advance of the monotheistic religions, which were (and are) based more around power politics than spirituality.

But this esoteric wisdom is once more streaming into the awareness of humanity as this great wave of evolutionary consciousness is urging us all to wake up and remember who we really are. We are being asked to step into a new level of spiritual maturity and reclaim our lost heritage.

The deep materialism into which our Society has fallen in the last few hundred years seemingly came out of a fierce struggle with, and backlash against, the deep superstition of an all-powerful patriarchal Church. In truth, it has all been part of a global one world agenda which has been planned and playing out for an exceedingly long period of time, gradually disconnecting us from our origins, roots and even our true humanity.

Now, however, the universal field of intelligence which underlies and pervades everything is breaking through the trance into which we have been placed and calling us back to our connection with our galactic families.

A new multi-dimensional human being is evolving, being re-birthed. Our very DNA is changing, being moulded by the vast energetic pulses sounding into our planet from the furthest reaches of our universe.

It is the task of all of us to begin to understand and reconnect with the true wisdom of our ancestors, and to explore once again the multi-dimensional world in which we live as we create the bridge between the old world and the new with as much grace, compassion and good intention as we can muster!

Gaia Consciousness

Our ancestors KNEW at a level they totally took for granted that the Earth was a living consciousness. It is something indigenous tribes today still know – we are in relationship with the Earth. She is called many things – the Great Mother, Gaia, Magna Mater, Ge – but one thing stand out, and that is that she is alive, she is conscious and she is aware.

The advent of Roman Christianity and its ever increasing grip on not only people's lives, but what they should think, saw this understanding begin to fade, as this grip on what people were taught, what they were allowed to know inexorably tightened.

In a bid to control Nature and dismiss the feminine principle, thereby bringing massive imbalance and disconnection in, not only were millions of women shamed, tortured and killed but little by little people were detached from their sense of the land as a living thing, instead being herded in churches and told that their only contact with the Divine could be through the rather sanctimonious offices of a priest, who judged and condemned anything that did not fit his narrow, misogynistic and controlling world view.

The advent of the Industrial Revolution and the so-called 'Enlightenment' made matters worse. God was dead, it was declared, the world was a machine, there was no such thing as miracles, and reductionism and materialism took hold.

Welcome to the Wasteland!!!!

Our poor, beautiful, generous and abundant Mother has been dishonoured and raped and pillaged by those with 'dead eyes'. They lack awareness of connection, of beauty, of the sanctity of life, of the miraculous found in the every day.

After the devastation of two world wars and the horrors of the atomic bomb – the ultimate wasteland – a shift in consciousness started to occur. The hippies and their 'flower power' heralded this. Then in the 1970s there came a scientist who dared to put his head above the parapet. He published a book called *'Gaia: A New Look at Life on Earth'*. He was, of course, James Lovelock. Gaia Theory was born.

It proposed the revolutionary idea that the Earth is a living, self-regulating, conscious organism. Every aspect of her, from trees to air, to creatures on the sea shore to climate is part of the way she regulates herself.

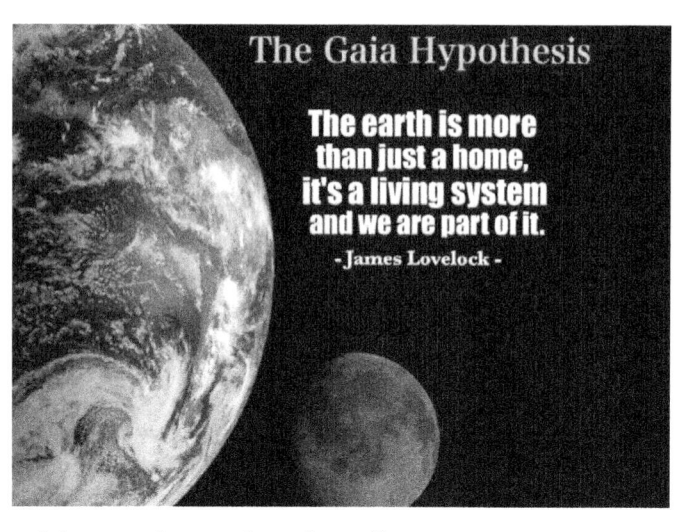

The debate has raged ever since. Those of us who know that Mother Earth is a conscious entity, are beginning the fight back against those who hold hard to the mechanistic and reductionist view of the world and see Her as just a resource to be used, a nihilistic and destructive view of the world which is anti-life.

Our awakening consciousness is going even further in beginning to understand once more the link between the consciousness of the planet and our own consciousness, how the wellbeing of one impacts the wellbeing of the other, and how our own interaction between the subtle energetic anatomy of the earth, which scientists don't even acknowledge, and our own energetic anatomy (ditto) is fundamental to both our purpose here and our ability to evolve.

In the following pages we are going to take a very basic look at some of the many ways in which we can begin to reconnect and interact with the Earth.

The Subtle Art of Geomancy

If you look it up the word literally means 'earth divination' and it is presented through the likes of Google as being some sort of medieval mashup of astrology and fortune telling.

In reality, by medieval times the true art of geomancy was all but forgotten except by a few. Some of the most visible ones from our point of view were the Knights Templar[3], although history omits to tell us their true affiliations and purposes.

When you understand that the Templar refers to the planetary energetic manifestation template or blueprint, including such structures as the grids, stargates and planetary shields, as well as being the name given to those who consciously work with these you start to understand them in a very different light.

Indeed, it is the heritage of the Grail lineages to act as Guardians to the Planetary Templar and to protect and repair the grids and other aspects of the Templar. They hold within their DNA templates the necessary light codings for this as well as for use with various portals and stargates. It is like a lock and key effect, and one of the reasons why these bloodlines have been hunted down with often the women taken and the men killed, as the DNA is prized by the fallen and intruder races. Without access to it they do not have full access to Templar mechanics.

This is really old knowledge that it is very clear our ancestors not only knew about, but were very expert in. Most of the ancient monuments that remain to us today from huge stone circles such as Avebury and Stonehenge, to more subtle aspects of the landscape such as sacred wells tap into 'power points' within the Earth's energy field.

There is a whole art to enhancing these energies – sometimes called 'riding the dragon' – that can help bring man and environment into

---

[3] Also known as the Luciferian Knights Templar. They propagated false teachings in relation to the Holy Grail, and worked to control many of the Earth's energetic 'power points'

harmony with the 'Spirit of Place', which is beneficial to the health and well-being of all involved.

The Knights Templar were just one of many groups that we see through history had a clear understanding of the importance of geomancy and the nodal power points in the land. If you had a control and domination agenda they were important places to conquer and hold.

Today, most geomancers know nothing of this and come to the work they do either through being extremely sensitive to earth energies or through the use of dowsing. Indeed, it has been dowsers over the last 50 years or so who have been mapping and sharing information around some of the important energy lines across the planet, work which is much needed and constantly being added to.

As we rebuild our understanding we are seeing many of the returning Indigo starseed races[4] who have been incarnating on the Earth for some time now, begin to step into what is called Gridworker roles. Many of these are from the old grail lineages and have returned at this vital time to help with the repair of the many damaged areas of the grids, and the unlocking of many portals and sites that were closed down.

They hold within their DNA much of the coding that is required to do this work at this vital time. Indeed, an aspect of the Grail Wisdom work is calling directly to those drawn to these areas of working to help build networks to heal and protect the Earth grids, whether they are aware of their lineage or not.

So geomancy is really all to do with the subtle relationship of man and his consciousness with his surroundings and encompasses such things as

---

[4] For more on this read *The Divine Human* by Saira Salmon

earth and landscape energies, earth energy balancing, earth acupuncture, spirit release and space clearing to name a few.

It would have been used in relation to finding the correct location, definition, siting, orientation and proportion for man-made structures and their interaction with the psychic or spiritual levels of the world around us.

Many of the important sites were originally very sacred as well as powerful and, as I have said, were targeted by those with control and domination agendas and have been used, abused and contaminated with very dark energies. Many of these sites are in an ongoing process of being recovered and cleared, but, as you can imagine, it is not an easy or simple process.

In essence geomancy as it is seen today has three main aspects to it: -

1. Dowsing of underground and surface energy meridians and the implementation of earth acupuncture to resolve geopathic stress.

2. Design and placement within the visible world and the design of human environments according to common sense as well as subtle methods.

3. Alignment with the time dimensions of astrology and astronomy.

In reality it goes much deeper than this as it also embraces knowledge and understanding of working with the Templar mechanics, an area of understanding we are just beginning to reclaim.

Geomantic practitioners tend to work in two ways:

- At the level of connection and witnessing of the subtle energies in Nature, helping to unblock or re-harmonise discordant areas or bear witness and honour our relationship with this invisible world.
- As a therapeutic art helping to deal with a client's problems, health issues, challenges, relationships and issues. They also help to mitigate sick building syndrome as well as negating the damaging results of exposure to harmful types of earth radiation and geopathic stress which affect human health.

Most of these work through the medium of dowsing, so contacting a local dowsing group can be a place to start if you are interested in learning more.

Gridworking tends to be another level on from this, and takes earth energy work to another level of opening up more into Templar mechanics.

Every culture has its own ancient geomantic traditions. In China it is the art of Feng Shui and in India it is Vastu Shastra. Western geomancy utilises dowsing and earth acupuncture amongst its techniques as well as assessing the best placement for something by reading the subtle earth signs and aligning or locating something so that it connects with or enhances the subtle energies of the earth.

Geomancy also involves keeping sacred sites honoured. Practices differ according to the underlying tradition but all are concerned with connecting to the sacred and protecting and enhancing energy portals in the land and 'between worlds'.

A term which is being seen in use more and more now is 'geobiology'. This is being used by some geomancers who wish to distance themselves from the more fringe practitioners and to ground this knowledge into current scientific models, where they exist, as well as providing demonstrable structures and constructs to help understand these phenomena.

Earth Energies

The term Earth Energies tends to be applied willy-nilly to a variety of phenomena relating to measurable lines of energy or grids that would seem to emanate from the earth itself.

These energies have been called different things in different cultures – the veins of the Dragon (China), The Serpent (India) Wonambi, or Crocodile (Australia) or the Wyvern (Christian). Again, deeper knowledge of the Grail Wisdom helps us begin to see why the Dragon or Serpent theme is so prevalent when talking of Earth energies as it hints at the deeper knowledge once known and its subversion.

This planet is made up of a wide range of natural energies, some of which can be measured by physical instruments and some of which are deemed to be 'non-physical' as they are not detected by current instruments (often not sensitive enough), but can be picked up by intuitive diagnostic techniques such as dowsing.

It would seem that, as yet, we don't have reliable enough technology - or perhaps it would be better to say refined-enough technology - to accurately measure what is going on with the so-called 'non-physical' lines to help us understand them.

This leaves us with all sorts of different interpretations and theories. Dowsing by skilled dowsers shows us *something* is going on, and indeed it is reproducible by other dowsers, but quite what is open to speculation.

Earth energies as a science is very much in its infancy.

Many of these lines of energy have been likened by some researches to the energy meridian lines that are found in the human body. These were pooh-poohed initially by scientists until sensitive enough instrumentation was produced that showed clearly the lines of invisible energy that run through defined channels in the human body – just as ancient Eastern sages said they did!

The resonance or frequency of these lines is also of interest to us. It has been shown that when people meditate and calm their mental chatter, their brains resonate at alpha frequencies in the area of 7 – 9 Hz. This is the same frequency as the energy field of the Earth!

This could be one of the reasons why meditation is said to be so beneficial to human health. In a relaxed state our energy field entrains with that of the earth.

The same has also been seen in human beings who live close to nature – their energy fields and that of the Earth are in synchronicity, with a resulting improvement in both mental and physical health.

Our increasing disconnection from these fields, and the daily exposure we now receive to a wide variety of frequencies through radio waves, microwaves and other electromagnetic frequencies are an unexplored potential cause of the rising levels of both physical and mental health, despite being at a point in humanity's history where we have never been so well fed and supposedly protected from a wide variety of diseases.

Indeed much of humanity has never been so sick and disabled.

We will look at this in more detail within the Home and Physical body sections, but for now let's have a look at some of the variety of earth energies which have been identified.

Physical Lines

ElectroMagnetic Frequencies

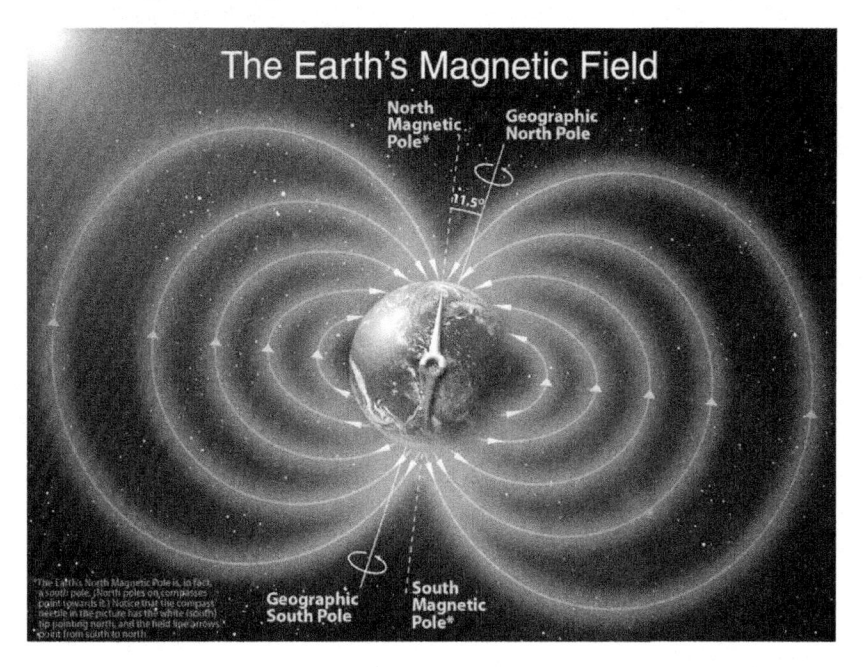

Schumann Resonance

It was only in 1962 that the USA National Bureau of Standards endorsed the work of the physicist W O Schumann that the Earth's natural electromagnetic field resonates at exactly the same frequency as the relaxed human brain emitting alpha brain – 7.83 Hz!

Called the Schumann Resonance this is closely monitored by scientists using laboratory equipment – in fact it is measured daily! Humans who live closely aligned with this resonance as said to experience much better health and general overall well-being than those who are dissonant with it. It has been poetically called 'Earth's heartbeat' by some.

In recent years increasing changes to this frequency have been reported, and it would seem to be an indicator of the levels of some of the increasing force of certain cosmic energy waves bathing the planet, with the frequency levels rising for periods of time way beyond the stable 7.83

Hz recorded since its discovery. Indeed, the monitoring stations for the Schumann Resonance show clearly the immense rises in this energy that have been more and more often recorded.

The Hartmann Grid
The Hartmann Grid was discovered by Dr Ernst Hartmann in the 1960s and follows the magnetic north/south and east/west. The lines of this grid are 6 –10 inches (15 – 25 cm) wide and are spaced 5ft 5 inches (1.6 m) apart. Where the lines cross what is called a 'Hartmann Knot' is formed.

Where there is a crossing of lines which carry negative charge – called a double negative – which on this grid occurs every 115ft (35 m) this is a geopathic stress point with implications for human health (we shall look at this more later on).

The Curry Grid
The Curry Grid was discovered by Dr Curry and Dr Whitman in the 1970, and runs diagonally at 45° to North, repeating every 8 ft (2.4 m) southwest to north east ad every 9ft (2.9 m) south east to northwest. They are wide at approximately 2 (0.6 m) ft and every 164ft (50 m) you get the occurrence of a double negative node or crossing point.

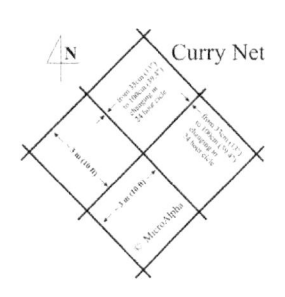

The existence of these grids was assumed to be hypothetical until an engineer in 2006, Hans Giertz, showed their existence using low frequency electromagnetics.

The Benker Grid
The Benker Grid is a 10 x 10 m (30 x 30 ft) grid named after Anton Benker, a German dowser who discovered this grid in 1953. Each grid line has a thickness of around 8 – 12 inches. He likened it at the time to a 'higher' version of the Hartmann Grid, to which it seems to correlate.

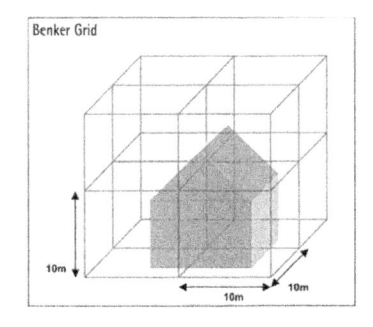

It is a radial grid (ie. 3-dimensional), built up

of cubes, which alternate in polarity. It is a magnetic grid system and has specific energetic qualities that it would seem our forebears knew about as ancient sites have been dowsed to find that stones are set within Benker squares.

It would seem, from anecdotal evidence that it is detrimental to health to sleep either on these lines or line crossing points, but not within them.

Other Grids currently being explored include:

Broad Curry Grid - 30° off north
Double-Curry Grid - 20° off north, with wide intervals of 410 ft (125 m) (many megaliths, sacred wells and springs, chapels, hill forts, and oak trees are found on this grid's lines.
Schneider – discovered by R Schneider in 1980s this grid is at 45° with repeating lines every 965 ft (294 m).
Angel Grid – discovered by Shaun Kirwan this grid has huge lines of etheric force which are connected to the golden section ratio.
Peyer or Solar Grid – said to be formed from natural energy which radiates up from the Earth's core in a grid of around 23 ft (7 m) square

Non-Physical Lines

There is a confusion of terms used around non-physical lines, made worse by different practitioner's interpreting them according to their own understanding or experience. As I said earlier, much of this work is in its infancy and is still in the process of finding a common language to work with.

Ley Lines

Accurately speaking the term ley lines was initially used to describe straight lines used to connect up different sites found on a map as first posited by Alfred Watkins in *The Old Straight Track*. The sites pick up a number of different types of features including churches, tumuli or ancient monuments, holy wells or springs, stone circles, burial mounds. They often follow the line of ancient track ways.

Ley Lines, in terms of earth energies, has come to mean an energy line, which can be dowsed in a way which is replicable (ie. can be dowsed and confirmed by others) and has a pair of earth energy lines attached to it. These are often referred to as a masculine or positive current and a feminine or negative current. So you have a straight alignment around which these two currents twine or snake. This is called a true ley line. Major examples of this are the Michael and Mary Alignment and the Belinus Line.

Another use of the words 'ley lines' can refer to lines of over-ground energy which follow the sinuous paths of underground water. Carrying what is called Yin Chi and Yang Chi, or negative and positive energy, they are also called 'spirit paths' by some (although this phrase is also used in other contexts) and frequently define processional routes to important places such as temples, cathedrals and palaces.

The first attempt at properly classifying different types of ley lines and their nodal points has been made by Rory Duff[5] along with a team of dowsers in his book *A Guide to Leylines, Earth Energies, Nodes & Large Vortexes*.

---

[5] www.roryduff.com

From a Templar mechanics point of view ley lines are the meridian axiatonal lines on the planet which conduct and transmit frequencies through the planet and transduce dimensional frequencies into the planetary systems (the same templating exists in our lightbody) and form part of the various planetary grid systems. In simplistic terms, while we might call the grids major veins or arteries, the leys are more like capillaries.

Telluric Currents

Telluric or Earth currents refer to an electric current which moves underground or through the sea. These form as the result of both natural causes and human activity and researchers say that they can be seen to interact in a complex patterns.

These are extremely low frequency currents and are found in both the Earth's crust and mantle, and are primarily geo-magnetically induced currents which are inducted by changes in the outer part of the Earth's magnetic field, usually caused by interactions between the solar wind from the sun and the magnetosphere or solar radiation effects on the ionosphere.

Because these currents flow in the surface layers of the Earth and we are able to measure the electric potential of the Earth's surface we can calculate the magnitudes and directions of telluric currents.

Telluric currents are known to have diurnal characteristics with a general direction of flow towards the sun. During the day they move equator-ward and at night pole-ward. Some are also influenced by the sun cycles, and others by lunar cycles.

Dragon Lines

You may hear some people talk about 'dragon lines' and this references the fact that many ancient cultures (including our own) often referred to some of the powerful telluric currents as dragons.

Indeed, the largest and most powerful energy lines on this planet, which in Rory Duff's classification table are Type 5 lines, he has named Emperor Dragon lines. There are very few of these on the planet, they are very powerful and are cosmic in origin.

In Templar Mechanics terms Rory may have tapped into the ancient understanding that Dragon lines are connected to stellar transmissions, and can reactivate once dormant sites.

The Dragon lines are considered the 12 main lines which transmit qualities of the Galactic zodiac and DNA codes into the planet and run Solar frequencies into the ley lines in their locality.

Ancient spiral vortexes imprinted into the Earth aeons ago are being reactivated by the increasing frequencies of these lines and act as massive sound (vibration) resonators to elevate human consciousness.

Those who work with telluric currents, or dragon lines posit that they have a consciousness and are a pathway of moving energy.

Dragon lines above the ground are straight and are influenced by and aligned to the sun or solar power.

Dragon lines below the earth are wavy in the way they move and follow water, and are influenced by and aligned to the moon.

Where these lines meet or cross are called nodes. The more powerful the intersecting lines the more powerful the nodes. Dragon nodes are said to be 'supernatural transformers of converging grid line energies'.

Rory Duff has found in his research that 3-dimensional energy shapes are formed at these points which can be symmetrical or asymmetrical in shape, and that the shapes tend to change over the course of a year. His research has also shown that our ancestors were aware of all of this!

Living on any of these lines (or nodes) can either be beneficial to human health or detrimental to it. It would seem that it depends upon the predominant energies that make up a line. The most ideal has been found to be 3 parts Yang or positive energy (male) to 1 part Yin or negative energy (female). The more Yin energy in a line the more draining it is! It has been shown that the 'happy' hormone serotonin is particularly affected by this!

Vortex

Vortexes are created by spiralling energy and energetically with earth energies can be electrical, magnetic or electromagnetic in nature.

Magnetic energetic vortexes attract energy, electrical energetic vortexes energize and activate and electromagnetic vortexes do both!

Where these are found in the landscape they are considered by scientists to be geophysical anomalies. Our ancestors knew what the scientists are missing – that these are portalways where it is possible to work with the energies to help raise consciousness as well as heal at the wholistic level.

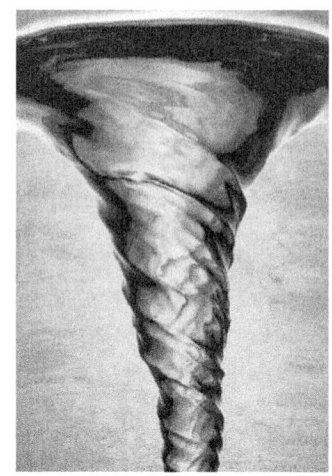

Vortexes are often to be found at old sacred sites as these places were revered by our ancestors due to their properties. There are also many dormant vortex points on the planet that were shut down or badly damaged by the artificial manipulation and interference of the Intruder races. Many of these are being powered back up as a result of Gridworker healing and repair missions to once more run energies into the earth and her grid systems.

Consciousness Grids

I want to touch lightly on what is a very extensive topic, and that is the planetary grid network. This is a living consciousness matrix within which is encoded the original planetary templating or blueprint, and relates directly to humankinds spiritual evolution.

The spiritual science of gridworking is referred to as the 'Templar' or Templar mechanics. As I have already said, this is also the title given to someone who comprehends and works with the planetary architecture and with earth consciousness.

When we use the term grid it is referring to the many layers which make up the morphogenetic field, and represents layers of crystalline blueprints woven into manifestation to support both form and consciousness.

As you can see from just this brief explanation it is waaaay beyond where our scientists are in their limited understanding of Earth grids.

These grids run through not just the geometric structures of the earth, but many run through into what is called Parallel or anti-particle Earth as well into higher dimensional levels of Earth imprinting into the further densities up. The stones or Pillars of Atlas, said in mythology to hold up the world were a metaphor for the concept that these grid lines hold our world in space and time and are 3-dimensional structures which act as an energetic 'skeleton'.

So you get an inkling of how complex they are. Different grids vibrate or move at different rates as we move around the sun, and there is constant interaction between stellar energies, the grids and the earth.

A couple of grids you hear mentioned are the following:

Crystalline Grid

The Crystalline Grid is a multi-dimensional light grid, a geometric lattice which encircles the earth and holds within it all the consciousness in the form of memories of all the beings of Earth.

This imprinting is done through the medium of crystals and this grid is effectively one which remembers human consciousness and emotions on the planet. It is this grid you are tuning into when you feel the resonant trauma remaining on a battlefield, or come across a haunting.

Everywhere you go you effectively leave an energetic imprint into this field. If it is strong enough, from massive trauma maybe, this remains resonant in the field. This is what the principles of Feng Shui refer to as 'Ancestor Chi'. This is where there is energetic imprinting into a room and object or environment. For example, a house where a bitter divorce has taken place needs cleansing before new people move in or the residue of the arguments and anger can leach into the new resident's fields and affect them negatively. This is also what psychometry is tapping into.

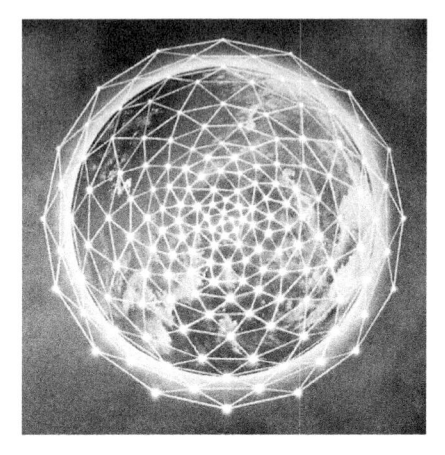

It is also this grid which holds the luminosity of many generations of heart-felt worship which imbues many churches and cathedrals.

The Crystalline Grid is said to be formed of light energy, and as the levels of photonic and other cosmic light is flooding the planet at higher vibrational levels, the grid itself is aiding the raising of levels of consciousness both on and in the planet.

We are all tuned to the grid at some level and will increasingly have to match this heightened level of frequency if we are not to feel ill effects from living within a dissonant frequency.

You may hear this grid referred to as holding the template for the New Earth, and it is this level of light frequency which is being referred to. By aligning with this frequency at the level of thought, desires, emotions etc it helps raise the vibrational level of our entire energetic anatomy, opening up access to forms of higher sense perception, including an understanding of the multi-dimensionality of who we are. It also enables us to download light code transmissions from this higher template.

This grid is also thought to be the means through which we will be able to tune into the multi-dimensional galactic communities which exist, many of which are aiding us right now, just inhabiting a different frequency band.

According to the channelled being Kryon, this grid remembers human consciousness and emotions and was seeded here aeons ago by beings from the stars. It is a multi-dimensional grid within which is found the 'Cave of Creation' also called the Cave of Treasures. This spans both dimensions and grids and is where the crystalline heart of Mother Earth is found, where all beings on death 'deposit' their memories before moving on. It can be deduced therefore that within the multidimensionality of this grid can be found the Akashic Records.

Kryon[6] states that all memories and past lives on Earth stay in the Earth, which is why accessing memories and lives on other planets is not part of this grids functions.

The Cave of Creation is NOT found within third dimensionality.

Earth's crystal structures in pentagonal symmetry

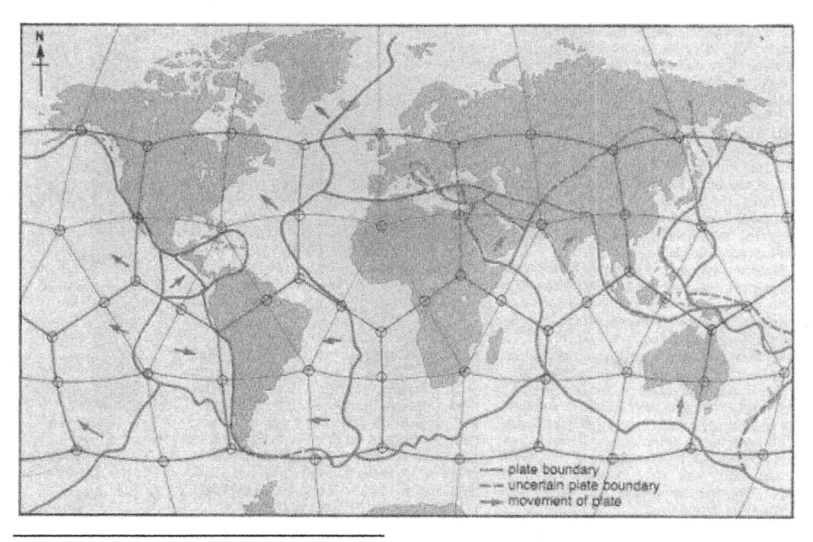

---

[6] Kryon is a channelled entity thought to be an aspect of Archangel Michael. As such he is a highly dubious source, although often his information is accurate. It is a question of sorting the wheat from the chaff, and maintaining due diligence.

The Gaia or Earth Grid

You may also hear this referred to as the Ancestor Grid.

This grid was also apparently implanted by beings from the stars, and interpenetrates and surrounds the planet. Indigenous peoples are very aware of, and work extensively with this grid which they treat as sacred. There is ample evidence to show that our ancestors were also tuned into this grid.

Like the Crystalline Grid, there is a multi-dimensionality to this grid, as all the elementals, and Nature beings and other benevolent helpers to the planet reside within the protection of this grid – as do we!

This is the grid that holds not just all life on Earth, but also the sentience of Mother Earth. It holds not just multi-dimensional life but also contains the wisdom of our ancestors, as distinct to the memory of all things which resides within the Crystalline Grid. Hence it is here that shamans will go to talk with Earth spirits or the ancestors to seek advice and guidance.

The Cave of Creation can also be accessed through this grid, as it spans both.

There are nodal points where the Crystalline and Earth grids, as well as the magnetic fields, interconnect at various places within the Earth, and these have been recognised for millennia by our ancestors as special places of interest.

Where the three fields overlap it gives a particular quality of amplification to the Crystalline Grid – Glastonbury is one such place, Machu Picchu another, as is Uluru in Australia.

There are also places where this crossing of grids cancels out, rather than amplifies, the Crystalline Grid. This leaves just raw earth energy so it is likely that awareness of the 'little people' and other elementals will be high in these places.

Another aspect of this cancelling out of the Crystalline Grid can leave what is called a 'null', which is a void in the grid and is generally an unhappy, unhealthy place to live due to geopathic stress and electromagnetic anomalies. The Bermuda Triangle is one such place.

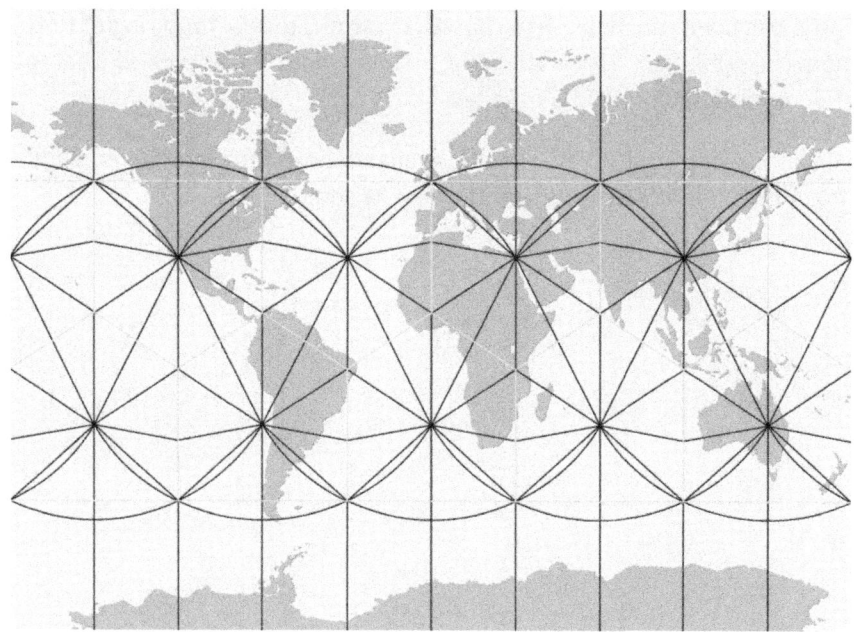

All the grids are being, or have been, recalibrated over the last few years, as human consciousness is being recalibrated. Given the tie between consciousness and aspects of these grids it is inevitable that their recalibration will affect humanity.

****

These two grids are both considered organic grids. There are other grid structures which have been installed at various times for various purposes. Some of these are for very benevolent purposes – indeed grids such as the Golden Eagle Grid and the Great White Lion grid saved the Earth from possible implosion at a time when huge damage had been inflicted on the planetary grids and fields.

But there are a variety of other artificial grids which have been installed at various points in fairly recent Earth history (75,000 years BC to 10,500 BC) by Intruder races for purposes of control and domination, that have caused immense harm to not just the benevolent and organic grids but also to humanity itself whose consciousness is very much linked into these grids.

There has been much damage caused at various levels, requiring at the moment immense repair, rebuilding and restructuring as well as clearance of demonic implants and blockages.

Much more information on these is available both through the ongoing Grail Wisdom body of work and the Lost Wisdom Library.[7]

---

[7] www.sairasalmon.com

Geopathic Stress (or Sad Dragons)

Geopathic stress is where a disruption or distortion to the natural energy fields and lines results in harmful radiation being given off, rather than that which resonates benignly with our own bodies.

Geopathic stress or land energy issues have been referred to as 'Sad Dragons' as the natural balance in earth energy lines is disturbed – the work of the geomancer or geobiologist is to make them into happy dragons!

There can be a number of reasons as to why energy lines and the surrounding land become disrupted:

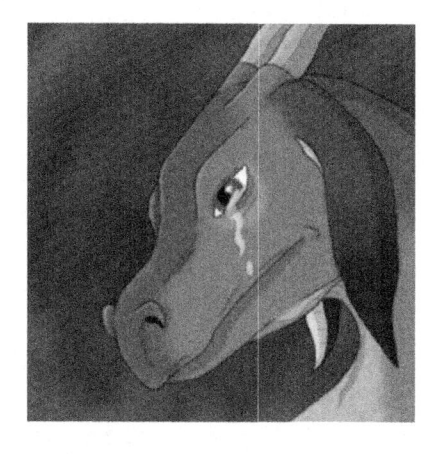

- Geopathic stress can be caused by harmful earth energies and underground water streams or geological faults
- Explosions, quarrying, tunnelling, mining etc
- New roads, railways, construction sites, deep foundations especially with steel footings, lampposts, cabling, power stations, electric cables, sub-stations, water mains etc
- Military bases
- Abuse of a space ie. old battle grounds and scenes of trauma
- Communication masts
- Emissions from all sources (manmade), mobiles, TVs etc
- Ring main wiring
- Energetic gridlock of the earth grids

Geopathic stress has a very real and recognised effect on human health. A lot of research has been done around this in some countries and in others (including Britain) there is little to no awareness of it in medical circles at all! In its milder form problems can include:

- Poor or disturbed sleep
- General fatigue and lethargy
- Headaches
- Irritability
- Illness ranging from reoccurring cold and infections and generally feeling life is an uphill struggle
- Nightmares
- If sitting on Geopathic stress, it may be difficult to concentrate or promote sleepiness.

Stronger Geopathic Stress has been implicated in some of the serious metabolic diseases:

- Cancers
- ME
- Wasting diseases (ie. MS, Parkinson's)
- Migraines
- Mental disorders (addictions, suicides, depressions)
- Infertility and repeated miscarriages
- Bowel disorders (IBS, Chrons)
- SIDs (cot death).

Babies and young children will often unconsciously move away from a source of geopathic stress – there may be an area of a room they won't use, or you may find them scrunched up in an awkward position in the bed or cot.

Another clue can be your pets – dogs will not lie in areas of geopathic stress, but will zero in on areas of good energy like a magnet! Cats on the other hand seem to be unconcerned by geopathic stress to the extent that their favourite place might often be on a line of geopathic stress.

Our farming ancestors were very aware of the effects of geopathic stress in the landscape on both their crops and animals. They worked to eliminate it wherever possible with the careful placement of standing stones, or even stone circles. Nowadays, you are more likely to find a farmer who will move these out of his fields, considering them to be a nuisance, as he has lost this level of connection to the land and the understanding of what these stones purpose was.

This loss of knowledge is fairly recent as I remember a conversation with a friend whose grandfather was a farmer, and how he used to be taken out into the field by his grandfather who would point out the directions of energy flow, and told how you should never plant a crop against or across a line of energy as it would not thrive!

How badly you are affected depends upon the strength of the geopathic stress, the exposure you have to it and your individual constitution. It is an ongoing stress on the body and the immune system and the weaker your constitution the more likely you are to feel affects quickly.

Geopathic stress has a physiological impact on the body, and because of this the best means of detection is ….. the human body! Dowsing has been practiced for over 4,000 years and is an ideal means of detecting harmful earth energies.

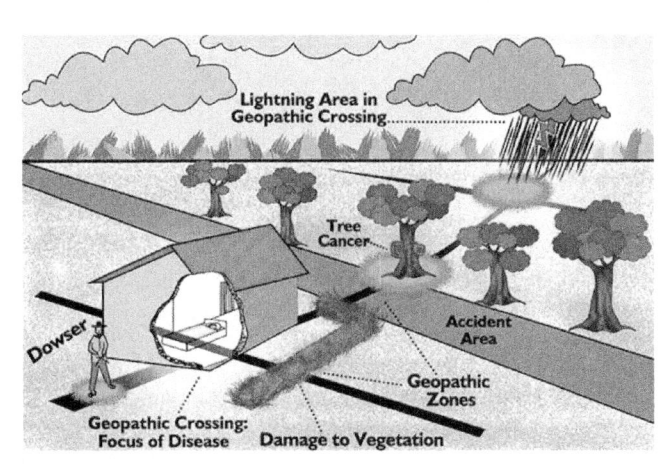

There are various ways to treat geopathic stress, depending upon where it is and the strength of it. Usually this cures it once and for all, but in certain instances it may reappear for a variety of reasons, not least of which is further disruption nearby.

There are geomancers and geobiologists who specialise in clearing and re-balancing areas of geopathic stress, and will check out and clear where you live. If you have the slightest worry that this might be affecting you it is well worth employing their services and getting it checked out.

I can speak from personal experience on this as my first introduction to geopathic stress came when I moved into a house which had a large, stagnant and blocked energy line running through the middle. Life was a struggle, nothing seemed to work and trying to make something happen was like pushing water up hill. When the line was cleared and got moving again life immediately seemed to shift into a different gear and hum along nicely…..

NOTE:
NEVER attempt to treat geopathic stress yourself as you may make matters worse – call in an expert!

Sacred Sites

Around the world geomancers have found the sacred sites of old temples, or religious meeting places are hotspots for earth energies – or rather, it is clear that our ancestors were fully aware of the various earth energies and their properties and harnessed them to great effect wherever they could.

It is also clear that many, if not all, of the structures used are not just placed on telluric currents - earth energy lines and nodes - but are constructed in such a way as to amplify the energy there.

It is also evident that the builders of these temples and structures incorporated certain details into what they build to harness certain energies – for example in stone circles there are entrance stones which channel the energy lines into the circle, and often lines are 'held' by prominent stones – tall thin ones for a male current, more rounded ones for a female current.

And it wasn't just our far ancestors who were tuned in at this level. Churches were either built over existing sacred sites, where this energy had been harnessed, or other sites where currents cross and node were found and the Church placed there.

The same is true for great medieval cathedrals built by Master Masons. Clues are to be found throughout the building for those who know what to look for as to the path of the male and female energy current, often with their nodal point being marked in some way.

So why go to all this trouble?

Our ancestors knew what we have forgotten. Not only are these energy centres places that can help us heal at a physical and emotional level, they can help us balance our spirit, and the more powerful they are the more they enable to commune with Source Energy and reach higher states of consciousness.

A group of monks chanting certain tones in these places could have an amazing impact on those present!

These currents and nodes have a direct effect on the physiology of our body. The electromagnetism of these lines affects the iron in our blood, the magnetite present in our skulls and can help us to access altered states.

Exploring these sites makes us question why they were made and marvel at the ability of those we consider vastly inferior to ourselves to produce wonderful monuments we would struggle to achieve today. Above all they make us ask ourselves 'What are we missing? What have we lost?'

The metaphysical world was far more real and immediate in humanity's past than it is today. With the cosmic energetic changes the planet is being exposed to at this current moment in time, many people are becoming more and more aware of what we seem to have been asleep to for hundreds of years.

Maybe one of the purposes of these sites was to keep just enough of us connected and aware, so with the help of the cosmic energies now flooding the Earth we can guide humanity into a new, more enlightened future once more!

Pilgrimage

Pilgrimage is defined as a meaningful journey to a sacred place and according to some commentators was once Britain's most popular expression of leisure and spirituality!!

You didn't go to the sea-side, you went on pilgrimage, whether you were a King or a commoner. It was just a question of whether you went on foot, horse-back, or part of a rich retinue.

Pilgrimage is still carried out today, very often for non-religious purposes. People will walk old pilgrimage routes in order to escape the everyday busyness of their lives, the pilgrimage offering an escape into a gentle rhythm of walking and quiet reflection.

Not only is this an adventure and an opportunity to meet new people, it is an escape from 'doing' into 'being'.

There is another aspect of pilgrimage though that many are unaware of – and that is as a simple, but effective, method of earth healing.

Just as the Aboriginals in Australia walk their 'song lines' in order to tune in to needs of their land, so walking or travelling along lines of energy in the land can help to enhance the flow of energy and bring greater healing and balance to the whole length of the line as well as the surrounding environment.

Undertaking a geomantic pilgrimage can be as simple as following an old pilgrimage route, or following an energy line across the land. You may find yourself drawn to certain areas, or offering healing energies and prayers in certain places, but whatever happens you will find yourself mentally and emotionally in a much better place because of your interaction with the land.

There is an old saying – that every pilgrim leaves a footprint of light that others might follow. As you walk the land, reconnecting to it and the energies of nature, it is a reciprocal relationship – as you are healed, so you too can offer healing to the land.

Elementals,

Most people who are deeply connected to nature, have some level of higher sense perception or 'psychic' abilities and have expanded their senses in such a way that they can tune into and even 'see' beyond the very limited levels of vision we are all channelled into as we grow up!

There are many beings who exist just outside our range of perception. Many of them are benevolent, some are not, but just because our limited human eyesight can't 'see' them doesn't mean to say they don't exist. They exist in a dimension and resonate at a frequency outside the standard bandwidth of normal human vision.

There is often a lot of confusion around the difference between elementals, nature spirits and faeries, so let's look at a very basic understanding of who they are and what they do.

As the name suggests the Elementals represent the forces of Nature and are beings who work with the four elements – air, fire, water, earth.

Elementals work at the junction between spirit and matter and each works with its specific element enabling the assemblage, cohesion and animation of physical matter on Earth. They permeate all matter and are the building blocks of nature.

All four elements are found in the material realm, as they sustain and create all matter. Indeed they enable the processes by which carbon matter manifests in this realm.

The different elementals interweave together to create all life and nothing would live if they did not – including us!

The interference of

intruder races in the Earth grids and their anti-human activities with regards to our planet have caused a lot of damage within the elemental realms – just think of what chem-trails alone have done! – but there is much support and help for the elementals at this time in the healing and rehabilitation processes.

Air Elementals

Elementals of the air are called Sylphs. Sylphs are the light-bearers in the etheric body of the planet and carry the light ether through the element of air and bring it into nature. They are highly sensitive to planetary alignments and information radiating from the sun.

Sylphs are enchanted into all forms of gas that are part of our earthly realm and are present in every breath of wind whether it be hurricane or breeze. They are also present in all forms of life energy, prana, chi or whatever else it may be called.

We interact constantly with air elementals in every breath we take even though we are largely unaware of it. They are also linked to the mental realm, the realm of thoughts, inspiration, intuition, dreams and ideas.

Water Elementals

Water elementals are called Undines. Undines exist in the flowing, moist, watery elements of the earth. They carry responsibility for the chemical ether within the Earth's etheric body. They have been described as dreaming 'the combining and separating of substances', as well as being the chemists of plant life and are continually binding and releasing themselves into the fluid element.

They can be found wherever there is a natural source of water – clouds, droplets of water, oceans, rivers, dew and mist.

They have a receptive nature and are responsive to waves of emotions as they surge through our body. They help maintain the astral body of humans and help awaken our feeling nature.

Earth Elementals

Otherwise called Gnomes, earth elementals are considered to be Earth's intelligence within physical matter, bearing it through every level of strata of the planet. They are to be found in every solid structure be it rock, building, crystal or plant. They mediate between the soil and plant roots and are considered to be the spiritual midwives of plant reproduction.

They love residing near metals, ores and crystals and permeate everything, every layer of the planet and live within the hollow spaces of planetary matter, the gaps between atoms. They act as a form of glue between spirit and matter, gravity and levity, as they form all the solid structures of the planet.

As they work to maintain the physicality of nature they also help us maintain our physical bodies – its composition, assimilation of minerals and nutrients etc. They also aid our awareness of our physical senses.

Fire Elementals

Fire elementals are called Salamanders and they are considered to be the oldest of all the elementals. Above all they are considered to be beings of transformation and their spiritual substance is the ether of living warmth they bring, and without them there would be no life as no heat would exist. Fire is considered to be a gateway to the spiritual world.

They are found in the flames of any form of fire, but also in the warmth of a summers day and have a luminous quality. They also work with the solar energy and both absorb and manage the vast range of solar data bathing the Earth.

Not only do they vitalise our being, ensuring we live with the warmth they bring, but they also invest every thought we have, bringing it into form. They stimulate the fires of emotional passion and spiritual idealism, and bring the inspiration for change, both destroying and creating. It is a spiritual truth that every thought creates form, and a salamander or fire spirit is enchanted into every thought to enable this to be so.

They work within our physical body to bring healing, aid circulation and maintain body temperature and metabolism.

The Fifth Element

You may also come across the element of Aether, or Quintessence. This is another word for Spirit, or the unified field of consciousness which permeates everything. It is sometimes lumped in with the Elements and

Elementals but in reality is not part of physical matter, although it permeates all of it.

I think the important thing to take away from an understanding of Elementals is that they permeate everything. The elements earth, air, fire and water are the building blocks of life here on Planet Earth, and these wonderful, hard-working beings are woven into all of our visible creation!

Devas, Nature Spirits and Faeries

The terms Devas, Nature Spirits and Faeries are often used interchangeably by those who have probably never stopped to questions the different role each have to play.

Nature Spirits

If the elementals are the building blocks of the world around us the Nature Spirits are Earth's building and maintenance team. Everything that has a consciousness which is unique to itself – just as each human being has their individual consciousness. And each species also has a collective consciousness – the collective consciousness of trees for example, or of humanity.

Nature spirits are everywhere, every plant, flower, tree and blade of grass has a nature spirit that can be communed with, communicated with. And they work alongside all the elementals who permeate every plant etc in order to nurture and care for it.

Devas

Each distinct place will also have an over-lighting being which we often called the genus locii, or a protective spirit of place. These are the devas, which are sometimes called landscape angels. They can go from small scale – a deva of your garden for example, to over-seeing large areas – a landscape temple (chakra-system in the landscape) or even a country. Each country has its own guiding and protecting intelligence.

Tuning into the your garden deva and asking it what is needed or it requires you to do is a simple courtesy, as is telling it what plans you have and why you may be undertaking tasks such as cutting things down or moving plants. It will help things at the energetic level settle down and thrive. And don't forget to listen – if it is resistant to something, find out why and see what kind of a compromise can be reached. Remember this is a relationship, not a dictatorship!

If you are in a new build home a deva for your garden might not have emerged yet. Particularly if build on land which has been meadow for many years. We don't live in a Society where the deva of the meadow is contacted and thanked for their guardianship of the meadow and told that this will no longer be necessary, and the new devas called in for each of the different plots, so the energetic template underlying a new housing estate can be resistant to what is being done. So you might want to consider doing this for yourself.

At the time of writing this I, for example, live in a house which is only 20 years old, and was built with one other on a meadow in a small rural community. The garden runs down to a brook (which has its own guardian) but was clearly still trying to be meadowland, and resisting the efforts of the previous owner to cultivate it to domestic garden. It had obviously become very hard work! Meadow weeds dominated the garden and brambles were everywhere.

I introduced myself to the local deva and explained that the meadow was no longer a meadow, but two garden plots, which needed their own genus locii, and the requirements I had for the garden, and why I wanted or needed to utilise the space in this way and although it initially required a lot of cutting and clearing of undergrowth energetically things started to flow as we both worked together to achieve the greater vision for the garden.

The garden deva also keeps a level of protection around the garden, letting me know if anything harmful was penetrating the boundaries, and generally helping to maintain balance and keep things harmonious. As a result the garden is full of birds and wildlife as they responded to the energetic qualities that the partnership of myself and the deva were creating.

Individual nature spirits and myself come into communication when I am planting or moving things – talking to your plants works! What are you doing? Why? What do they need? As you tend and care for the space, dialogue with the nature spirits as they do the same and work together.

This is an old skill that most have lost. Having green fingers relates to this partnership of man and land spirits working together. What has become really clear to me is that the nature beings WANT to work with us, and despair at the wanton and unnecessary destruction promulgated by so many, completely unaware of what they are doing.

Learning to come into resonance with all the different aspects and levels of nature in order to open up a dialogue with it is a basic shamanic technique that is quite simple to learn and just requires patience and application.

Faeries

Faeries are their own distinct group of beings, which are very much a part of Nature but do not have the same role as nature spirits. You could say they inhabit a different level of the hierarchy.

There is a bewildering array of faeries, and one thing most who are in contact with them say is that Faerie is a law unto itself – it does not follow human codes and ways of being.

That is not to say Faerie is against humans – many faeries welcome contact with humans. Some do not. And to think of them as the tiny, childlike, gossamer winged sprites of children's fiction is to do them a disservice. They are much more complex – and interesting – than this!

Elves, pixies, leprechauns, goblins, spriggans, sprites, brownies, kelpies, dwarfs, phookas – the list goes on and on. For those wanting a flavour of the many types and appearances I can do no better than refer you to the books and paintings of Brian Froud.

Faeries can be large groups or 'courts' – often living in hollow hills – small family groups and even solitary individual faeries. It is said that thorn trees growing on a hill was a good indication that faeries lived there!

There is a hierarchy within the Faerie realm, and their aristocracy are called either the Trooping or Heroic Faeries. These are organised into two courts – the Seelie and Unseelie Court. There is a perception that the Seelie Court is the 'good' faeries and the Unseelie Court the 'evil' faeries, but this could well be a Christian overlay.

There are many, many stories and legends concerning the faeries. They are implacable enemies if you upset them or invade their habitat uninvited. If you are invited be cautious and whatever you do never accept food or drink. Be polite, but decline. Be wary also of kissing a faery on the lips. Even should you return to the surface world, a piece of your soul may remain behind!

And faery time works differently to time in this world. A few weeks in Faerie can be several hundred years in ours.

The Fae

Many of you may also refer to faeries as the Fae. This is not really correct. In the Grail Wisdom the Fae are understood to be one of the Grail bloodlines, one which all but disappeared from the planet at a time where they were being hunted down mercilessly.

In Irish lore they are immortalised as the Tuatha de Danann and are said to have retired to the 'hollow hills' (another dimension maybe?), and it is known that the last throw of the dice to keep the Grail teachings fully in public awareness, undertaken by a figure captured in myth and legend – and the Grail stories – as King Arthur was of the Pendragon bloodline, which was a Fae lineage.

Legend surrounding Guinevere, Arthur's heirogamic partner and queen, also speaks clearly to her Fae Grail lineage, as well as to the trickery that was enacted around her to break apart her union with Arthur. Arthur's mission, to re-establish the Grail and Law of One teachings was largely a failure due to this sabotage and Earth (and humans) fell into a very dark time, from which we are still struggling to emerge.

Some of the Starseeds from a system called Eridanus who are incarnating here on the Earth at this time to be part of the 'boots-on-the-ground' lightworkers would also appear to have a connection into the ancient Fae bloodlines.

Gwion Bach & the Ceridwen Mysteries

I want to give you a flavou of some of what can be found in the old myths and stories. This is a myth from Welsh lore that gives us a glimpse of an initiatory process, into the mysteries of the elements, being told in a story. Those who had been taught the inner mysteries would be aware of what it alluded to. To everyone else it is just a story.

Long ago, there lived a powerful goddess called Ceridwen. She had two children – a son Afagddu or Utter Darkness and a daughter Crearwy.

Her daughter, Crearwy, was beautiful and clever, but her son was ugly and stupid and shunned by all. Ceridwen decided to create a potion to make him wise. This potion took a year and a day to make, with different herbs which had to placed in the cauldron in different seasons.

For a year Ceridwen gathered the herbs and brewed her potion. A blind man, Morda, tended the fire beneath it to ensure it didn't go out, and Ceridwen found a poor boy called Gwion Bach, to stir the potion continuously.

According to legend the first three drops of this potion conveyed wisdom, the remainder was poison.

As the potion neared completion Gwion Bach stirred the cauldron. As it bubbled over the fire three drops sprang up and fell onto Gwion's hand, burning him. He instinctively put his hand to his mouth and ingested the drops.

Immediately he became wise, gaining great knowledge and magical wisdom.

And he knew that the goddess, Ceridwen, would not forgive him for taking the potion destined for her son….

He began to flee, turning himself into a hare to run faster.

And as this happened the cauldron cracked and the poisonous liquid left behind began to leak onto the land, devastating it.

Ceridwen returned and seeing what has happened looked around for Gwion Bach, and using her mystical vision sees him in the distance as a hare. Immediately she turns herself into a greyhound and gives chase.

As she begins to catch up with Gwion Bach, in fear he leapt into a river, turning himself into a salmon as he did so. Ceridwen followed him, turning into an otter.

Just as she is about to catch him, he leapt from the water and became a bird and flew up and away as fast as he can.

Ceridwen followed, becoming a hawk and pursued him fiercely.

Tiring and frightened Gwion sees below him a huge pile of grain on a thresing floor and diving towards it became a piece of grain, hiding in the pile.

Ceridwen turned herself into a hen, and piece by piece pecked up all the grain. And that, you might think, was the end of Gwion Bach.

But no! the grain that was Gwion Bach had taken root in Ceridwen's belly and she found herself pregnant.

Nine months later she gives birth to Gwion and has planned to finally kill him. But once she sets eyes on the babe she sees a child so beautiful, and so full of light, who shone like the sun that she is unable to bring herself to do this.

Instead she set him in a leather bag and casts him out to sea, where the tides washes the bag into a river mouth and onto a weir, where it is found by Prince Elphin who is blinded by the light radiating from his brow and cries out Taliesin! Meaning 'how radiant is his brow!'.

And thus was born Taliesin, a great poet, prophet and wise man who is the most famous bard in all of British history.

When you look more closely at this story you see it is a teaching tale of initiation into the elements as a journey back to Source.

We have the time of preparation as Gwion stirs the cauldron....

Then he experiences first earth (hare), water (salmon), air (bird) and then fire (grain) before being swallowed (sacrifice) and gestated to be reborn clothed in the elements as light (quintessence) in the form of Taliesin.

There are other deeper levels of teaching also that can be found here. Many stories were layered in this way.

Cycles and Rhythms

I want to touch on another aspect of Earth Wisdom which is the understanding of her cycles and rhythms.

I am not going to going to much detail here as my booklet *The Wheel of Life – Geometry of Time and Space* goes into more detail on this aspect.

However, our lives are defined by a series of cycles and rhythms many of these set by nature or even great cosmic cycles and not only is this an important way of reconnecting into nature and the cycles that define our lives, but it speaks to one of the ancient and universal archetypes – that of the Wheel of Life.

We are all aware of time cycles such as that of 24 hours to a day, 60 minutes to an hour etc. These are clearly man-made cycles that fit within the natural cycle of day and night. Then of course we have months and years, or nature cycles such as the seasons, the definition of solar cycles here on earth with the solstices and equinoxes and also lunar cycles with the waxing and waning of the moon.

I'm going to touch on just a few here, but if you look there are many, many more playing out at every level of our lives, some of them manmade such as our clock-based cycles, but many of them natural.

Solar Festivals

The Solar Festivals celebrate the rhythm of the sun's rise and fall each year and is based on the cross points of the solstices and equinoxes which shape the cycle of the year.

Annually the earth makes one great circle around the sun – this is a solar cycle - and within this cycle are eight specific points which mark the changing aspects of the seasons. The solstices and equinoxes mark the mid-point of each season, whilst what are called the cross quarter days are the gateways into each season.

Our forebears saw these as important power points within the year and marked them usually with celebration and feasting. The Christian church then went on to 'take over' these pagan festivals and they became festivals within the Church calendar, disconnecting them – and us – from the nature cycles they intrinsically are.

Marking these in a way that is meaningful to you can be a lovely way of reconnecting into this ancient rhythm once more.

Some form of fire, be it in a fireplace or firepit, a candle or bonfire is at the centre of any celebration as a reminder that it is a solar cycle that is being recognised.

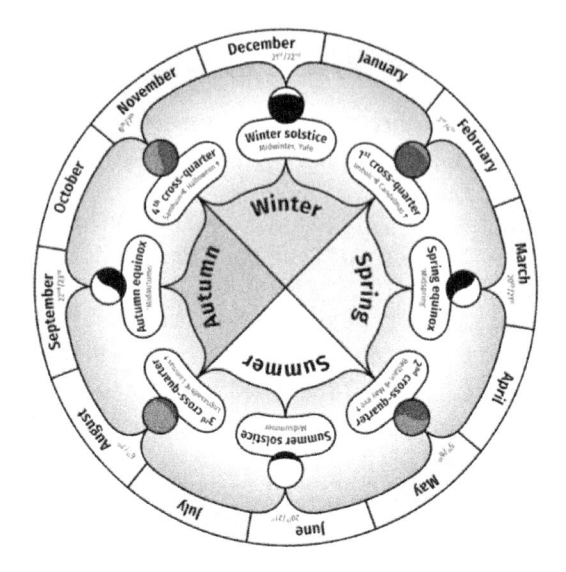

Lunar Cycles

Lunar cycles are marked by the phases of the moon. During a (solar) year there are 13 moon cycles and our ancestors were very much in tune with the waxing and waning of the moon as it influenced almost every area of their (and our!) lives – from hair cutting to crop planting and herb gathering.

There is a lot of Moon lore held by tribes, indigenous cultures and even in the old wives tales of our own. When the Roman Church took control of our lives here in the West we lost access to so much old wisdom, but it is gradually being re-discovered and remembered and usually, when subjected to scientific testing is found to have validity.

We are all familiar with the cycles of the moon, from New to Full and back to New moon approximately every 28 days or so. We have dropped the linkage between our months of the year to the moon in favour of having 12 months only, which has necessitated some jiggery pokery with the number of days in each month to make it work. Incidentally 12 is considered a masculine number, whilst 13 is feminine. Did this have anything to do with it?

The effect of the moon on Planet Earth and all of her inhabitants is all pervasive – from holding the planetary axial tilt in place to the effect of planting of crops, the potency of herbs gathered during different phases, how easily we detoxify and even the efficiency of healing from surgery or trauma at different phases.

It is astonishing in just how many ways the Moon affects us daily in our lives, and well worth looking into further. There are some excellent books available such as *Moontime* and various books that take you through the process of gardening according to moon phases. There are even some farmers who quietly pay attention to this – because they find it increases crop yields.

Food for thought!

Part 3
The Grail and the Home Domain

The Grail of the Home Domain

Our home should be our Sanctuary. It is where we go to relax, recharge, feel safe and where we are most likely to feel we can be who we are – no facades, pretences or Oscar-winning acting efforts required!

So it is important that we ensure that our home environment nurtures and sustains us to the best possible degree. It is the chalice within which our physical body resides and our mental and emotional well-being should thrive.

And yet, all too often, for many of us our homes might be making us sick – or at least not supporting our health and overall well-being. In this section we are going to look at some of the many ways our home environment does NOT support and enable us to be the best we can.

Again, it is very much about energy and how it flows and moves, or not, in some form or another. The more we understand the many ways in which energy works, how it becomes disharmonious, what we can do to increase levels of beneficial energy, how things interact with our own personal energy fields and how we can measure our own response to this, the more we can manage our environment to become a field which sustains us and contributes to our optimal well-being, supporting our consciousness at every level to expand and evolve.

It is not something that should be left to chance.

First and foremost is the understanding that every home has its own spirit or guardian energy. At an energetic level when a home is created, it creates an energetic blueprint and an energetic being inhabits that blueprint. We might call it an angel, or the Spirit of the Home, or whatever term you might prefer, but in an ideal world we would all connect to, introduce ourselves to and ask assistance from this being as both a courtesy and a way of ensuring that we don't bring disharmony into the space.

The only time you might not find this being there to connect to is with a new home – housebuilders to the best of my knowledge don't do any ritual of consecration of a new home, calling in a guardian energy, so you might have to do this yourself.

New housing estates are usually built on fields and meadows, and the land can be traumatised by the process and also unaware that in the human world its future has been divided into small plots rather than the whole it was, so a conversation at this level can be helpful and ensure energetically things fall into place. The same is true for gardens – you might have to invoke a deva into your plot, explain the land is no longer a meadow, show them the boundaries and ask them to look after and nurture the space with you!

In the following pages not only are many of the things we are going to look at harmful to us, some are downright dangerous and therefore if we are to create a safe, harmonious and secure home environment that nurtures and sustains us both energetically and physically we must be aware of them.

It is up to each of us to be wise and informed in the choices we make within our intimate environment. In an ideal world Government agencies would do the job we think we are paying them to do, to ensure materials and substances are safe and not damaging to us in any way. But this is not what is happening, the interests of big business always seems to trump health and safety for the individual.

For example, statistics tell us that over 80% of the physical toxicity we are exposed to each day comes from our home environment.

80%!!!!

There is clearly a lot of room for improvement…..

Sick Building Syndrome

We are going to start with something some of you will have heard of - sick building syndrome. This is recognised particularly in relation to big office blocks, but most who work within them are blissfully unaware of what this is.

And how many of you have considered that your home environment might also come under this heading?

So what is sick building syndrome?

The term relates to various non-specific symptoms that occur in people who work within a building. They experience acute health issues that would appear to be directly related to the time spend in the building in question.

Nothing specific is identifiable. Sometimes it will be limited to a certain area of the building, sometimes to a whole building. Often the symptoms are relieved within a very short time of leaving the building.

Everything that applies to a workplace, potentially applies to our homes. There are heart-breaking stories of people who have had to leave their homes as they just make them ill, or who have been told they have a 'mental illness' because the medical establishment won't recognise or acknowledge their malaise comes from their home environment. And yet it is recognised as a potential workplace problem!

Just one example of the many disconnects in our Society!

For many companies this is becoming a serious issue as levels of absenteeism are high, productivity is low and staff turnover is also high. The company sees a very real cost in terms of its bottom line, and therefore attention is being paid to this, but more important surely is the impact on both the health and the quality of life this has on each of its employees?

A variety of things have been identified as potential, or contributing, causes but as well as the obvious there are several things which are rarely thought of.

But first let's look at some of the symptoms that occur:

Headache	Dizziness
Nausea	Fatigue
Eye, nose or throat irritation	Dry cough
Dry or itching skin	Allergies
Cold or flu-like symptoms	Hoarse voice
Personality changes	Asthma attacks
Concentration problems	Sore eyes
Chest complaints	Skin rashes

Some of the possible causes include:

Chemical Contaminants
When it comes from outdoor sources such as air pollution entering through air intake vents it is difficult to do much about – although good filters on air intake vents can be a big help. The indoor sources are usually the bigger issues.

The most common contaminant are VOCs or volatile organic compounds which are difficult to avoid. They are found in paint, adhesives, soft furnishing, carpets, manufactured wood products, cleaning agents, pesticides, printers to name just a few. Offices are full of these things...but more to the point, so are our homes!

Other problems can be tobacco smoke, synthetic fragrances, and 'respirable particulate matter'.

Biological Contaminants
These include mould, fungus, pollen, bacteria and viruses and insect and bird droppings. Airborne diseases can be spread very quickly through offices by air-conditioning and heating systems.

Mould can be a serious problem, although this is often more likely in poorly heated and ventilated homes and have an extremely detrimental effect on health. Living in a damp

CENTRAL NERVOUS SYSTEM SYMPTOMS:
Headaches, fatigue, difficulty concentrating, lethargy
Skin itching and irritation
Diarrhoea

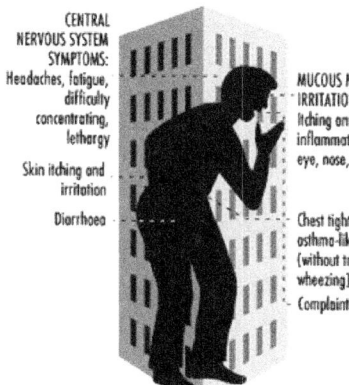

MUCOUS MEMBRANE IRRITATION:
Itching and inflammation of the eye, nose, and throat

Chest tightness and asthma-like symptoms (without true wheezing)
Complaints of odours

climate does not help in this regard.

Poor Ventilation
The ever increasing cost of heating has led to buildings being made more and more airtight, and ventilation levels being reduced, and as a consequence fresh air (such as it is!) is at a premium and indoor air pollution is on the rise.

As is so often the case, building controls and standards are established with cost in mind, rather than the well-being of the human inhabitants.

Electromagnetic Radiation
This covers a whole host of things that weren't on anybody's agenda a couple of hundred years ago. Electricity circuits are just the start of this one. Then we have computers, televisions etc emitting radiation, microwaves from not just microwave ovens, but also from cordless phones, mobiles phones etc. We shall look at this kind of technostress in more detail shortly.

Suffice it to say that we currently live and work in a sea of unseen energies that can affect our immune systems directly.

Poor Lighting
And by that I don't just mean poor light levels, or the absence of sunlight, but exposure to such things as fluorescent lighting as well as too much exposure to artificial lighting. It has been shown that limiting our time under artificial lighting is vital to good health as it messes around with our body's circadian rhythms. The rising and setting of the sun influences every cell in our body – it is part of our neurobiology – but the advent of the electric light bulb changed our relationship with light and we are just beginning to realise the potentially profound effect this has on human health.

One of the things you don't see listed is Geopathic Stress. We touched on this in the previous section and talked about *what* it is, so here we are going to look at *how* it affects our health, as this imbalance in earth energies can cause life-threatening illnesses and can be dealt with, or at least mitigated, by experts who know what they are doing.

So many of the problems with 'sick buildings' are really caused by poor building practice and lack of attention in the design and choice of building materials to what it is that makes humans thrive.

For example it has been shown:

- ✓ That workers have 25% better memory function when they have views from their building
- ✓ There is a 10% overall performance amongst pupils in schools where there are good levels of daylight, as well as 20% faster progression in maths and 26% faster progression in reading skills!
- ✓ Office plants can increase staff productivity by 38%, boost staff well-being by 47% and increase creativity by 45%
- ✓ Offices with fresher air have an 11% productivity gain
- ✓ Offices with good levels of daylight and opening windows have an 18% increase in productivity

Think about how this applies also to our hospitals, and schools as well as our homes…..

None of this is 'news'. Man is a part of nature and deeply connected into her cycles and rhythms. Modern workplaces (and homes) often ignore this fact and then wonder why there is a lack of well-being in their workplace!

Sick Building Syndrome can apply as easily to a house as to an office block. New build houses in particular, which tend to be draught proof and air tight, are more likely to be prone to these types of problems due to off-gassing of newly-installed building materials. Sometimes, simply opening a window and airing the house can work wonders!

Geopathic Stress

We looked briefly at what geopathic stress is and the general causes in the previous section. Now I want to look at how it affects us specifically in our homes, as it can be devastating to health here.

Geopathic Stress (GS) can be defined as a disruption to (or distortion of) the Earth's natural energy fields causing harmful radiation to emanate from the Earth's surface.

There are two natural causes – underground streams and geological faults and cavities – and a whole host of man-made causes, including mines and quarries, old battlegrounds, industrial tree felling, railway and road cuttings, major earthworks, steel pylons and even building foundations.

So you can see that the possibility of man-made geopathic stress is HUGE – particularly as very few are looking out for it and trying to re-harmonise what has been made disharmonious!

The Effects of Geopathic Stress on Humans
Humans are bioelectrical beings and the healthy functioning of every cell depends upon these processes.

GS can interfere with this functioning as well as the ability to repair cells, and it can also significantly affect the immune system so that the whole body system weakens and is more prone to illness and disease.

Mild Geopathic Stress – its effects include poor sleep quality, irritability, prone to colds, nagging illnesses, lethargy, tiredness, arguments.

Stronger Geopathic Stress – wasting diseases such as Motor Neurone, Parkinson's, Multiple Sclerosis, mental disorders including addictions, suicides, depression and obsessions, bowel disorders including Chron's and IBS, anxiety, infertility, ME and cot death (SIDS). Research also points to cancers of all types where there is stronger GS.

The following illnesses have all been linked to GS, as a result of the breakdown of body function and immune system damage:

Cancer	Aids	Arthritis	Rheumatism
Asthma	M.E.	Migraines	Insomnia

Stomach disorders	Kidney disorders	Gall stones
TB	Meningitis	Multiple Sclerosis
Heart trouble	Diabetes	Osteoarthritis
Sinus problems	Uterine problems	Adrenal issues
Thrombosis	Eye problems	Ear problems
Inflammation	Varicose Veins	Leukaemia
Nervous disorders	Mental and emotional problems	

There is also strong evidence to link it to depression, suicide, divorce, alcoholism and high blood pressure. Children can be particularly affected and have sleep disturbances and night terrors as well as bed wetting.

It has even been claimed to ruin your sex life! So definitely something to be taken seriously!

The effects on a Human depends upon the strength of the stress, the amount of time exposed to it, and your individual constitution and outlook.

Lines are classified in strength from 1 – 16. Strength 1-2 will cause milder issues, 4+ will cause ME and other chronic diseases with 9+ being implicated in serious disease such as cancers. Most GS lines are in the region of 4 ft (1.2 m) wide.

In countries such as Austria and Germany a huge amount of research has been done into the connection between illness and geopathic stress. In the UK it is considered 'fringe' at best – despite the growing body of evidence!

It is not uncommon in those countries where it is recognised for doctors to call in dowsers when a patient is diagnosed with cancer as it is recognised that treatment outcomes are severely impaired unless the underlying cause is corrected.

The problems with GS were proven as long ago as the early 1930s by Gustav Pohl. In more recent experiments Dr Otto Bergmann (University of Vienna) carried out tests on 985 people, having them sit on geopathic stress for 10 minutes. Thorough tests were done both before and after and the effects on health were noticed within just a few minutes.

'One can image the dire consequences which exposure to geopathic stress over many years could do' wrote Natural Medicine magazine.

A world renowned cancer specialist, Dr Nieper stated '92% of all my cancer patients and 75% of my MS patients are geopathically stressed'.

I could give you many more examples but hopefully you are getting the idea!

Geopathic Stress Clues
There are some things you can look out for that might give you a hint that geopathic stress is an issue.

In your environment you might want to look out for areas where mushrooms, mistletoe, ivy, bindweed, foxgloves, nightshades, medicinal herbs, elder trees, nettles and docks thrive as all these plants love geopathic stress!

Another clue is stunted or twisted growth in trees or plants.

Fruit trees that fail to thrive or fruit.

Animals are generally very good at picking up GS and will avoid it, especially birds. You will never find a dog sleeping on GS - so if your dog avoids an area pay attention! Cats, on the other hand, as well as owls, slugs and snails all love GS!

Accident blackspots can be down to GS, as can sick building syndrome, constant electrical breakdowns, poor neighbourly relations, a quick turnover of businesses in a particular building and lightning strikes.

Earthbound spirits are also more likely to be found on GS lines.

So how do you find it?
The most sophisticated and sensitive instrument for

Tree affected by
Geopathic Stress Zone
Geopathology

finding Geopathic Stress is the human body! Learning to dowse is quite straightforward so once you know what to do and the protocols for finding it the process is quite simple.

Clearing it is really the province of a trained earth energy worker. There are a variety of measures which can be taken. A trained dowser will find and know how to fix the geopathic stress problems that might be affecting the health and well-being of you and your loved ones. Contact your local dowsing society or body to find someone to help you.

If you don't know what you are doing don't mess with it! You could make matters worse….

And bear in mind that new GS can always re-appear if there is building, quarrying, mining work etc on the earth energy line that affects you. So if you know you are living on a line, particularly if there is a crossing node of one or more lines, get it checked regularly!

EMFs & Technopathic Stress

EMF is short for Electro-Magnetic Frequencies, which permeate our environment.

Man himself is an electromagnetic being living with his own individual fields, which is part of the larger whole of the planet, which itself is part of the great fields of the cosmos.

As Dr Patrick MacManaway, a subtle energy practitioner, so beautifully puts it:

'We ourselves are electromagnetic beings, living within our own mini-magnetosphere generated by the spark of our heartbeat, holding within that resonant space all the frequencies of our thoughts and feelings, our metabolism and physiology'

We cannot escape the electro-magnetic field within which we live

' surrounded as we are by the dancing, ever shifting tides in the geo-magnetosphere, played into resonance by the drumming of the solar wind and the long slow music of the spheres.'

We have evolved in harmony with the environment which we are part of, and the range of frequencies within human physiology is a part of who we are.

The electro-magnetic environment has changed considerably however in the last 100 years or so – and the unseen and hidden effect on human physiology is one of the elephants in the room regarding the rapid expansion of technology.

There is a lack of willingness to admit that as electromagnetic beings we are going to be affected, often negatively, by the different range of frequencies that we are now all bathed in daily.

Electricity has only been used domestically for just over 100 years, and only in great quantities since the 1950s. Our bodies are now bombarded with several million times more EMFs than they were 100 years ago – it is madness to think there won't be some consequences to this playing out!

The term coined for this is technopathic stress and particularly refers to the explosion in the last 20 years or so in the levels of pulsed microwave radiation from mobile phones, wireless devices etc

There are well over 10,000 published studies and official reports which suggest that there are measurable biological effects from alternating electric and magnetic fields, and yet they do not seem to be taken into consideration when new technology is rolled out – and this is before you consider that the Government safety levels for exposure were by and large based on 1960s research so bears little relevance to the electromagnetic soup we now find ourselves in!

For example, Prof Ross Adey (Loma Linda University Medical School, California) in 1992 summarized the physiological effects as follows
- compromised immune competence
- production of melotonin and other essential hormones affected
- cell respiration and enzyme production affected
- brain wave rhythms (EEG) and DNA reproduction affected
- effects on foetal development

In 1995 a draft report by an important American Scientific committee was leaked which concluded that millions faced an increased risk of cancer and other degenerative diseases from exposure to fields from power lines and electrical appliances and that mobile phones also give rise to great cause for concern.

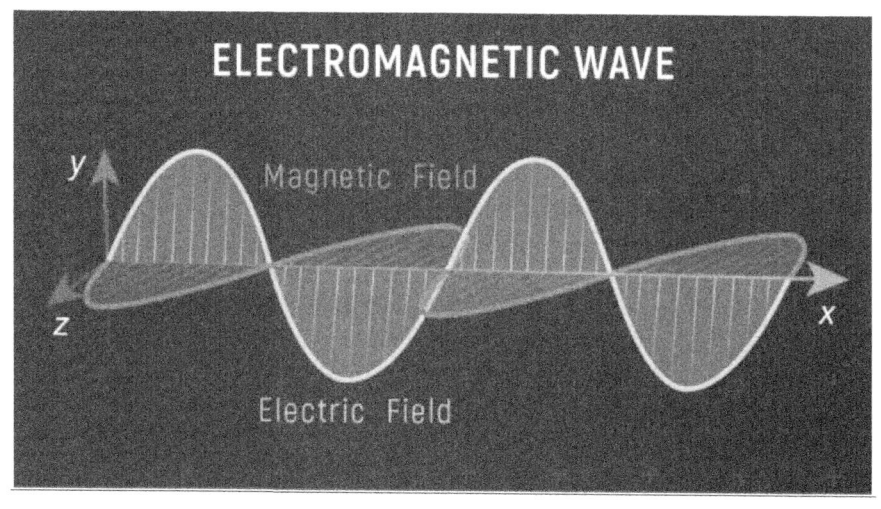

The eminent scientist Dr Roger Coghill of Coghill Research found the

incidence of leukaemia to be 4 times greater when the electric field was 20v per metre (average is 5 v per metre), ME to be 3 times greater and there was also a high correlation with cot death (SIDS).

GP Dr Stephen Parry found links between home exposure to magnetic fields and depressive illness, severe headaches and suicide.

Symptoms include:

> Headaches, insomnia or poor sleep quality, sinus congestion, memory loss, difficulty concentrating, brain fog, skin rashes, ME, irritability, neuralgia, nosebleeds, tinnitus, light sensitivity, MS and even cancer.

Sceptics (and those with a vested interest!) claim that all so-called problems are purely psychological, but more and more studies are beginning to be published which suggest long term exposure to any of these radiations (let alone all of them!) effects the functioning of our immune system, and causes serious health issues.

Some more forward thinking governments are taking preventative action, or advising citizens to limit exposure, but most ignore it. There is big money to be made from selling licences for the continual upgrades of existing technology grids.

Even in the last few weeks the media have reported that a big study on the dangers from this kind of exposure in the United States being undertaken by a Government agency has been cancelled as the results being found were so negative.

Huh!

Results not what you want so you shut down an official study? You can't make this stuff up! What this tells you more than anything is that you cannot trust the official line that this is all safe and hunky dory.

Always, always *DO YOUR OWN INVESTIGATION!*

Exposure - Outside the Home

Power transmission cables – even at ground levels reading can be 50 kV, and directly underneath cables as high as 400kV! Some governments have stopped positioning schools near them.

Electricity sub-stations – the magnetic field can radiate up to ¼ mile from these. Walls and trees between can shield from the electrical field but not the magnetic.

Radio transmitters and radar – potentially a problem, therefore it is wise to read the fields.

Mobile Phone Masts – maximum fields at ground level usually occur between 30 and 150 m from the mast.

Railway lines – cancer clusters are common near electrified railway lines

Digital mobile phones – when transmitting they pump out between 900 – 1800 megahertz

Exposure - Inside the Home

Mains supply - frequencies normally in 5-60 Hz range. Fuse boxes give off high fields, do not sit, sleep or work next to this.

Smart Meters – quite simply, don't have your meter changed for one of these. If it is too late and you already have one be aware there is huge controversy regarding their safety, their effectiveness and longevity. Claims that they reduce electricity bills are false and those already sensitive to technology could find this tips their health over the edge.

Light switches and wiring – ideally should be in earthed metal conduits although this rarely happens.

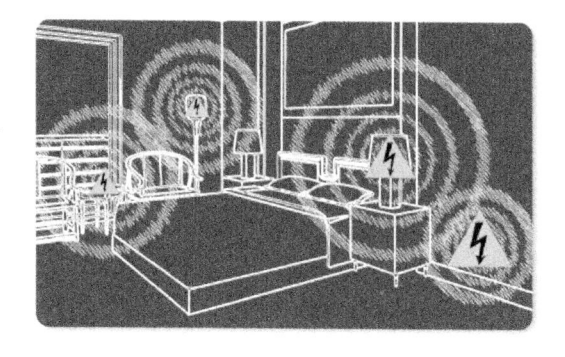

Power sockets and

extension cables – power sockets always give off high electric fields as do extension cables.

Electrical equipment - ie. electric blankets, bedside lamps, clock radios, mains adapters, microwave ovens, Baby monitors, burglar alarms, games consoles, induction hobs, etc. Our homes are now full of gadgets. Many of these now use wi-fi or microwave technology to make then wireless.

DECT cordless phones – transmit high levels of microwave radiation even when not in use. Often the greatest level of EMF exposure in a house!

Digital mobile phones – high fields when in use and even when only switched on emits 2 megahertz(2 million hertz).

Computers and televisions – keep laptops off your lap, sit as far back from computer as practical.

Microwave ovens – ideally don't have a microwave – safer for you and your food! – but if you must don't stand anywhere near it. All microwaves 'leak' to some degree. Think about leaving the kitchen entirely when in use – particularly children!

Electric Cookers – gives off high electric fields when operating. Don't stand near whilst in use.

Magnetic Induction Hobs – give off high EMFs, not recommended.

Storage heaters – these have a high magnetic field when charging. Ensure always at least a metre away from beds.

Bluetooth and 'wearable' tech – now forms part of many tech gadgets. Claims that it is safer than standard wi-fi are not based on facts – in reality there has been almost no research done on safety! You will however find plenty of anecdotal tales of harm from high blue-tooth usage individuals.

Microwave smog from neighbours - most of us can pick up at least one, if not more, neighbours wi-fi and DECT signals. Most likely to be a problem if you live in a flat, terraced house or tightly packed housing estate.

Dirty Electricity
This is a term applied to higher-frequency interference which is carried on

mains wiring, with the levels of frequency involved typically lying between power-level EMFs and microwave bands. The alternating current carrying the electricity becomes distorted and can exacerbate any electro-sensitive problems individuals are experiencing.

Meters to monitor, and filters to clean the main supply are available to fit.

Measuring EMF and Microwave Exposure

These fields can be measured in your home using an EMF meter or a microwave meter. The evidence suggests that a safe threshold is 5 v/m for electric fields and 50 nanotesla for magnetic.

These meters can certainly be bought online, or some places will rent you one. It is an eye-opening exercise to take meter readings around your home and see just how high some of the fields are. Particular note should be taken of your bed's readings, especially on the pillow, and where you sit and/or work most of the time.

Solutions

Man is an inventive creature, and as a result there are solutions to many of the problems that are found in the modern home. Beyond 'prudent avoidance' they include:

- manually switching off circuits
- installing demand switches
- installing shielded cables
- EMF blankets
- Microshield protection case for mobile phones
- ECOS paints
- Microwave netting

- Non-measurable devices such as essences, crystals, RadiTech, monstrosos cacti etc.

I give some more information in Appendix 2 but for more information on what these are, where to find them and how to use them, either go online or read books such as *Technopathic Stress, Killing Fields in the Home* or *Safe as Houses*? (see Further Reading)

Toxicity in the Home

Back to earth with a bump now as we look at some tangible aspects of things that can affect us in the home.

As I have already mentioned a shocking 80% of the toxicity we are exposed to comes from within the home environment. Far from being a safe sanctuary, it can be a health nightmare if you do not get up to speed about the many forms of pollution you can be exposed to within the modern dwelling.

There is hidden danger in the everyday things around you.

Are you aware of them? Do you know how to avoid unnecessary exposure and protect your health?

The next few pages are far from comprehensive, but we are going to look at some of the worst offenders, and some of the simple things you can do to duck this particular missile....

When we talk about toxicity in the home we are primarily talking about our exposure to chemicals.

How many of us think as we go through our morning routines of the dangerous chemicals we are routinely exposing ourselves to? Not many of us, I'm sure as we have tucked away at the back of our mind the 'fact' that our government wouldn't let harmful things be sold to us – there are laws to prevent this aren't there?

And yet....it is clear that something isn't working. There are over 84,000 chemicals in everyday use that we are potentially exposed to on a daily basis and yet the number that have been robustly tested for 'consumer safety' only numbers in the low hundreds.

Why? Because the number of different chemicals being produced is too huge, and the lobbying power of the chemical industry too strong, for consumer safety to be the first priority. Things tend to work on a 'we'll sort things out if there seems to be a problem' approach. They are considered safe until they are shown not to be!

And the guinea pig is.....You!!!!

We all know that certain chemicals are immediately toxic to the human body and would not willingly swallow or exposure ourselves to them, right? But what many people are unaware of is that low levels of toxicity can build to cause long term problems.

VOCs

Your carpets and the paint on your walls are just two of the things which are likely to be oozing what are called VOCs or volatile organic compounds, which are emitted as gases from both solids (such as chipboard furniture) and liquids (such as cleaning fluids) into your home. They are recognised as potential health hazards, affecting both short and long term health.

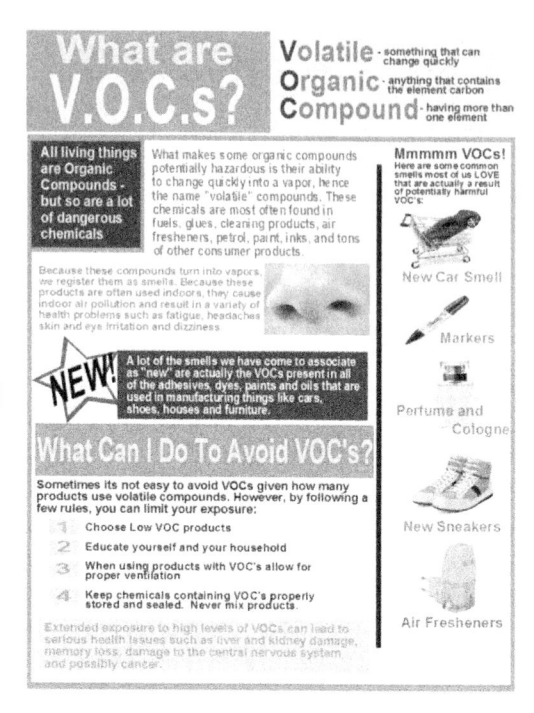

Thousands of products emit VOCs, and the levels of these compounds in the home is consistently found to be 10 times higher than outdoors. And if your home lacks good ventilation then levels risk being even higher as they can build up unchecked.

Fire retardant finishes on soft furnishings, carpets etc are another source. They emit, amongst other things, bromide gases, which affect the ability of the thyroid gland to utilise iodine. Most of us are walking around with quite high levels of bromide in the body.

Natural fibres should be your first choice. Synthetics, although usually cheaper, are a potential health hazard and the various finishes you can find on fabrics, including stain resistance etc all carry health consequences.

Household Cleaning

From there we can move to household cleaning and laundry detergents – it has been found in various studies that women who work primarily in the home, and therefore spend more time cleaning than those in the workplace, routinely carry much higher chemical loads in their body from their increased exposure to these chemicals. The same is true for people who work as cleaners. Who would have thought cleaning a house could be so hazardous? So look for the more ecologically friendly alternatives in your choice of cleaning and laundry products…

Personal Care Products

Personal care products such as toiletries are another huge source of pollution, and often not thought of, yet the majority of the toiletries you have been using since you were a tiny tot contain a cocktail of nasties.

The skin is a huge sponge, so much of this cocktail ends up **inside** you! Up to 500 dangerous man-made chemicals have been found to be present in a single fat cell (a single fat cell from an Egyptian mummy was found to contain none by comparison)! Every day you are unknowingly and unwillingly exposing your body to this toxic overload and little by little it begins to tell on your health.

Consider also that this cocktail of chemicals – and every women (and man) using standard personal care items daily applies over 170 of them! – have never been tested *in combination*. So on its own something might be ok (or more likely not!), but when it mixes with a chemical from a different product it causes a negative reaction.

And when you've been using it every day for years….well who knows? Certainly not the Government regulators!

Food

Think next of the food you eat, sprayed with pesticides and insecticides. It is estimated that if you eat a non-organic diet you will consume about 150 mcg of pesticides **a day**! Think of those luscious strawberries we so love – grown using methyl bromide, a category 1 acute toxin! And then there's the monosodium glutamate, aspartame, saccharin, growth hormones, colourants and additives, and let's not forget genetically modified foods, and irradiated foods, and foods high in levels of cancer-causing glyphosate…..

It goes on, and on, and on. None of us are free of toxins in our body, because even the best diet now can't avoid some level of exposure.

Mould

Mould and other fungal toxins can be devastating to health. It is estimated one in three people have an allergic reaction to either mycotoxins or other moulds found in homes. Damp areas in the home are always a potential problem for this – try to dry things outside or keep humidity levels down – but also consider how easily the spores get into the atmosphere and can move through the home in air conditioning and heating ducts.

Plastics

Plastic is found in use in every area of the home and garden now, from food packaging to vinyl flooring, children's toys, storage containers, wires, fixatives etc. It is now a ubiquitous part of daily life….BUT many of the chemicals found in various plastics have been shown to cause endocrine damage and are hazardous to health. Chemicals such as phthalates and PVC can leach from containers into food and water or be ingested and build up in the body.

And then we have the more recent introduction of micro-plastics which seem to be in the most unlikely products – and we are all carrying some level of exposure and build-up of these.

Heavy Metals

Our bodies are not very good at detoxing heavy metals and so, on the whole, the body tends to stick any exposure to them into 'storage' to hopefully be dealt with at a later date when it can figure out the problem. Unfortunately, modern life keeps on exposing us and exposing us….

Health concerns include cancer, neurological disorders, Alzheimer's disease, foggy head, fatigue, nausea and vomiting, decreased production of red and white blood cells, abnormal heart rhythm and damage to blood vessels.

Our exposure comes from a wide variety of sources – seafood, vaccines, dental amalgams, antiperspirants, building materials, lead paints, pesticides, preserved wood to name a few......even Teflon cookware is a culprit!

Gardens

And then there are the chemicals we use in the garden – lawn treatments, sprays for roses, weed killers - Roundup (glyphosate), for example doesn't damage just plants but wildlife, pets and children as well as adults exposed to it, is deemed to be carcinogenic and takes many years to break down in the soil – yet STILL it is on sale in the shops and widely used by farmers. Does no-one care? It is madness.

And then there's furniture – paints, varnishes, finishes etc.

And it doesn't end here.... Many people get high levels of exposure to toxic fumes in their work environments – mechanics, hairdressers, painters, nail technicians, potters, cleaners and others.

Frightening isn't it? But frightening you isn't the point of this – you need to be informed, and once armed with the right information you can then make choices to ensure you are not compromising your health and well-being without even realizing it!

In many ways the general advice is quite simple

- first identify the hazards in your home, and then eliminate them, or at the very least, minimise your exposure to them
- ensure there is plenty of fresh air in the home and air all rooms regularly, especially in winter
- ensure there is clean water for drinking, cooking and ideally bathing that is free from contaminants and chemicals
- use natural materials both in the building and furnishing of the home
- ensure good levels of natural lighting in all rooms
- ensure good levels of humidity and temperature
- protect the home environment from EMFs and other radiation
- avoid harmful earth energies such as geopathic stress

Is it just coincidence that there has been a steady increase in serious diseases such as cancers, heart disease, diabetes, Alzheimer's, Parkinson's, multiple sclerosis, kidney disease, liver disease, asthma, infertility, birth defects and the many other chronic diseases that are so prevalent in modern life? What do you think? For a clever species we seem to remarkably stupid when it comes to maintaining our health.....

A recent study found traces of 350 man-made chemicals in breast milk – would any mother knowingly feed this mix to her child? Would she knowingly feed it to herself? And what effect is this having on both adult health and the vitality of children?

No-one knows – and at the corporate level very few care, as long as shareholders dividends hold up!

And whilst some of these chemicals might be safe others are known endocrine disruptors, carcinogens and neurotoxins – and yet they are still allowed to be used! Again - madness!

The American College of Obstetricians and Gynaecologists reported in 2013 that there is 'robust' evidence linking 'toxic environmental agents' to 'adverse reproductive and developmental health outcomes', and yet nothing changes.....

The National Institute of Occupational Safety and Health found that 884 chemicals used in personal care products are **known** to be toxic. So in all this madness YOU have to look out for yourself, and arm yourself with the information to at least mitigate your – and your family's – exposure.

Remember, you will never be able to be the best version of yourself if you are ill and suffering. Awakening your Grail Wisdom means being alert and *taking action* on all threats that may limit your ability to tune in and evolve your consciousness.

So what are the major culprits to look out for? Here is just a partial list:

- ❖ **Sodium laurel sulphate and sodium laureth sulphate** – used in most shampoos, bubble baths, shower gels, toothpastes and cleansers it is also used to clean garage floors and degrease engines! If it gets in the eyes it can permanently impair their normal functioning, it irritates skin tissue, corrodes hair follicles, can cause cataracts, hair loss, mouth ulcers, flaking skin and urinary tract infections. It can react with other chemicals found in products to form potentially carcinogenic (cancer-forming) cocktails. It also enters, and is residual in, the heart, liver, lungs and brain.

- **Formaldehyde (formalin, formal and methyl aldehyde)** – used as a disinfectant, fixative, germicide and preservative in deodorants, liquid soaps, nail varnish and shampoos. It is a carcinogen and neurotoxin, an irritant and sensitizer. It can cause damage to DNA, irritate the eyes and lungs, is a leading cause of contact dermatitis and is implicated in asthma and headaches. Sweden and Japan have both banned its used. Look for **bronopol, quaternium 15, imidazolidinyl urea and DMDM hydrantoin** as these break down to release formaldehyde.
- **Propylene Glycol** – a cosmetic form of refined crude oil it is also used as anti-freeze and brake fluid. Found in hair conditioners, deodorants, cosmetics, after shave, body lotions, skin creams, baby wipes, sunscreens, and toothpaste and – increasingly – human and pet foods. It is implicated in contact dermatitis, kidney and liver abnormalities, eye and skin irritation, nausea and headaches and can be found in even hypoallergenic and baby products. It gives the 'glide' factor to creams, but is in fact, robbing the lower layer of skin of moisture, causing skin to age faster than if nothing was used.
- **Phthalates** – also called 'gender benders' they are a family of industrial plasticizers banned in the EU from plastic toys but still used in hair sprays, nail varnishes and perfumes. They can cause damage to the liver and kidneys, lungs and reproductive system. Some studies have linked them to male infertility.
- **Parabens (alkyl parahydroxy benzoates – butyl/methyl/ethyl/propyl/isobutyl paraben)** – used as a preservative they have been found in breast cancer tumours. Found in the majority of personal care products they are oestrogen mimics and thus linked to testicular cancer and low sperm count also.
- **Fluoride** – found in the majority of toothpastes and many drugs it is lethal at a dose of 5 mg/kg. One tube of toothpaste will kill anyone weighting up to 4.5 kg! It is also bio-accumulative and is linked to cancer, fertility problems, thyroid issues and

neurological conditions such as hyperactivity, attention deficit disorder, increased aggression and reduced IQ. It is also directly linked to fluorosis (fluoride poisoning) which causes blotching on teeth and skeletal problems. In areas where the water is fluoridated the number of hip fractures in older people can double.

- ❖ **Toluene** – found in nail enamels, hair gels, hair spray and perfumes it is a neurotoxin and can lead to liver damage, asthma and disrupt the endocrine system.
- ❖ **Diethanolomine (DEA), triethanolomine (TEA) and monoethanolomine (MEA)** – common ingredients in many toiletries they accumulate in the body's organs and induce cancer.
- ❖ **Alpha Hydroxy Acid (triple fruit acids, lactic acid, sugar cane extract, glycolic acid)** – used for exfoliating they remove not just damaged layers of skin but the protective barrier as well and can lead to long term skin damage. This in turn leads to more chemicals being absorbed and more sun damage.
- ❖ **Alcohol** – found in mouthwash, it has been linked to mouth, tongue and throat cancers.
- ❖ **Talc** – a recognized carcinogen it is linked to ovarian cancer.
- ❖ **Perfumes/scented products** – mainly synthetic compounds made from petroleum and linked to allergies and breathing difficulties.
- ❖ **Aluminium** – found in deodorants and linked to Alzheimer's disease.
- ❖ **Hair Dyes** – particularly darker colours are associated with an increased risk of cancer, particularly lymphatic and myeloma

The list could go on and on……..And this is just the toiletries!!!!!!!!!

Wise up! Don't take anything for granted, check it out, and find alternatives. There are always alternatives – sometimes not as convenient as something full of chemicals but you have to ask yourself - What price health?

And if you don't think you should make your health your number one priority, then just go and talk to people who have lost theirs- you'll realise just how limited and how much of a struggle life is without it! And it's too late when it's gone…..

The Art of Feng Shui

Many of you will have heard of the term 'Feng Shui' but only in terms of shifting furniture or keeping toilet seats down!

Whilst these things are (potentially) part of Feng Shui practice it is really about the subtle flow of energy (chi) in our environment and how this affects human health and wellbeing, and as such takes in everything from the placement of buildings in the landscape to the placement of furniture in the home.

It distinguishes between 'nourishing' energy and 'detrimental' energy, with the emphasis on increasing levels of nourishing energy and negating detrimental energy or 'chi'.

It has been described as an art, rather than a science, as the practitioner has to be aware of and sensitive to energy at many different levels, and read the many clues around him or her – both in Nature and within the home and the lives of their clients. For those attuned to both see and feel the environment there are many hints to be gleaned as to what might be blocking or depleting the flow of beneficial energy and affecting relationships, flow of health and money, family relations and even luck.

It takes a lot of time to study and understand the principles that contribute to Feng Shui. The practice developed over 5,000 years ago in China and, like Chinese medicine, is based on centuries of observation as to how energy flows, the effects of stagnation and blockage, how different energies are attracted to certain areas and how certain configurations can either hinder or help this flow of energy.

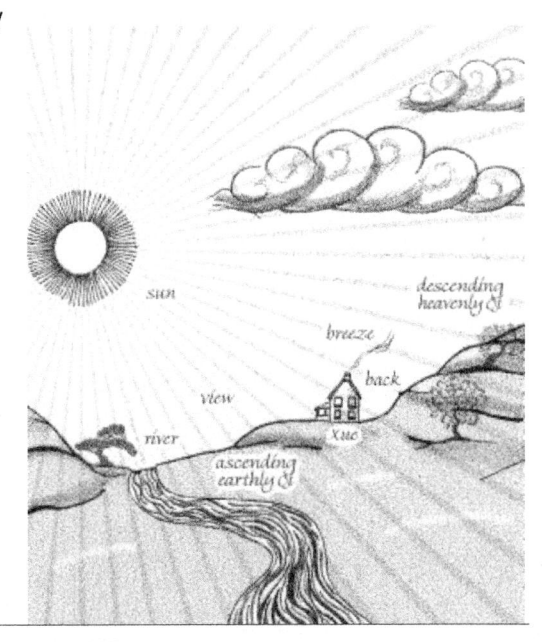

For example: sharp corners can send energy shooting out with a 'cutting' effect, clutter can cause energy to pool and stagnate, open doors in a line can allow energy to race through in too fast and frenzied a manner, a blank wall can stop it in its tracks, sinks or toilets can drain energy...

What are called 'cures' are often used to correct this flow of energy and can include such things as wind chimes, use of certain colours, placement of crystals, use of water or certain objects, mirrors and even plants.

For example, a plant can be placed in a corner where energy is pooling to help move it along, or mirrors can be placed to 'bounce' energy down a long corridor, slowing it down, clutter can be cleared to enable energy to flow.

Yin/Yang

It is important that you have an understanding of Yin and Yang energy. These are two different types of chi or energy which are mutually dependent but opposite.

The interdependence of these energies is beautifully illustrated in the yin/yang symbol. Nothing will ever be wholly yin or wholly yang, but a mix of the two.

There are two main continuums to consider for yin/yang – active and passive and sedating or energising. Ideally it is about achieving balance, a harmony of the two.

Words to describe yin energy – cold, wet, dark, interior, feminine, slow, still, passive, descending, sedating, soft, contracting, moon.

Words to describe yang energy – hot, dry, light, exterior, masculine, active, fast, moving, hard, ascending, energising, expanding, sun.

Within the home yin features would be – fabric, carpets, rugs, soft furnishings, curtains, soft, indirect, downward lighting, softwoods, blue and green or muted colours. Yang features would be hardwoods, stone, marble, glass, mirrors, sculptures, blinds, bright upward lighting, red and orange or bright colours.

Five Elements

Feng Shui works with the concept of elements, which are seen as being different manifestations of chi – Earth, Wood, Fire, Metal and Water. Western traditions more normally acknowledge four elements – Earth, Air, Fire and Water – although some add in a 5th called aether or quintessence.

Ideally there should be a balance of the elements within a space. A lack of a certain element, or the dominance of one can bring in certain difficulties, and much of the art of Feng Shui is understanding how to bring the balance back!

The elements move in a pre-determined way and follow either:

> **the supportive cycle** – Water helps Wood to grow, which enables Fire to burn, which gives ashes to enrich the Earth, which forms Metal which feeds Water
> **the destructive cycle** – Water extinguishes Fire which melts Metal, which cuts Wood, which exhausts Earth, which muddies and blocks Water
> **or the exhaustive cycle** – Water weakens Metal, which weakens Earth, which itself weakens Fire, which destroys Wood, which weakens Water.

Each element symbolises certain qualities:

Wood – spring, growth, optimism, vitality, initiating, changeable, expansive, nurturing, versatile

Water – winter, stubborn, diplomatic, secretive,

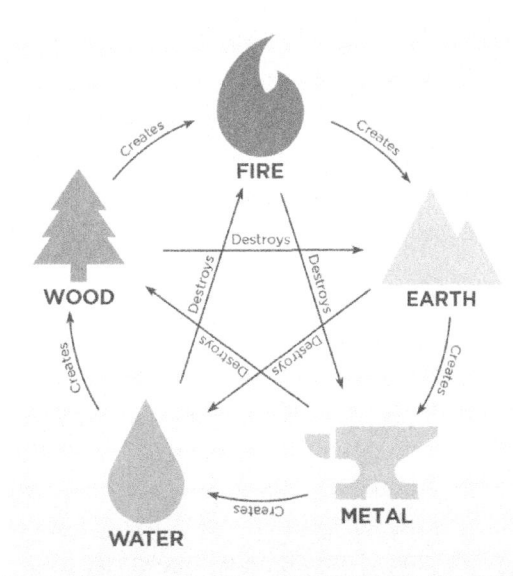

tranquillity, flexibility, progress, flowing

Earth - nurturing, supportive, warm, maternal, grounded, steady, fairness, instinct, receptivity

Fire – summer, heat, light, bright, clarifying, expansive, excitement, passion, recognition

Metal – autumn, strength, solidity, rigidity, intuitive, organised, refined, leadership

The Bagua

A template, or 'bagua', is used to put over a room or house or building plan, which is divided into sections. Each section equates to a life area and also an element. Items should avoid being placed in areas where they are destructive and supportive items placed in life areas where help or a boost is needed – for example place something representing the water element (fish tank, bowl of water, small fountain, tortoise, picture of water, blue carpet etc) in your wealth area to energize this.

The bagua is based on the magic square and represents the journey of life in the nine principal aspects. A good balance is required in each area. When applied to the house, garden or office we can see which area rooms fall into and how that area of energy on the bagua is being represented in our lives – is it being diminished, nourished or dominated? This then leads you into looking at ways to harmonise the imbalances.

The nine aspects of the bagua are:

1. North. Career, Life journey, day-to-day duties, life path, beginnings.
2. South West. Relationships, life partner, marriage, friends.
3. East. Ancestors, family dynamics, elders, past.
4. South East. Wealth, finances, abundance, good fortune, blessings,

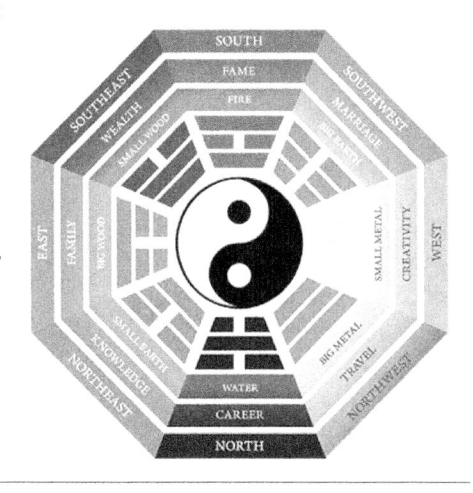

self-empowerment.
5. Centre. Health, well-being.
6. North West. Helpful people, travel, benefactors, friendships.
7. West. Creativity, children, hobbies, projects.
8. North East. Knowledge, wisdom, learning & study, quiet contemplation, self-knowledge.
9. South. Recognition, fame, project or journey's end, illumination, plans for future.

There are two different ways to place the bagua over your house or office plans:

Compass: this is aligned with the compass, so Career/Journey faces North etc.
3-Door Gate – this method aligns the northern section of the bagua with the front of the property or main entrance into the property.

Other important aspects of Feng Shui are geopathic stress/EMFs, space clearing, symbolism, directions and clearing clutter. An understanding of the I Ching can also be helpful.

If you wish to start to apply some of the principles of Feng Shui to your home you can make a start using the help of some of the excellent books available, but if you can afford it I highly recommend the services of a trained Feng Shui practitioner as they will quickly and easily pick up many things that you will miss and bring change and improvement more quickly to your life!

Remember, this is all about the flow of energy and bringing more harmonious energy into your home and life. The more you can sensitise yourself to being aware of the way things flow around you the more tuned in you will become to the greater whole.

Space Clearing

This takes in a lot more than most people realise and is an important part of keeping your domestic space clean, energised and supportive.

Space Clearing is the term used to define the art of cleansing and consecrating space.

Why would you want to do this?

We know that everything in the Universe is comprised of energy, and all the seemingly 'empty' spaces are full.....of energy.

Energy needs to flow and move, it should not be static. And it is this constant flow and movement that energises and brings change. Chaos theory maintains that a butterfly beating its wings in the Amazon will create a storm somewhere else on the planet. Whether that is true or not I don't know, but it speaks beautifully to the fact that small movements and changes in the great web of energy we live in ripples out to have effects elsewhere. It does not necessarily need big actions to create lasting change.

If energy gets caught or stuck, it stagnates.

Equally so, as energy radiates out from something – an emotional outburst perhaps, or a trauma – that energy imprints itself as it moves out.

Think of walking into a room where an argument has just taken place – we often say 'You could cut the air with a knife' meaning the negative energy of the argument had created an energetic density that was almost tangible.

This energy gets imprinted into the fabric of a building, the bricks and mortar, as it ripples out. The residues accumulate and build up – much like dust does – and then stagnates, affecting the future flow of energy within this space.

And the lives of everyone working and living within this environment are also affected, often negatively.

Strong emotions, traumas, repeated action and behaviours become deeply imprinted into the fabric of any structure, or landscape. Think of an old battlefield. Those with any sensitivity can feel the trauma that has seeped in the ground and rocks, held there and deeply woven into the fabric of the space. It can be cleared, but requires working with consciously by those who know what they are doing.

Our homes in particular are mirrors of ourselves – our hopes, our dreams, our emotional highs and lows, our traumas, our joys. All are held within, and express themselves in the flow (or not!) of energy and the things and symbology of what we choose to surround ourselves with.

We are sensitive creatures when it comes to reading energy – we can all pick up 'atmosphere' in a place. Some homes we walk into and just love the feel of them, others we can find difficult to be in for very long and are energetically unwelcoming.

Space clearing cleans, clears, raises and revitalises the energy in a space, and in doing so raises the quality of the lives of those inhabiting those spaces. It is a powerful technique for clearing and harmonising energy in a home or creating sacred space.

It is a very simple principle, but can make a profound difference, as it allows our personal spaces to become collecting points for vibrant and positive flows of energy that ripple out into the wider world, instead of the energetic equivalent of a grubby, stagnant, stinking swamp!

Which would you rather live in?

Space clearing can be done on its own, but is particularly effective when combined with conventional Feng Shui. By combining the two, in the hands of a trained practitioner who can 'read' all the energetic and physical clues, you can uncover many of the stuck and difficult areas of your life and be given tools and understandings to work consciously to change them.

I give you a simple but effective space clearing method in Appendix 3. Use it regularly to clean and clear the energy in your home, particularly after arguments – and always use it when moving into a new house!

Clearing Clutter

Clearing clutter is ideally something you do on an ongoing basis, as if you leave it too long it can become overwhelming. The longer you put it off the more impossible the job becomes....little and often is usually best.

We live in a Society where most of us have lots of 'stuff' (particularly compared to our forebears). So how do we define clutter?

This is a simple but effective definition:

> Clutter is anything which is not - genuinely useful
> - genuinely cherished or loved
> - orderly

You could add to that household paperwork, tax records etc that you need to keep – but keep it organised!

Broken or unfinished items also count as clutter – you need to decide if they are worth repairing or finishing by the above criteria. If not, get rid of them!

Physical clutter in the home creates a blockage to the flow of energy and an area where energy can pool and stagnate. A Feng Shui practitioner would look at where this clutter was within the 'template' of the house as it usually reflects blockages within the client's life.

Why Do We Hang On To Clutter?

- ➢ 'Might come in handy someday'
- ➢ Sentimental reasons
- ➢ Unwanted gifts – sense of obligation/duty to hang onto them
- ➢ Inherited attitudes from parents – conditioned patterning
- ➢ Status & ego – feel items make you look good/trendy/upmarket in others eyes

- Good advertising and marketing – buying things we didn't really want/need
- Time poverty – can never find time to sort things (this is really procrastination)
- To keep busy and avoid taking a closer look at what is not working in our lives

Whilst clutter clearing is not rocket science, it can be very difficult for many people. Hanging onto 'stuff' is a pattern that is likely repeated in many areas in their lives – hanging onto old attachments, hanging onto old traumas, hanging onto unhelpful behaviour patterns. Someone who has chronic clutter problems is likely stuck and stagnant in every area of their lives.

It is a discipline to address clutter in a timely manner, just as much as washing your face in the morning or putting away the washing up.

Clutter Clearing Tips

- Don't even open junk mail – put it straight in the bin
- Get a friend to help you – they will likely have a more dispassionate view
- Start small – choose just one area or room to begin with
- Throw anything that can't be recycled or sold
- Ask yourself 'Is this useful? Is this loved? Is this necessary?' (ie. tax returns etc that you legally have to hang onto for a number of years)
- A 'might be useful someday' pile is strictly forbidden!
- Anything you can recycle or pass on to charity shops – put it in car and do so quickly
- If you have lots of notes and scraps of papers clear them onto a calendar, a day book or journal, so you have everything in one place

Understanding why you are hanging onto stuff, and the psychology of clutter can be helpful in giving insight as to what is going on within your life, but is not a necessary part of taking action.

Remember, it is a simple choice you have to make – firstly to decide that clearing clutter and bringing more space and energy for new things to come into your life is important.

Then doing it!

Predecessor Chi

It is not just buildings and spaces that accumulate old energy – objects do to. Many people love to buy old furniture, jewellery etc but never stop to think of how much of the previous owners energy is still imprinted into it and being brought into their space, potentially bringing with it deep unhappiness, sadness, trauma and negativity.

Predecessor chi refers to both this energy in your space but also the energy on things in your space. It is the residue of human thoughts and emotions from predecessors (and also yourself).

You can clear predecessor chi from objects and furniture in much the same way you clear it from the space around you. Smudge all around the object with desert sage and/or use sound vibration from bells, cymbals or drums and/or clear with specially designed clearing and purifying essence sprays.

Then you can wear the necklace Aunt Maud left to you without any concerns of tapping into any of Aunt Maud's emotional stuff!

Presences

Something that is not often considered when doing basic clearing is also the presence of earthbound souls or other presences. This should not scare anyone, nor is it spooky. We are surrounded by lots of unseen beings. We just need to ensure that those we share space with are appropriate and benign.

Presences can include thought forms. Thought forms are mental constructs that have received so much mental energy that they take on an energetic 'presence'.

An earthbound soul is a soul whose physical body is no more, but their soul has not left the 3rd dimensional plane and journeyed on as should happen. Other presences might include interdimensional beings or other forms of entity. It is rarely appropriate that they are here.

Portals

Portals act as a gateway into this dimension from other dimensions. Just as humans can stumble into something quite unexpected so can other beings, and find themselves in the wrong place and unsure how to return.

There are also beings which quite deliberately engineer the ability to come to this plain as they 'feed' off dense, negative energy and human beings can provide plenty of that! (This is another reason for clearing and energising your space – so it is not attractive to other entities!)

Portals can be created by vortexes or sinkholes at places where energy lines intersect – if the lines are toxic this is not good! There are other areas in the landscapes that both our ancient ancestors and modern dowsers know to be portals where the ability to tap into an interdimensional energy is known about.

But portals can also open up in the home. The most common sources are mirrors, fireplaces and toilets.

Again, if you are not confident and clear in what to do this is not something that you should tackle yourself, but get in someone who is trained in finding, clearing and closing these energetic portals and ensuring that all beings and entities are returned to their rightful place (both sides of the portal!).

For both portals and presences a professional space clearer trained in removal of such things comes into their own, or a shamanic healer or dowser also trained in such work. You should not tackle this sort of thing yourself if you don't know what you are doing as you can accidentally make matters worse by not following correct protocols or connecting into the appropriate interdimensional help.

Symbolism

This is a fascinating aspect of getting the balance of harmonious energy correct in your home, and once you have understood the principles and trained your eye to look carefully you will start to see the symbolic impact of many items in your physical environment that are giving you a subtle message.

Your home environment is a metaphor for your life, a reflection of you. Unconsciously many of the things we choose and the way we place them have a story to tell us about ourselves and our lives, our beliefs and our behaviour. We dress the interior of our homes and the beliefs and attitudes embodied in these things reinforces the original patterns – a potentially vicious circle ensues…..

Symbolically, what we see around us, much of which we take in at a subconscious level on a daily basis can either lift or depress our energy, can reinforce a sense of well-being…or conflict,

Here are a few simple examples:

Restrictions – restrictions above your head are symbolic of restriction of opportunity in your life. Examples include low beams, sloping low ceilings, cupboards above bed. Are these things manifesting problems in your life?

Dripping taps – symbolizes financial or energetic loss. Where are you feeling this drain?

Broken Items – can symbolise things which are broken/not working in your life. What is the item and what does it represent? Which life area is it in and how is this energy showing up in this life area?

Mirrors – what are they reflecting? Is it something that is subconsciously not wanted or draining to that life area? Does it take all of you in or is it broken/cuts off top of head/shoulders, or does it split your reflection (think cupboard doors)?

Sticking Doors – Which doors are these? Is this a seasonal thing? Can represent struggle – energy finds it hard to get in or out.

Doors Banging – are there arguments/clashes?

Unused rooms – where are they on the bagua? Does this represent an under-utilisation of your skills etc in your life?

Double bed – if used by a single person who wants a relationship is the bedding for one or two people?

Artwork and Ornaments
This can be very informative. Our choice of artwork and ornaments is highly personal and the artwork we allow on our walls can reflect back at us aspects of who we are or what is happening in our life that we might otherwise miss.

They are also images that we see again and again every day (often unconsciously) and that can reinforce certain messages…..

Very generally natural, beautiful and joyful scenes have a positive effect.

Stormy, war-like, conflict scenes can have a negative effect.

Abstract art is not very beneficial either way.

For example, you might have the conditioned belief relationships end in pain. Unconsciously the images you chose to surround yourself with are either of single people or people ignoring each other or back-to-back…..

There are several questions you need to ask:

>What is actually happening in the picture – be objective!
>What is the energy of the picture – yin/yang, 5 elements, movement, colour etc
>Is there any predecessor chi – previous owner, reproduction, artist
>What do you see/feel when you look at the picture –this can be very subjective
>Under what circumstances did you acquire it?

You also need to look at:

>What is the subconscious message from a picture?

What life area is it in?
Does it dominate or nourish the element of that area?
Does it enhance/block/control/diminish the energy of that area?

Also….think about both sides of the coin – something damaging can in some instances serve as well as block.

Look at the two pictures below – one is a lone ship on stormy seas, the other bright and warm and full of symbols of abundance. They tell very different stories and have a very different feel. Take a moment to feel into them and the difference energetically and what this means to you…..

In an ideal world you would ensure that the pictures on your wall are supportive to the life area to you have them in.

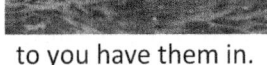

For example:

1. Journey/Career. What is wanted is a sense of harmonious progress and flow. You want the flow going away from you into the distance, free of obstacles. Example: pictures of a free flowing river, open calm sea, long view to distance…

2. Relationships. Harmonious close, receptive, loving and caring personal relationships are desired. What do you want from your relationship? For example: stability (images of swans or mandarin ducks who mate for life). Passion (red). Romance (pink/peach). Communication (yellows). Pictures of couples, objects in pairs….

3. Elders. What are wanted is harmonious relationships with our parents/our past. Are there family issues? Not just parents but ancestors, ethnic culture etc. Examples: Trees (strong, evergreen), pictures of parents/grandparents, culture, tribe etc, group of friends…

4. Good Fortune/Wealth. What is wanted is to feel fortunate, experience good luck, money and income flowing in. You want the flow towards you, so think of water flowing towards you, or a waterfall, trees in leaf signifying abundance or evergreens, by lakes, the Spring – season of abundance……

5. Health/Well-being. You want a balanced picture, to feel physically, mentally, emotionally and spiritually balanced. Think of natural scenes (balance of 5 elements), healthy places to be or someone exemplifying the qualities of good health….

6. Helpful People. What is wanted is to have friends/people who show up when needed, mentors or support, to be giving and helpful to others. Think of what this means to you….ie Mentors, angels, gurus, friends having a good time….

7. Creativity/Children. You want a flow of good ideas/projects or artistic creativity and to have good relationships with children. Yang is the creation of children, yin is artistic ability. Think of pictures of your kids, or others, lakes (depths of creativity), artistic picture or activity that speaks to you of what you want to create…..

8. Quiet Contemplation/ Knowledge. The desired outcome is to get to know oneself, learn what is necessary. Yang is outer knowledge, yin inner knowledge. Think of pictures of mountains, a place where you achieve quiet contemplation, guru or spiritual leader, or things which represent the knowledge you want to acquire…..

9. Recognition/Illumination. What is wanted is to gain internal illumination and external recognition. Yang – external, yin – internal. Think of pictures of sun, yang energy, fire, fiery colours

The above are just a few suggestions which may or may not resonate. Remember, it is what it symbolises *to you* so can be very personal. Don't just take someone else's interpretation but feel into what it is saying to you.

The Language of Colour

There is a whole language to colour that we understand at a subconscious or even archetypal level.

Most of us understand it, even if we are not fully conscious that we do. Understanding this language and using it in our home environment to give us the desired effects can be very nurturing and supportive.

The vibrational rate of the visible spectrum of light gives us colour – the longest wavelength and slowest frequency of vibration is red, the shortest and highest is violet. There are many wavelengths we can't see (yet!). Some maintain that as mankind evolves we are seeing ever more colours as our bodies adapt to a broader visible spectrum of light!

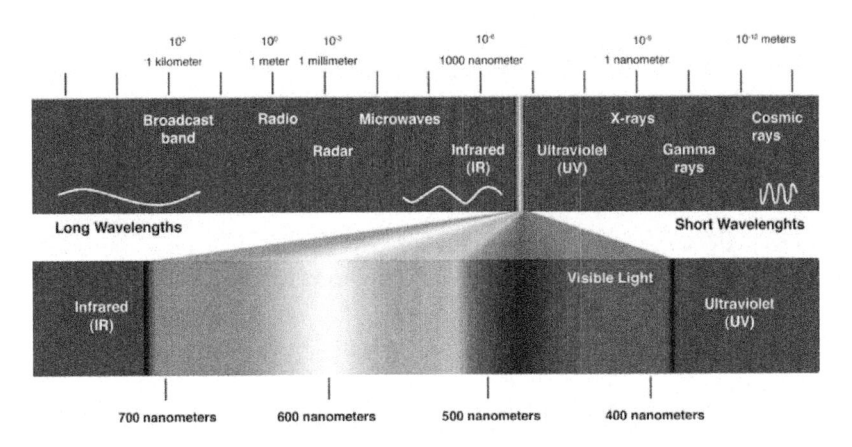

Let's look at each of the main colours in the colour wheel in turn and see what we can discover about them. There are tints and hues. The tint is a hue with a lot of light, or white, added to it – for example, pink is the tint of red. The tint is always seen as representing a higher level, or intensification, of the colour due to its higher levels of white or 'clear' light.

The colours described are either primary, secondary or tertiary. Secondary colours are created by mixing two primaries together, and tertiary colours are combinations of primary and secondary colours.

Red - Primary
Red is the most physical of all colours, and can be used to counteract

physical apathy. It also raises blood pressure, or can be used to treat low blood pressure. Red stimulates the adrenal glands and helps us build stamina. It represents life force, the blood, is a colour of passion and vitality and high energy and is seen as being very grounding. In the negative this can turn to aggression and anger, and it is the colour for danger and sacrifice.

Use red in your clothing, your walls, your ornaments etc if you are too tired to want to do much, or to bother with taking care of yourself properly. Red also energises the emotions where they lack depth or are weak. For those who are over-stimulated, or highly stressed, red should be avoided.

Pink - Tint
Pink is the tint of red – it is red with a lot of white added (or light in it!). As a consequence it is much gentler and less stimulating. It is also seen as being the colour of compassion and unconditional love and caring but can also be seen as sweet and fluffy and smothering. It is the colour most associated with the feminine – the strength and passion of red distilled into something gentler and more caring.

Coral - Tertiary
Coral is associated with community and balanced independence and interdependence. As such it opens the way for networking and cooperation at this level.

It refers to the new consciousness which is emerging within humanity, and is a grounding emotional energy and said to represent the new Christ or Christos energy.

There is also a delicacy and fragility to it, helping make us aware of the fine balance we walk between harmony and disharmony, much as a coral reef thrives within a narrow band of parameters, and starts to die when these are breached, and teaches us to recognise and respect this.

Orange - Secondary
Orange is another stimulating colour as it contains red, but this is softened by the addition of yellow. It is the colour of assimilation, of testing, of judgment. It is seen as being a happy, genial colour representing joy and happiness and as such can be used to combat depression.

It helps to stimulate the appetite – both sexual and for food. It has a beneficial effect on the digestive system and the immune system and also has a releasing action on body fluids. It is also seen as being a spiritual colour and worn by some monks.

Wear orange to brighten your mood and as it is said to help break down barriers it can therefore be good in social situations, as well as being the colour of luxury and also giving courage to change unhappy situations.

Gold - Tertiary
Gold represents a higher octave of orange. It is the colour of wealth, wisdom, high spirituality and real luxury. In the aura it is said to attract positive energy, and it is the colour of the Holy Grail and of Divinity. It represents innate wisdom or gnosis that is not learnt but comes from within and in our Society has come to represent material wealth.

Yellow - Primary
Yellow wavelengths of light are known to stimulate the brain, so it is easy to see why yellow is associated with the workings of the mind and learnt knowledge as well as focus and concentration. It is also symbolically associated with speed – including speed of thought and decision making, which is why it is the colour used to offset confusion or uncertainty. If you have an important decision to make and are unsure, try wearing yellow to help you!

Yellow also helps to strengthen the nervous system and helps to activate the motor nerves and lymphatic system. It is also associated with enabling the correct uptake of calcium from the blood and resonates with the digestive system, gall bladder, liver and pancreas.

There is the obvious association with the sunshine, brightness and happiness, but yellow also has a darker side. Historically it was often used by the Catholic Church to symbolise heresy against its doctrines, revolutionary France used yellow to daub on the doors of those thought to be traitors to the new regime and Jews were forced to wear yellow in Medieval times, as well as yellow stars in Hitler's Germany.

Olive Green - Tertiary
This sits between yellow and green and, much like the hardy olive tree, it speaks of strength of character, able to endure and turn the bitter to sweet. It is said to be the colour of feminine leadership – the leadership

of the heart, caring of the feelings of others, able to overcome emotional pain and turn it to benefit, strong yet flexible, and able to handle things with sensitivity.

Green - Secondary

Green is the colour of nature and as such represent growth, fruitfulness, new beginnings and natural abundance. It is the most important healing colour with this association with new life and growth – indeed green is the colour of the archangel of healing, Raphael. It is also the colour of the faeries, powerful beings whom it is not wise to cross!

Green is the colour of balance and harmony both within our bodies and in our external environment. Wear it when you feel things are out of balance at any level. It helps us connect with empathy to others and our environment and can lessen stress – and thus promote healing!

It can help to give us a much needed sense of space when the world is pressing in on us, and also help us establish healthy boundaries.

Green is also connected to the heart. It is the colour of the heart chakra and represents kindness, openness and generosity

Turquoise - Tertiary

Turquoise is one of the colours of the New Age. Along with blue it represents communication, but in the case of turquoise it is mass communication which is enabled by new technology and multimedia.

It is a creative, artistic colour about freedom of expression and intelligence linked with feeling. It brings an openness to new ideas and its link with the blue-greens of the ocean make it not only both invigorating

and calming, but also lifts us and has a child-like playful positive quality.

Within our body it helps stimulate the immune system, being in resonance with the thymus gland, and can act like a tonic to frayed nerves.

Blue - Primary
Deep peace, calm and serenity are some of the signature qualities of blue. It soothes, cools and calms. It is considered a colour of higher consciousness and wearing this colour can help calm the mind and bring tranquillity. It can also give a feeling of protection, maybe because it can bring calm in the chaos!

Blue is also the colour of Truth, the higher mind and the thinker. It is said to inspire mental clarity and creativity, and promotes faith and trust in Life.

It is also the colour of communication, being the colour of the Throat chakra, but this is interpersonal communication not the mass communication of the turquoise.

Blue is also the colour of authority. It is our own natural, innate authority, which is often devolved to institutions of Society, so has both positive and negative connotations.

It also represents the Mother principle, and the Mother Goddess as Queen of Heaven, or the Virgin Mary, who is usually depicted clothed in blue.

Within the body blue is linked to the throat and thyroid gland, and can help to calm and lower high blood pressure, and reduce stress. Its calming function can help promote sleep, and it is said to have an anti-inflammatory effect.

Indigo – Secondary
Indigo is a combination of blue and violet and, next to violet, considered to be one of the most spiritual of colours, combining harmony of the mind and the body, heaven and earth.

Its link to the Third Eye chakra associates it with clarity of inner vision and psychic senses and intuition. It is the colour of witnessing, where we find the detachment to watch the Self, and not indulge in knee-jerk reactions, seeing the wider picture and our part in it.

This can bring often painful insight, but also great learning and compassion and self-acceptance with it.

In its darker tones it is representative of the creative void from which inspiration sparks to bring light to the mind and the world.

Violet - Secondary
Violet is associated with the veil between this world and the world of spirit, and therefore spirituality and the mystical. It is a powerful colour of transformation and service to humanity and can help to bring a calm and reflective state of mind.

It can help to open us to new growth and high ideals, and the red hidden within it can hint of hidden passion.

Violet can depict grief and suffering, but it also holds the potential for transformation within this, as it is in emotional extremis that old patterns and beliefs which hold us back can be shattered, allowing new growth more aligned with who we are to come through.

At the level of the physical body it affects the brain and nervous system and can be cleansing. It also helps to suppress hunger and balance the body metabolism.

Magenta – Tertiary
Mystics tell us that this colour was once 'unseen' within the colour spectrum, being just outside the visible spectrum for us. Humanity's evolving senses have expanded now to encompass magenta. Whether our forebears could see this colour or not I can't say, but it is the colour of the 8th chakra, awareness of which has emerged only recently.

Considered a spiritual colour it is practical in its application, being representative of nurturing, caring, supportive and compassionate. It is showing our love to others (and ourselves) in the little everyday things, building up a state of Grace which helps all who come into its field.

White/Clear

The full spectrum of colour is contained within white. It represents ultimate purity, transparency and light. It has the quality of reflection and can help to open up a space for this. Too much white, however, can seem sterile and isolating, as if we are caught in a spotlight with nowhere to hide!

Black

Black is contradictory in that it symbolises the dark, and is linked with death and mourning, and the occult. Black sits at the other end of the spectrum to white, and absorbs light, so it can also be said to contain all the colours too.

It represents the void from which all creation came, and can therefore also represent unrealised potential, either good or bad, waiting to be birthed. It is the colour of mystery and the feminine creative force. As a species humanity fears the unknown and this is probably why it is connected to negativity and bad things.

Spiritually it is considered psychically protective and it is worn by many people often as a blank cloak behind which they can hide themselves.

Using Colour in the Home

Understanding the psychology and meaning of different colours and the way they affect us at a subconscious level means that we can begin to use this understanding in both the way we dress each day, and within our home environment to our benefit.

For example – don't paint a room where you want to relax or sleep red! Use yellow or orange colours for areas where you eat, dress in yellow if you are doing study work…..

It's not rocket science – it just requires a moment's thought!

Orgone Energy

What is orgone energy?

We have to start by looking at the concept of orgone energy – a concept which many scientific circles refuse to acknowledge.

Which is strange as orgone energy is another word for the bio-energetic life force, and I think most of us would agree that exists, even if science can't yet explain it!

Called Chi, Prana or Qi in other traditions it is the life energy which flows through every living thing and can be captured photographically by Kirlian photography.

The term was first coined by Dr Wilhelm Reich in the 1930s and he proposed the key to physical and mental health was the correct balance of orgone energy within an organism.

He discovered that he could accumulate this energy by layering organic and non-organic materials. Furthermore he posited there were two types of orgone energy – positive (POR) and deadly (DOR). DOR is generated by disturbed energy from electrical machinery, radio and microwave towers, nuclear plants etc.

Positive orgone energy is structured, organised and coherent, whilst deadly orgone energy leads to decay and entropy for biological life. In traditional health systems this would refer to blockages which impede the flow of life energy.

Reich build what he called 'orgone accumulators' and would sit patients within an orgone accumulator box where they were bathed in high levels of orgone energy. He ensured this was positive by siting his laboratory well away from disturbing influences and had so much success with treating even the so-called 'incurable' diseases that he attracted the attention of powerful people who went all out to discredit him.

Key Benefits of Orgonites:

- Transforms electromagnetic smog to positive Chi.
- Protection from Mobiles, TV, WiFi Broadband, Computers etc.
- Protects from geopathic stress such as ley lines and water veins.
- Clears and harmonises the energy of your space, room or office.
- Removes stagnant energy from the body.
- Amplifies personal intentions, mind power and manifestation.
- Enhances psychic abilities.
- Helps to raise consciousness and vibration.
- Balances chakras, the aura and harmonises mood.
- Shields against negative energies and entities.
- Restructures and energises water and food.
- Helps the growth of plants.
- Charges and cleanses crystals.
- Strengthens the organism and adds vitality
- Improves sleep, accelerates regeneration and healing
- Helps to remove physical and psychological stress
- Anchors higher dimensional frequencies into 3D reality!

For a theory and practice which is supposedly 'nonsense' his laboratory was destroyed and he was imprisoned in America where he died broken and destitute. Both the American Food and Drug Administration, and the Nazis and Communists in Europe all marked anything Reich had written for incineration. Four separate book burnings took place in America alone.

For something that is apparently nonsense, the Establishment went to a lot of trouble to cover it up!

Today, there are many people producing what are called 'organites' which are devices made from resin, metals and crystals. The use of crystals, which are programmable with intention, and also the sacred geometrical forms many use, help to ensure the DOR or the deadly orgone energy is not produced by exposure to negative environmental energies.

It was discovered by Don and Carol Croft that the addition of small quartz crystals to the mix of organic and inorganic material ensured that the deadly DOR energy was transmuted to the highly beneficial POR energy. The resin used in an orgonite shrinks during the curing process, permanently squeezing the quartz crystal inside which creates a well-known piezoelectric effect inside the crystal, meaning its end-points become polarized electrically. It is believed this is also what causes the orgonite to function so effectively as a positive energy generator.

The field of positive orgone energy produced by these devices absorbs negative energy from our aura and our surroundings, and help to accumulate and magnify the helpful POR energy, bringing harmony and helping with health issues, ensuring the Chi or life force which surrounds them is pure and clean.

In a world where we are continuously bathed by ever increasing levels of electromagnetics, and other forms of human-generated energy which is either untested, or known to be detrimental, a few orgonites in the home, car and office can be a simple way of helping to even out the balance.

And many of the orgonites now produced are things of great beauty also!

www.orgonistesart.com

The Ancestors

Home is the heart of family, but our families are often challenging and our biggest teachers. And here in the West we have forgotten what many other parts of the world still remember – it is not just our living family, but those who came before us in our family lineage that might be responsible for many of the challenges we face. What Western Society has become disconnected from is a sense of their lineage and ancestry.

Many ancient and indigenous cultures honoured their ancestors as a part of daily life. In the East, for example, the Ancestors still have an important part to play in everyday life, with many homes having an altar to the Ancestors and various festivals dedicated to their memory. Mexico and South American indigenous cultures, Native Americans, and the Maori are just a few examples of cultures which acknowledge and honour the Ancestors.

And it is not just honouring the memory of your ancestors which is important – it is understanding the legacy they have handed down to us, both good and bad, in the influence of beliefs and behaviours, traumas that encode our DNA, and even what is called family karma.

And this is not just mumbo jumbo or old wives tales. Science is now beginning to understand how our DNA gets altered by exposure to trauma and a wide variety of outside influences – and these changes are passed onto the next generation……and the next…..

Epigenetics, a relatively new field of science, is clearly showing us that within our RNA (an aspect of our DNA) we carry cellular memory of our Ancestor's experiences mapped into our genes – trans-generational trauma carried down over 40 generations. War, famine, oppression, slavery, deep personal and collective trauma embodied within us.

So how can these Ancestral wounds show up in us?

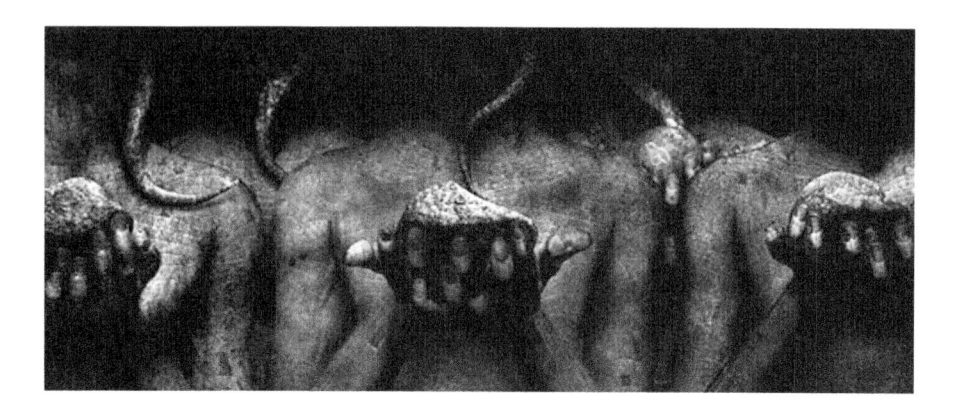

- Disease, illness and chronic conditions, triggered or exacerbated by today's stressful and polluted lifestyle
- Emotional issues, fears, beliefs, phobias, etc that are not born out of our own personal experience
- Mental issues including depression, anxiety, low self-esteem, addiction etc
- Sense of 'not belonging', deep feelings of lack, feeling unworthy, abandoned, irrational fears of something around our neck, or being drowned, not wanting to be 'visible' and to play things small, never feeling safe…..this list is endless and the roots trace back to generations before us
- Unhealthy or damaging patterns of behaviour that we recognise ourselves repeating from our parents and grandparents

These inherited wounds can run our lives and desperately require us to undertake ancestral healing work to free our lineage from these burdens.

Any healer who takes their healing practice to this level will tell you that at a *minimum* at least a third of the issues physically, mentally and emotionally that afflict us and that we struggle with are from our family lineage and karma – a huge proportion of our energy is enmeshed with them. Sometimes, healing and acknowledging these problems can bring HUGE shifts in well-being, not just for the person being treated but for other family members as well.

None of us is an island – we are the sum total of the stream that we arrived here on – our lineage, our ancestors. Much of who we are is defined by both our DNA and the energetic family field that we chose to be birthed into.

There is a saying 'You can't chose your family, but you can chose your friends' which ignores the fact that we *did* chose the family we are birthed into. When our Soul decided to reincarnate, it chooses a country, family and potential life path that would give us the best chance of teaching us what we need to learn to progress our Soul's evolution.

If you find yourself born into a total dysfunctional family, or abject poverty, or an abusive situation or even worse, you might refute that, but try to take what I call the eagle's eye view and stand back and think what *might* be the lessons that could be learned from situations like this – maybe to not let others define you, maybe to learn determination to walk a different road to those about you, or to learn forgiveness, or (big one this!) self-love, or maybe yours is a teaching path where you overcome adversity to stand as a light to inspire others….

There are many potential explanations, but only you truly know what qualities your Soul needs to develop – and you can rest assured your family will likely be part of helping you to undertake this quest! Not that they are likely to be aware of this –just being who they are will test you to the limit! Or you will have inherited certain family behaviours or patterns of being which give you the ideal opportunity to step up and change them into something healthier – and help heal your family line of this issue at the same time!

Benefits of Ancestral Healing

When we have a clear understanding of, and intrinsic connection to our Ancestral lineage there are many benefits which accrue to both us and potentially other members of our family:

- ✓ A real sense of the stream we arrived here on and the support it can give
- ✓ Reclaiming of skills or strengths that are part of our lineage
- ✓ Releasing of trauma that is part of our lineage
- ✓ Releasing of illness patterns that have become encoded from previous generations
- ✓ Clearing of any patterns or emotional challenges that come from the ancestral lineage
- ✓ Greater sense of belonging and being part of the whole
- ✓ An ever-present well of ancestral support and good will to call on

So how might you do this?

Some people are self-aware enough to see and do this work for themselves, but the majority of us tend to find getting clarity around our own (and Ancestors) wounds very difficult. We might see it mirrored back at us by others around us, if we know how to do shadow work, but otherwise it is best left to a trained ancestral healing practitioner. They will use a combination of ritual, energy work and shamanic journeying to heal, release and reconnect us in such a way that allows us to go forwards free of the burdens brought to us on our ancestral stream, blessed with its gifts and free to rewire and rewrite the story of our lives.

Your Garden

Your garden is an extension of your home space and just as you would seek to make your home a harmonious and relaxing space, the garden itself should reflect these qualities.

But here you have to work in partnership with Nature if you are to achieve this.

Most of the time we are so disconnected from any sense of the land as a living Being that we don't even think about our responsibility to make a relationship at this level, let alone consider that we need to work in co-creation with the land and its nature spirits when we work on a garden.

So, as has already been explained, first and foremost introduce yourself to the deva of your garden and ask them to work with you in partnership to make the garden a beautiful and harmonious space for both you and Nature to thrive.

And like any relationship, there is an element of compromise here – your needs with regards to how you want to use the space have to be set by the side of, and balanced with, the needs of the deva and the energy of the garden.

Co-creation – not dictatorship. It means we have to get very good at listening and not ignoring what we hear/feel in response to the plans we have.

I also find invoking the help of the nature spirits to look after and nurture the plants very helpful – it helps even the most unlikely specimens to thrive!

Chakra gardening
I wanted to just mention chakras in relation to a garden. There are two ways of approaching this. If you have an established garden you may well find that if you take the time to tune in there is already an established chakra system, or one in the process of

forming – remember chakras are an energetic archetype, and there is an energetic blueprint for this space.

If the garden is new, or one has not yet formed you can help it establish. You obviously need a good understanding of the chakras and what each relates to (a good understanding of all the energetic archetypes is VITAL to all of this work), and again it is not about imposing something on the space, but working with it, feeling into where the root and its energy might be etc. Then you can work with plants, colours and features that will enhance this, and use the space accordingly.

For example, the root area might be where you grow vegetables…..or it might be where you have family entertainments. The heart might be a beautiful peaceful spot where you can sit quietly. Unless you have a blank canvas you may have to work with the existing garden features and this becomes easier when you realise that chakras in the landscape don't HAVE to be in straight lines – they can curve and spiral – so keep your senses well-tuned in to see how the energy wants to move.

Incorporating elements of sacred geometry into the design of your garden will also add to the sense of balance and harmony.

Below are some plants for each chakra area you might think of including (these are based on colour – if you are a plants person you might want to also consider how the qualities of the plant suit the chakra in question).

Root Chakra – Red
Red rhododendron, skimmia, Oriental poppy, flame creeper, red hot poker, ribes, red geranium, cannas, red tulips, red zinnia

Sacral Chakra – Orange
Potentilla sunset, black-eyed Susan, tiger lily, ranunculus, marigold, California poppy, crown imperial, helenium, physalis, nasturtium

Solar Plexus Chakra – Yellow
Forsythia, yellow tulips and primula, daffodils, cowslips, winter aconites, sunflowers, witch hazel, mahonia, kerria japonica, winter jasmine, broom, St John's Wort, evening primrose, rudbeckia, welsh poppy

Heart Chakra – Green or pink
Grasses, ferns, box, palms, euphorbia, hostas, diorama, magnolia, carnation, cherry blossom, phlox,

Throat Chakra – Blue
Blue hydrangea, ceanothus, ceratostigma, kingfisher daisy, lobelia, bluebells, morning glory, ceratostigma, campanula, Canterbury bells, cornflowers, delphiniums

Third Eye Chakra – Indigo
Hyssop, grape hyacinth, allium, cyclamen, aubretia, forget-me-not, lithodora, monkshood, wild indigo,

Crown Chakra – Violet or white
Snowdrops, white hyacinths, mauve lilac, white camellia, myrtle, spirea bridal veil, yucca gloriosa, Hibiscus Blue Bird, wisteria, aster, lavender

And, of course, there are species such as roses, clematis, chrysanthemum, dahlia, tulips etc which come in a rainbow of colours!

Part 4
The Grail of the Physical Body

The Grail of the Physical Body

Next we come to the container of the physical body, this envelope within which our consciousness resides.

You may think you know all about your body as
- a) you have one
- b) you did biology at school

But I can promise you that you don't.

The understanding we have of our bodies is very limited because not only are we taught a small fraction of what it is about/can do, but also most of us are more in touch with our heads than we are our physical bodies.

We look back to our ancient forebears and we see an understanding of the body that was based very much in the perspective of the human spirit, of human life force – and they must have got at least some of this right as otherwise humans really wouldn't have made it this far! Here in the West, having thrown out all the wisdom of our ancestors we are not doing very well are we? Depressed, sick, anxious people everywhere....

But modern medicine throws its hands up in horror at the mention of life force and spirit. Instead the body is regarded as little more than a machine which needs fixing, much like a car.

The endemic levels of chronic disease are probably a clue to us that this approach is really not working that well!

For many people the amazing experience of being in a physical body is more of a nightmare than a blessing! Our consciousness inhabits the most exquisite form which is an amazing electro-chemical antenna which not only receives and transmits information constantly, but can also connect to different dimensional domains.

This is so different to what we have been taught it can take a moment to get your head around it. As more people are re-awakening to the true realities of who we are, many new modalities for helping us begin to reclaim our original blueprinting and abilities are starting to come on line.

The new model of healing which is emerging is very much an integrated approach – when you break a leg the mechanistic approach is fine, but a more nuanced approach is required for any form of disease.

This new body of understanding is being loosely grouped together under the heading 'Vibrational Medicine'. What this means is that both scientific understandings around the nature, energetic and otherwise, of the atoms and molecules which make up our bodies is combined with ancient observations around the body as a life-energy system, and every aspect of our make-up is factored into the picture – energetic, emotional, environmental, mental etc

So this model comes from the understanding that whilst bugs and germs *might* have a place to play, a big contribution to illness is chronic dysfunctional spiritual, emotional and mental energy patterns and behaviours and beliefs, as well as what is called Terrain theory.

So it is essential we begin to understand our bodies energetically, their energy anatomy, as well as understand their physical anatomy.

This is going to be the new medicine more and more, particularly as we advance further into the energetic changes which are unfolding. I myself have seen big changes over the years I have worked in the holistic health and well-being fields, with it becoming more and more apparent that the underlying causes of health problems lie substantially at the energetic level and the physical issues are only clear symptoms of this.

The table below gives you an idea of the differences between the two modalities of medicine.

Conventional Medicine	Vibrational Medicine Model
Based on Newtonian Physics	Based on Einsteinian & Quantum Physics
Views the body as a biomachine	Views the body as a dynamic energy system
Sees the brain as a biocomputer with consciousness as a by-product of the brain's electrical	Mind and Spirit are true sources of consciousness (the actual operator

activity	who runs the brain/biocomputer)
Emotions thought to influence illness through neurohormonal connections between brain and body	Emotions and spirit can influence illness via energetic and neurohormonal connections among body, mind and spirit
Treatments with drugs and surgery to 'fix' abnormal biomechanisms in the physical body	Treatment with different forms and frequencies of energy to rebalance body/mind/spirit complex

*Thanks to Richard Gerber

Important points I came to understand include:

> Your body never works against you

> It is always seeking to find balance, to re-establish a healthy blueprint, energetically and physically.

> It is always doing the best it can for you, given the circumstances it finds itself in

Ultimately your body is the vehicle for your consciousness. The ability of that consciousness to expand into its potential can be severely limited by not looking after that vehicle. Mental and emotional balance require a certain degree of physical balance and junk food, copious quantities of alcohol, recreational and medicinal drugs, a toxic environment both physically and energetically, and lack of care and consideration for the basic needs of the body ie good food, water, movement, do not give you the best chances of success – far from it!

In the coming pages I am going to briefly cover two aspects of the Grail of the Physical Body – first the energetic aspects which form and constantly interact with us in our physical body, and then we shall look more at enabling a better understanding of the matter/physical body.

Within the Grail Wisdom body of work is a much deeper understanding of the role energy plays, and its different architectures and geometries that enable not just the birthing of matter forms, but also spiritual ascension mechanics. It is complex and requires that you have a basic understanding of energy and the many simple ways we enact with it and how it shapes our world as a foundation, hence this book which will help you begin to perceive the world in this way, before diving deeper into the Grail teachings should you so wish.

By taking in these basic understandings and re-forming your world view to incorporate these it will immediately begin to transform the way you understand the world around you and interact with it. You can then begin to build, step-by-step upon this foundation with the more and more complex layers that follow.

Inevitably you are lead back to your heritage as a Divine Human and the true miracle that is our Creation all around us.

But every journey, as they say, starts with the first steps, so let's start by looking at aspects of the human energy system…..

The Morphogenetic Field

We are going to start at what I call the 'below the line' level ie. the energetic template and blueprints that define our physical form, before we move in the more physical aspects of the matter container which holds our consciousness.

Form comes into matter from out of the energy fields, but there is nothing random or chaotic or chance about this. There are a series of 'templates' which step down higher levels of frequencies and consciousness into the earth fields, and our body form is then manifested or built upon the instruction sets contained within those templates.

At the universal levels there is a templating which every structure in our Universe, from the architecture of our Time Matrix[8] to the smallest bird here on Earth shares, it is just a question of scale. This is called the Kathara Grid or the 12-Tree Grid or the Tree of Life.

I want to make VERY clear here that when we talk of the Tree of Life, which you might also see described as the organic Tree of Life, this is NOT the same as the base 10 Tree of Life of Kaballah/Qabala teachings – this Tree is the *Artificial* Tree of Life and is a result of deliberate misdirection and corruption in the knowledge. I dive deeper into all of this in my upcoming book *The Tree of Life*. At this moment, just be aware that we are talking about very different outcomes and understandings, when working with the organic Tree as opposed to the artificial Tree.

The organic Tree is the base manifestation template of all Creation, and is an architecture of crystalline energetic substance composed of patterns of frequency. From this comes the many layers and layers of morphogenetic fields that exist wherever matter has manifested, regardless of dimension.

---

[8] The Cosmic structure contains six 15 dimensional Universal time matrices for the purpose of consciousness individualization into dimensionalisation, in order to experience the perception of time, and to which are collectively referred to as the Time Matrix.

The morphogenetic field is best understood as a form-holding blueprint which contains the information as to how each individual form of consciousness will manifest itself into matter.

These are templates made up of conscious light and sound, and are instruction sets that direct, through the movement of scalar waves, form to be created according to the blueprint. This in turn creates a holographic projection within that frequency band that we perceive as form – our body, the world around us and so on.

You will have heard before, I am sure, that we live in a holographic reality. This is giving you a glimpse of what that means.

The instruction sets in the morphogenetic field contain intelligent energy that is connected and relays information to our consciousness. Depending upon our training and sensitivity we can either translate that information through our senses, which are a rather blunt instrument, or perceive it directly through our conscious self.

Morphogenetic fields are layered into the consciousness architecture of the planet, which also includes the collective mental and emotional energy body of humanity. It is this collective consciousness field that manifests the reality of the world we 'see' and experience around us. Hence the need for a collective shift within the mental and emotional bodies of a critical mass of humanity in order to bring about change to the current collective experience.

This is not as hopeless as you might at first think, as those who can and do move themselves into higher vibrational frequency ranges exert a greater influence on the collective fields than someone stuck in a very low vibrational state. It has been estimated that just 8 -10% of humanity can influence the direction of travel, and the greater the number of those who come on board with a higher vision

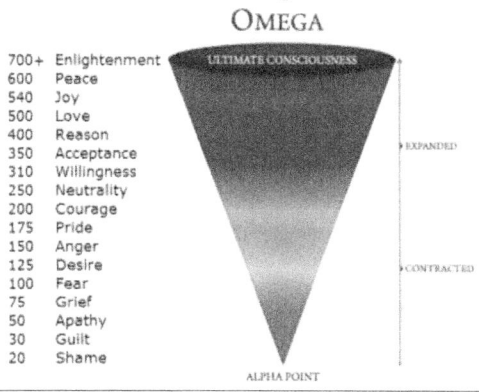

OMEGA

Level	Name
700+	Enlightenment
600	Peace
540	Joy
500	Love
400	Reason
350	Acceptance
310	Willingness
250	Neutrality
200	Courage
175	Pride
150	Anger
125	Desire
100	Fear
75	Grief
50	Apathy
30	Guilt
20	Shame

ULTIMATE CONSCIOUSNESS
EXPANDED
CONTRACTED
ALPHA POINT

for the New Earth, the better the outcomes will be.[9]

It is easy to see if you look around you that this process is well underway, and if you chose to come deeper into the Grail teachings you will be part of this great movement into a higher version of humanity.

---

[9] See the work of David Hawkins *Power v Force*

Diamond Sun DNA

The next step down into matter, as it were, works through our DNA. Our understanding of DNA is currently in a fairly primitive state, and there is a lot more to be uncovered and understood about it.

DNA contains a genetic language which is the blueprint for all life. It is the bridging point at a cellular level between energy and matter. It effectively decodes information into 3D realities, acting to organise matter into the biological form corresponding to the information.

Found in the nucleus of every physical cell, it draws in information from the morphogenetic fields and introduces it into manifestation.

It is made up of 4 nucleic acids and metaphysically each of these is connected into one of the base elemental substances we are familiar with – earth, air, fire, water.

There is nothing fixed about DNA, it is always forming and re-forming according to the energetic exchanges taking place, responding to the vibrationary fields within which it finds itself. So it is interesting to note that the genetic code of our DNA isn't fixed and static but works very dynamically, constantly responding to information coming in not just from the cosmic fields through the morphogenetic templating, but also from our environment around us – toxins in food and environment, ideas and emotions that flow though us and so on, working to absorb, interpret and shape it all.

There is a lot more information to share at this level, but I don't want to get too complex here. Suffice it to say that some scientists are beginning to recognise that there is a highway of light information that penetrates down through the heart of the DNA double helix as it forms and reforms, responding to the information fields around it.

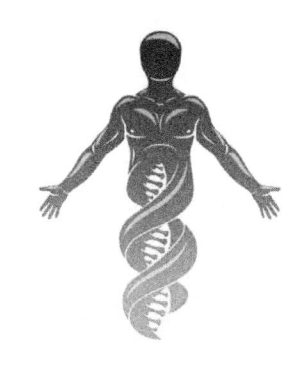

There is even more than this going on with our DNA templating though. DNA as we currently understand it today is not the *original* DNA blueprint recorded in the planetary energy grids. The two active strands of DNA which we have been told about, and which much of humanity is still working with, is an unplugged and reduced form of our original DNA, and the higher blueprint is still sitting within the planetary architectures waiting for us to realign and re-integrate with it.

Remember the so-called 'junk' DNA that scientists talk about? 95 -98% of our total DNA depending upon the source you look at, inactive and apparently useless.

Well, it's not. It has been deliberately unplugged and switched off, many, many thousands of years in our past, in order to turn us into the amnesiac, unconscious and unaware version of humanity we became as a result. That is a long story for another time, but know that our original template is a high frequency 12th dimensional, 12-strand diamond sun DNA templating which is called the Angelic Human templating or Diamond Sun template.[10]

Diamond Sun DNA
12 Strand

The original design of our DNA not only opens up a whole new range of senses and abilities within us, but is also designed to work in alignment with the consciousness grids of the Earth, as well as enabling us to embody 12 dimensions of consciousness.

This template is waiting within all of us to be reactivated strand-by-strand. The great energetic shifts and rising frequencies we have experienced over the last few years have been enabling many to begin the process of re-activation, and we have been joined by many Indigo starseeds[11] incarnating here at this time to help us who already have their 6th strand activated.

---

[10] Picture thanks to www.energeticsynthesis.com

[11] See my book *The Divine Human*

Once we have fully embodied and activated this 12-strand DNA template not only will we be able to travel interdimensionally without deterioration of our biological form, but it opens up pathways into what are called the God Worlds – into many other levels of Creation.

We are truly amazing, powerful creator beings at our core and that legacy is just waiting for us to wake up and begin the process of reclaiming it.

Chakras

The next level we are going to look at is the chakra system. Many of you will already be aware of chakras and the chakra system. I have written a very comprehensive book on chakras[12], and there are a plethora of others available to read also, so I am not going to go into great detail here as for those who are unaware the information is easily available.

What we will look at here is how the chakra system is the anchor point for the energies being brought through from the Source fields/Zero point fields into your system.

Chakra is a Sanskrit word meaning 'Wheel of Life', and the Chakras are viewed as an archetypal map to human consciousness. The awakening and unfolding of each individual chakra within the human energy anatomy is a part of every person's growth process, and therefore working with them consciously can be a considerable help to the awakening of our consciousness and our self-development. Once all the chakras are understood, experienced, opened and connected harmoniously they act as a bridge between matter and spirit, a clear and unimpeded connection between heaven and earth, if you will, or our higher and lower consciousness.

So you can begin to see why a good working knowledge, and experience of our chakras might be helpful to us!

Let's just take a moment to consider why knowledge of the Chakras might be considered important. Your Chakras are part of the silent communication that goes on between you and the Universe. The chakra system is also the anchor point for the energies being brought through

---

[12] *Complete Chakras* Saira Salmon

from the Field into your system. There are at least seven layers to the energy body which surrounds us, rather like an egg. Each chakra interpenetrates and passes energy through each layer of the subtle bodies, stepping it down in frequency before bringing the energy/information field into our body.

There are seven major chakras – although there are numerous smaller ones as well, but it is these seven which mirror the archetypal emotional and energetic issues we need to master and a working acquaintance with them can help us with these lessons. Even a cursory study of them will uncover that they are a profound mapping of universal principles and levels of consciousness and growth. They equate to seven sacred truths found in many religions and wisdom teachings and to seven distinct stages of individual maturation.

Each Chakra has a different emphasis and includes our foundation and survival instincts, our relationships, our vitality and emotional sensations, personal will and empowerment, our ability to give and receive love, creative expression, psychic awareness and spiritual connection. They also help us to navigate and integrate the seven archetypal levels that impact our lives.

So, in short, the Chakras give us a map that helps us explore our connection between the physical plane and the higher, deeper and more spiritual planes of existence.

When each of these centres is balanced and working harmoniously we feel grounded and connected, emotionally safe, have mental clarity, are open and loving and have a clear sense of purpose and vitality.

When one or more falls out of balance we start to become dysfunctional in all sorts of ways, and fail to hear our Divine guidance correctly – or maybe not at all! We lose touch with who we are and our purpose and become incongruent.

Each chakra works at a specific frequency, depending upon its role. As a consequence, although all chakras contain all colour frequencies (remember light = colour), each individual chakra has a specific colour associated with it, depending upon its frequency.

Amongst the many benefits you will start to see, as you work to open and balance each Chakra are:

Root Chakra – you will be more grounded, feel safe, have a greater sense of 'belonging' and be able to manifest life's necessities with ease and achieve your aims.

Sacral Chakra – become more creative, more sexual and attract the opposite sex more easily, as well as creating a better level of connection with individuals

Solar Plexus Chakra – become more self-empowered, look and feel more confident, and see your will power and tenacity increase

Heart Chakra – connect to your higher purpose, achieve deep, loving relationships and become more compassionate

Throat Chakra – communicate more effectively, be unafraid to stand up for your truth and be respected for your authenticity

Brow Chakra – manifest eagle eye intuition, rely on your 'gut' feeling, be open to new ideas and inspirations

Crown Chakra – know beyond a shadow of a doubt that you and the Universe are One, maintain a strong connection to higher guidance and deepen your spirituality

And for those who are thinking this all sounds a little woo woo, I think it is worth saying that modern science is beginning to recognise what is very ancient knowledge.

Japanese scientist Dr Hiroshi Motoyama has conducted research that confirms the presence of chakras in human energy fields, and also that certain humans can project energy through their chakras. He devised electrical instruments to measure the comparative 'charge' around each chakra and through the *nadis,* energy channels within the body, and found that practitioners trained in Chakra Healing showed a considerable increase in activity within a Chakra when they concentrated their attention upon it.

Dr Valerie Hunt, Professor Emeritus of Physiological Science at UCLA, has also carried out further work. She conducted experiments with electromyography, which is used to measure electrical activity of muscles and discovered that emanating from the sites traditionally associated with the Chakras were strong levels of radiation.

And then we have Itzhak Bentov, a researcher of physiological changes associated with meditation, who has duplicated Dr. Motoyama's findings regarding electrostatic energy emission from the chakras.

This is just part of the increasing interest and research that is being done that now supports the existence of chakras, but it is important to realize that whilst science may provide us with some intellectual understanding, it is only direct experience of, and working with, chakras that allows us to truly know them. It is the difference between rational knowing, and real experience.

If you are curious to know what a chakra looks like, we have some idea given to us by those who see energy – this is a skill that according to energy pioneers such as Barbara Ann Brennan can be taught to most of us!

Each chakra is rather like a cone, with the tip or point of the cone connecting into the body along the main energy line or current which pulses up and down the spinal cord. In Hindu wisdom this is called the *sushumna,* which is wound around by two energy channels called nadis.

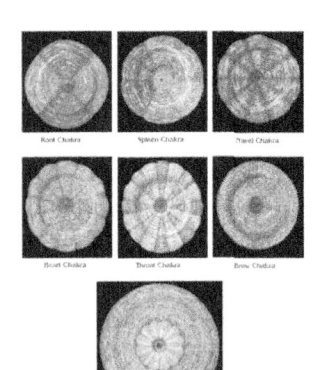

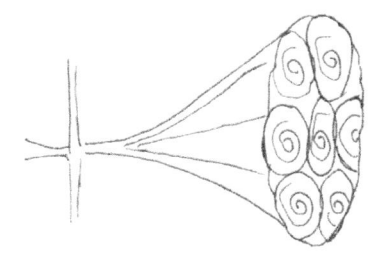

Chakras Illustration *L W Leadbeater 1927*

The Subtle Bodies

I want to just touch on these so you have an awareness of the energy 'egg' which surrounds us.

The physical body we see is just one of the several layers that make up the vehicle within which our consciousness resides.

The Human Energy field surrounds and interpenetrates the physical body. The collective name for the layers, which make this up, is usually called the aura, or auric field, and those who can see it describe it as having a luminous, radiant quality. Indeed, through the advent of Kirlian photography, aspects of this can be captured on camera.

Based on their observations, both historical and modern, researchers provide us with an understanding of the many layers, which make up these so-called subtle bodies. The different layers interpenetrate and surround each other, with each succeeding body composed of finer and finer substances and vibration.

You will find, according to the source you use, that some commentators speak of five subtle bodies, some of seven and some allude to more beyond this. Although this may seem contradictory, practitioners who 'see' the various levels of the subtle body use what Barbara Ann Brennan, one of the modern explorers and an acknowledged expert on these fields, refers to a Higher Sense Perception or HSP. As one's HSP is tuned to different vibrational levels or fields, so different levels of the auric field become visible, and more clearly defined. The more experienced the practitioner the higher the range of frequencies they will be able to 'see'.

The following understandings of the various energy bodies are based on the work of pioneers in this field such as Barbara Ann Brennan and Donna Eden.

There are seven layers of subtle energies surrounding the body, which can be broken down into three categories, much as the chakras can – indeed each layer has its own chakra system within it. So in reality, when we talk about the seven chakras, we are really talking about each chakra being made up of seven 'nested' chakras each, rather like a Russian doll, which connect each layer of the subtle bodies to each other and the physical body.

Having said that, each layer is more specifically associated with an individual chakra – the first layer with the first chakra, for example, the second layer with the second chakra, and so on. This is as much to do with the resonance of each layer of the field and each individual chakra and os associated with and gives a sympathetic vibration between the two.

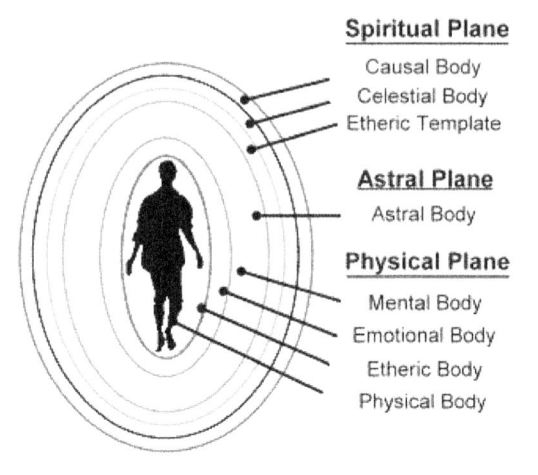

Spiritual Plane
Causal Body
Celestial Body
Etheric Template

Astral Plane
Astral Body

Physical Plane
Mental Body
Emotional Body
Etheric Body
Physical Body

Each of the three categories is a plane of the gradations between the physical world and spiritual plane, from physical existence to spiritual knowing.

The layers of the aura or subtle bodies can be categorized as

Physical: Etheric
Emotional
Mental

Astral: Astral (This is often called the bridge between the lower and higher bodies)

Spiritual: Etheric Template
Celestial
Ketheric Template or Casual

They flow from more dense to more subtle, as they progress out from the physical body, with the denser layers being easier to 'see' for those who have the ability. The higher, or subtler the layer the more expanded is the consciousness that is required to 'see' it, as it is accessing finer and finer fields of vibration.

I am not going to go into much more detail about these here. More information can be found in my book *Complete Chakras* or by reading one of the experts on this topic such as Barbara Ann Brennan's books or there are various courses available which will take you through this in more detail.

There is another level of energetic architecture and templating that is more complex again and goes beyond this. As part of the deeper Grail teachings I do not want to go into this here as it may confuse but did want to ensure you understand this is the tip of the iceberg.

Truly, we are amazing beings!

The Meridian System

This is probably the system that is most recognised within the world of Western medicine and forms the basis of the practice of acupuncture, an Eastern healing modality that often brings spectacular results and has Western science scratching its head as to how this is achieved!

The meridians are a network of energy lines which are associated with various organ and body systems and carry life force or 'chi' energy. The source of this energy is said to come from three places – our parents, our nutrition and directly from our environment.

These rivers of energy, or light, interconnect our cell tissue with the outer world. They are energetic in nature, but influence us at the physical level. There are acupuncture points at various points along each meridian where the channel of energy comes close to the surface of the body and can be accessed by either pressure (acupressure) or very thin needles (acupuncture).

Interestingly, modern science now has sensitive enough instruments to thermographically, electronically and radioactively map the meridian paths around the body, and research has shown that they transport chemical, electrical and etheric energies.

There are 12 major meridians and several minor. The 12 major are:

- Lung meridian
- Large intestine meridian
- Stomach meridian
- Spleen meridian
- Heart meridian
- Small intestine meridian
- Bladder meridian
- Kidney meridian
- Pericardium meridian
- Triple Warmer meridian
- Gallbladder meridian
- Liver meridian

They form a complex series of pathways around the body, transporting life force energy throughout. Where problems, traumas or blockages build up there can start to be long terms issues that may result in a chronic condition if not addressed.

Here in the West we rarely think about the effects of say surgery or a broken bone or other trauma on our energy meridians, but going to a practitioner who can reconnect severed pathways, or unblock stagnant channels can make a big difference to both initial healing and long term health.

Human body meridians

The Electrical Being

It probably comes as no surprise to you when I tell you that we are bio-electromagnetic beings. Medical science has known this for many years.

Electrocardiograms, electroencephalograms and electromyographs are all used routinely – and the latter has even been used to measure the human energy field.

So the fact that our bodies use electrical energy (and therefore must be generating it) has long been known. Our nervous system is the primary communication route through which these electrical messages are sent, with electrical impulses being carried throughout the body via nerves.

Our nerves are the equivalent of electrical wiring and are the relay system between our brain and the organs and muscles of the body. A kind of Morse code of dots and dashes is used as the 'language' to carry this bioelectrical information both to and from the brain.

Recent studies have shown the electrical control systems within cells and tissues are even more complex than that used along the nerves. It has been discovered that cells have the capacity to function just like tiny integrated circuits and it is thought that our cells can communicate with us using not just light-based and chemical signals but also electronic ones and it is looking like this might be an extremely important communication system which controls whether cells divide or not.

Follow this through and you can start to see that this may well have serious implications in our understanding of problems such as cancer, where cell division has got out of control. It is like the signal these cells receive is giving the wrong message.

Work has also been done by a scientist called Robert O Becker, who was a pioneer in the field of regeneration and its relationship to electrical currents in living things. Not only did he demonstrate the regeneration, for example, of a human figure tip (I give you the before and after photos on the next page) and the effect bioelectrical currents can have on healing at many levels, but he also investigated the effects of power frequencies and radio wave fields on human health.

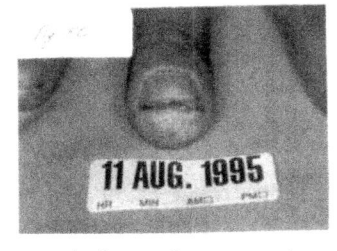

He was nominated for a Nobel prize twice, but his warnings about the problems of electromagnetic frequencies (EMFs) not only lost him his research funding and ultimately position, but also the Nobel prize. This is what happens when you come up with research findings which are against the greed of powerful vested interests unfortunately and is a not uncommon story.

But he demonstrated clearly that the human body was an electro-chemical organism which relies on the earth's magnetic field and internal cell energy for health and repair, and not only was human healing compromised by the high EMF fields radiating from power lines, radar, microwaves ovens, satellites, radios and other electrical equipment and within which almost all of us reside to some extent or other, but also the negative impact they have on health, with this type of radiation correlating to increases in cancers, birth defects, depression, learning disabilities, chronic fatigue syndrome, Alzheimer's and even increased levels of suicide.

He also demonstrated how acupuncture taps into this electrical energy as well as homeopathy, visualisation, hypnosis and electrotherapy.

His work is fascinating as it gives us a whole new perspective on the possibilities for a different kind of healing to that based in often dangerous drugs, but also the ability of regeneration of spinal cords and lost limbs. His warnings about the dangers of EMFs have been repeated time and again by other researchers but are largely ignored by the mainstream and the public as they aretotally unaware of the sea of harmful energies we all reside in – and getting ever more powerful as new generations of cell phone masts are introduced. The clear evidence is ignored and we are all the losers.

Another fascinating insight he had was that extra sensory perception could occur from extremely low frequency (ELF) waves. It is just this type of wave energy that is beginning to affect the earth!

We covered in the previous section some of the problems with EMFs in the home. Now you can clearly begin to appreciate the effect it might be having on us as a bioelectrical organism.

Technopathic Stress
This is where we start to look at the impacts of man-made technology on us as bio-organisms. It has been shown clearly enough that we rely on our internal electromagnetic environment for health and when this gets out of balance problems arise.

Technopathic stress is a recent problem. When electricity first started to be used, going back to the 1760s we start to see the first instances of those who engaged with this new form of energy to conduct experiments etc showing signs of electrosensitivity. It was called such things as telegraphic sickness which afflicted telegraph operators. The history of the development of electricity has a narrative running alongside that of individuals exposed to these currents having a variety of health problems, which all fit the description of neurasthenia or electrical hypersensitivity. So much so that by the end of the 18th century it was generally acknowledged that electricity could make people ill.

In the 19th century however the psychiatrist Sigmund Freud stated that all those suffering the effects of exposure to electrical fields were in fact suffering from 'disordered thoughts and poorly controlled emotions'. The effects of electrical fields were left to wreak havoc. As a result you are now likely to be medicated rather than helped with the effects of the electrosmog within which we live.

In 2001 the Canadian astronomer Ken Tapping showed that influenza pandemics over the last 3 centuries occurred when there were peaks in solar activity and breakthroughs in electrification or the introduction of ever more powerful radio transmitters can also be linked to the waves of flu epidemic we have seen in the last century, starting with the Spanish flu in 1918 which killed so many. The story continues with powerful radar surveillance systems being installed, then military satellites and so on till we come to the present day when ever more powerful radio masts and satellites are being used to bath the planet is increasingly powerful fields.

And everywhere we see sickness – humans, animals, nature…..

Technostress is not taken seriously by the mainstream however – think how inconvenient it would be to admit that our use of powerful electrical, magnetic and radio currents are having a devastating impact on living systems.

So we all live within the effects of this and have to find some way of mitigating it and keeping our organism as balanced as possible within this. This is something we are all going to have to get wise to.

So reading up on technostress and taking some steps within the home to mitigate it is important for health and even doing something as simple as switching off your wi-fi router overnight can help with brain fog and sleep problems.

The Light Being

This is where things start to get really interesting. It has been clearly shown that our cells have light-communication systems.

The cells of our body emit weak bursts of ultra-violet light, and this is part of a light-based control system that our cells appear to use to communicate with each other. In fact, the human body literally glow, but at a level which is 1,000 times less intense than that to which our human eye is sensitive. But we emit visible light in levels which rise and fall during the day according to scientists who are researching this!

It is important to understand this as not only is light in the form of colour a potentially powerful healing mechanism (see previous for the Language of Colour) – and one used by our ancient ancestors successfully – but links into the fact that along with the great energetic changes happening on this planet we have also fully entered what is called the 'photon belt' – something that happens about every 11,000 years – and we are all being bathed in a much greater number of light photons. These occasions have been linked in the past with big leaps forward in human understanding and evolution.

But there are certain conditions which are needed in the body in order to make best use of the light energy – there needs to be sufficient of the beneficial fatty oils and also sufficient hydration.

Pioneering work has been done around this by Barbara Wren who, like many pioneers has felt the full weight of the Establishment against her in order to discredit her work. But she is very clear that healing and enabling the mechanisms within us which contribute to being able to access this light energy are clearly linked to each of us being able to reach into our full potential as well as access the deep well of universal wisdom which we all have the potential to tap into.

Take a moment to think about the fact that everything in the universe is energy, and each and every form of energy has a unique resonance. We are a vibration, a form of light being, which has slowed down its resonance to the extent that we are matter.

Also consider that light carries information. A healthy body will allow the full spectrum of light to move through it, permitting the cells to receive the information it carries. An out-of-balance or toxic body starts to refract light, not channel it. The implications of that are huge.

Consider also that our DNA, the double helix which defines who and what we are, has also been found to have a communication highway of light running down the centre of it – and this clearly brings to mind the depictions of the channels of energy both in the land (Ley lines) and in our bodies (shushumna, ida and pingala).

All of this should lead us to the conclusion that keeping our body fit and healthy and properly nourished so it can maximise its ability to utilise and create light is very much a part of being on any spiritual path or quest.

Our physical bodies are the container for the grail essence which is our soul, our spirit. For us to be able to express the full magnificence of the container for this essence needs to be looked after and respected.

The Placebo Effect
Or the Power of the Mind

Just about everyone has heard of the placebo effect.

This is defined as a phenomenon in which people experience a benefit from a substance or treatment, even though that treatment or substance is to all intents and purposes inactive and therefore shouldn't work.

There are countless experiments and studies which demonstrate the placebo effect and what these show is that the mind can have a powerful influence on the body ie. our beliefs can influence our physical reality.

Any metaphysician is familiar with this, and why this might be, but scientists stuck in the world of Newtonian physics struggle with this concept, even though they can see it is real.

They talk of 'fake' treatments and how the mind 'fools' us, really missing the point that our mind shapes our physical reality from the field of energy we are all part of.

It is an incredibly powerful fact when you grasp it – by changing our internal wiring or belief system we can change our external reality. Literally!

Of course, it isn't easy as patterns of belief and behaviour are deeply conditioned into us, as is our world view on what is possible and not possible. If you have been taught from an early age this can't happen or that is real, then unpicking that can take time....but it can be unpicked.

I will say it again – our Mind defines our reality. Really sit and think about that statement for a moment, and all it implies. Then think of the many ways or areas in which your life is less than what you might wish it to be.

How do ingrained patterns of belief and thought contribute to this? What can you do to change this, starting now?

We are all shaping our brain, our body and our external environment from the thoughts and emotions which we generate. Gaining mastery of these, being fully aware of their frequency and the consequences of that is a powerful game changer.

The great universal laws speak to this and it is a Truth which is being rediscovered today by lots of people.

The Energy of Water

Water is something we very much take for granted. But we shouldn't. Not only is freshwater a very scarce resource - it makes up only about 2½% of the total water on the planet, and most of that is frozen into snow and ice – but we are beginning to understand what a fundamental imprinting and communication system it is due to the work of pioneering scientists.

The humble water molecule is, quite simply, miraculous!

No-one needs any introduction to water, but there is a sense in which it is so much a part of our daily lives that we take it utterly for granted. In fact, water, when you look into it is quite extraordinary.

Given its chemical makeup it doesn't behave in quite the way scientists think it should to follow the rules of physics, and this alone starts to alert you to the fact there is something more going on here.

Water has both a higher boiling point and lower freezing point than it should. It can exist as a solid, liquid and a gas ie water, steam and ice and there are various other things going on with it. It is an extraordinary element.

But the thing I think that is most miraculous about it is its receptivity - water can be programmed!

Water can hold messages. This has been clearly shown by a scientific researcher called Dr Masaru Emoto. He published a ground-breaking book called 'The Hidden Messages in Water. Having researched the properties of water for many years Dr Emoto clearly shows the consequences of all sorts of things on the integrity of water – pollution, for example, chemicals and so on.

But even more fascinating is the impact

Love and Gratitude | Honesty | Love of husband and wife | Happiness

Hope | I can't do it | I can do it | Eternity

our thoughts have – his experiments showed that thoughts directed at water affected it in different ways. The more positive and beautiful the thoughts the more beautiful the resulting water crystals were. The more negative and discordant the more of a blob the water crystal became!

The pictures say it all. And he has repeated this time and time again. He has even demonstrated that it is not only a question of saying something positive, but thinking it from a distance, or writing it on paper and sticking it to the sides of a container holding water are equally as effective. Words carry vibrations. The water picks them up and changes accordingly.

His research even shows the ability that prayer has to improve even polluted water. Imagine that! Praying to clean and purify water!

Interesting as all this is – and believe me, it is! – it is the *implications* of what he has discovered which are so profound at a variety of levels.

First is the fact that you are 70+% water (the amount varies depending upon how dehydrated you are). When you think a negative thought about yourself – I'm not good enough/pretty enough/intelligent enough for example – how do you think that thought, and the subsequent emotions it produces is affecting your body? You are programming the water in your body with it, and affecting the health of that body. If the fluids within your body become sludgy and muddy and incoherent it inevitably affects the health of that body.

Implications for health = huge!

Then think of homeopathy, which drug companies have spent a lot of money trying to discredit. It uses the *memory* of water to deliver treatments for health problems. All of the so-called scientists who pooh-pooh this have clearly not read Dr Emoto's work or understood the implications of it, let alone read the many, many properly conducted scientific studies which show its efficacy.

Dr Emoto experimented with food also – this picture is of a rice experiment. Rice, of course, has a high level of water when cooked. Loved rice lasts much longer than hated rice. Can you imagine? Again the implications are huge. Not just for you and the food you eat – you can easily see how blessing a meal can have a real effect – but also for extending shelf life. Can you imagine the staff in a supermarket lined up every morning offering love to the food on their shelves to ensure greater health-giving properties and longer shelf life.

What a world that would be!

So you can clearly start to see that water is an extraordinary element and understanding this and then the knock on effects this will have on anything which contains water could be a huge game changer.

How does water hold messages? That, to the best of my knowledge, hasn't yet been unravelled, but it is intriguing to think where this might go in the future.....

Another aspect of water which it is worth mentioning here is that it has the ability to heal a wide variety of problems – or at least, if we drink enough of it problems can be averted.

We all know that we need a near constant intake of water in order to survive. In fact, so critical to life is it that a body can survive no more than 2 -3 days without imbibing water as we lose water almost continuously through breathing, sweating, tears, urine and faeces. We only have to lose 15% of the water in our bodies for things to hit critical.

Even mild dehydration affects the ability of our blood to function well. As anyone who is familiar with the work of Dr Batmanghelidj[13] is aware increasing your water intake is a simple remedy to anything from thick, sluggish blood leading to high blood pressure and cholesterol problems to stress, asthma and some forms of pain. Powerful indeed!

It becomes even more intriguing when you look at the research around how, generally speaking, as a population we start to dry out as we age.

I was taught many years ago in my naturopathic training that when we feel hungry it is often a signal that we are thirsty, and we eat instead of drink.

Look at this diagram of the average amount of water we contain as we grow up. You can see that from the moment we are born we start losing hydration. Every system in our body is clearly designed to work within a high water content environment and yet that water keeps diminishing.

You begin to understand the mechanism that Dr Batmanghelidj was tapping into when, by putting more water into someone's system imbalances started to balance out. Many people say 'I'm not thirsty' but the thirst mechanism is notoriously unreliable and the more dehydrated you are the less it works, which is very unhelpful!

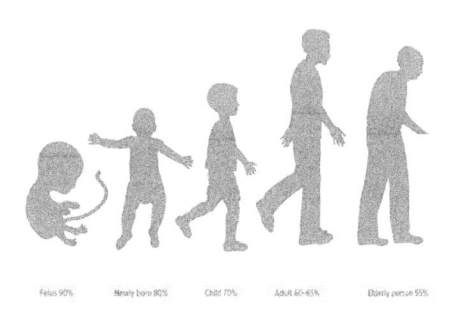

So to help all the physical, electrical and biological systems within you work at their optimum just drink more water every day – pure, clean water that is, not something heavily adulterated by chemicals.

There are many different types of water purifiers available which strip out contaminants. It is always wise to have a system which re-introduces beneficial minerals to the water and if it vitalises the water, so much the

---

[13] *Your Body's Many Cries for Water* Dr F Batmanghelidj

better. But remember, you can always just bless it before you drink a glass – Dr Emoto's work shows us how powerful this simple mechanism is.

Sound & Vibration

Everything is made up of energy. Energy vibrates and it depends on the frequency of vibration as to what the energy becomes. That is very simplistic in many ways, but if you can remember this simple principle then a lot of new ideas and concepts open up.

The Universal Cosmic Laws[14] talk to this principle of vibration and how fundamental it is to the world of both matter and energy.

The benefits of sound and vibration are not new. Pythagoras, the Greek philosopher for example was well aware of the benefits of sound and he taught that musical instruments, particularly the lyre, were capable of tuning the soul to the singing rhythms of the universe, the 'music of the spheres'.

Everything has a frequency, even emotions, and we are constantly being vibrated on a cellular level by sound frequencies both at and outside the levels we can hear. Every cell in our body picks up and resonates to the frequencies they are exposed to. The right sounds harmonise, calm and transform. The wrong frequencies create disharmony and harm.

Sound has been used as a healing tool to right disharmonious frequencies for much of mankind's history. Sound has also been used as a means of connecting to the Divine and from the chanting of the Perpetual Choirs to that of Benedictine monks, the sacred has been bathed in sound.

Gongs, from as early as 4,000 BC, have been used as sacred instruments and other instruments as well as voice has been used in sacred ceremony as far back as we have a written historical record.

So you can see this as a means of raising your frequency, improving meditation and touching into the numinous, or you can also see it as a means of balancing the body, bringing deep peace and relaxation and healing.

Modern day sound healers will use their voice and their instruments to boost your energy, release energetic blocks and limiting patterns, induce

---

[14] See *The Universal Laws* Saira Salmon

relaxation, reduce stress, help you to find inner peace, get in touch with creativity and help you align to your potential.

When we are healthy, everything in our body is vibrating in harmony, the whole resonance is harmonious and balanced. Disease or dis-ease results when a part of the body starts to fall out of this harmonious resonance.

What sound healers do is to approach the body as if it is whole and complete – they are talking to the energetic blueprint of health we all hold in other words. The body is then filled with vibrations that 'talk' to the body at this level, vibrations and frequencies which emphasize wholeness . The body knows where these frequencies are most needed and will pull them to that area, bringing resonance and harmony back in.

Through the process of entrainment, disharmony is brought back into harmony. It is a question of restoring the harmonious vibrational frequencies.

This potentially works at several levels:

- by entraining the body toward homeostasis or balance
- by helping to restore regulatory function which has fallen 'out of tune'
- by altering cellular functions through energetic effects such as influencing neurotransmitters etc

If sound can have that profound an effect on us, just take a moment to think of the impact that disharmonious noise may have. How it will impact us at the mental/emotional level as well as the spiritual…..

Sound healing is only part of what can be achieved through vibration though. In fact almost all forms of energy healing and many of the so-called 'New Age' healing modalities (some of them are very old!) are found under the heading of Vibrational Medicine.

Why? Because energy is vibration.

Here are just a few of them:
- homeopathy
- acupuncture
- flower essences

- tissue salts
- colour healing
- magnet healing
- radionics
- distant and hand-on healing

And it is likely, as our awareness of the energetic world continues to open up, that healing modalities will more and more switch in this direction as we begin to truly understand what it is to be human.

And for those who choose to dive deeper into the Grail Wisdom than this simple introduction will come to understand how everything in our Universe is birthed from sound, light, frequency and vibration, and the many architectures and geometries that are formed as it all comes through into creation and the world of matter.

Earthing

It's been called the most important health discovery ever....and there is good reason in our day and age to think so. But it really is nothing new – our ancestors were doing it all the time!

It's earthing!

So obvious, so simple – common sense really – and yet so overlooked. Particularly as we now live in the age of energy. We are immersed in an invisible sea of electromagnetic waves, microwaves and other energy fields generated in a variety of ways.

When I learnt about this some years ago I was fascinated to discover there are various natural energy 'grids' that surround the Earth (see Part 2). They have been measured ever since the necessary instrumentation was invented, and they 'vibrate' in most areas of the world at a similar level to that of the human body – we are in harmony with them. That makes sense, right?

We are a part of the overall ecosystem so it's no surprise that we resonate harmoniously with it. Where we don't the incidence of degenerative illness shoots up!

From a health point of view, the man-made energy fields we are now surrounded by build-up in our body. And due to synthetic-soled shoes, floor coverings etc we rarely are ever directly connected to the Earth anymore, so most of us don't discharge this energetic build up.

The result – the development of inflammation and the chronic pain that goes with it, poor sleep and energy levels, higher stress and tension, poor healing outcomes, out of balance body rhythms, hormones and so on. The list is a long one.

Does this sound fantastic? There is good research to back this up!

The following is taken from a research paper into the effectiveness of earthing:

> *'Emerging evidence shows that contact with the Earth—whether being outside barefoot or indoors connected to grounded*

conductive systems—may be a simple, natural, and yet profoundly effective environmental strategy against chronic stress, ANS dysfunction, inflammation, pain, poor sleep, disturbed HRV, hypercoagulable blood, and many common health disorders, including cardiovascular disease. The research done to date supports the concept that grounding or earthing the human body may be an essential element in the health equation along with sunshine, clean air and water, nutritious food, and physical activity.'[15]

There is something to do with our connection to the earth and the exchange of ions which occurs and 'grounds' us and synchronisation with the earth's electric potential and frequency which has a direct effect on our health and is profoundly healing.

Amongst the many studied benefits are : improved blood sugar control, improved cortisol (stress) levels, improved thyroid function, better balance of electrolytes, better circulation, lowered blood pressure, improved blood clumping, improved quality of sleep, less joint pain and stiffness, rapid reduction in inflammation and pain, improved healing of wounds, fibromyalgia, arthritis, back pain, psoriasis, jet lag, improved sleep, cramping, restless legs….the list goes on…and on.

There are even reports of autism symptoms improving and there being anti-ageing benefits.

Earthing is Simple

At its simplest earthing is easy – walk barefoot on the earth for a good 10 minutes a day. In reality, if you live in northern climes frozen feet can become a real issue!!

So there are various ways you can earth yourself daily without stepping outside and risking frostbite! Earthing sheets can be used on your bed, earthing mats can be used with a computer or when sitting down, and earthing bands can be attached to wrists or ankles whilst sitting still.

---

[15] Earthing: Health Implications of Reconnecting the Surface Electrons. Gaétan Chevalier, Stephen T. Sinatra, James L. Oschman, Karol Sokal, and Pawel Soka Jan 2012

All of them are either plugged into a grounded circuit within the house, or a spike is driven into the ground outside via a wire run from the blanket/mat/band.

Whilst earthing sheets are not cheap I can attest to their benefit, having used one for many years.

And using an earthing mat as a mouse pad for the computer does improve the exhaustion and sense of depletion which a day in front of the computer inevitably brings.

So investigate this further if you wish – there is plenty of research now, a book available and even a movie has been made about it (search YouTube)!

It may be one of the simplest and most profound ways you can help yourself to protect against the electro-stress we are all exposed to.

Dowsing for Health

Dowsing for health can be an easy and interesting way to either diagnose an area of the body where there is a problem, or find out what is going to be the most effective form of help for you. It is as specialist an area in its own right as dowsing for earth energies is.

I was first introduced to this may years ago when, after two years of struggle and feeling more and more like death warmed up each day, and being told by doctors that their panels of tests showed I was a 'well woman', when I clearly wasn't, a friend told me of someone they had heard of who got good results. Desperate, I booked an appointment.

I was slightly bemused, to say the least, when the first thing she did was whip out a pendulum, but within 10 minutes she had an answer for me and told me what to do. Proof of the pudding is always in the eating, and following her instructions I recovered my health.

Case closed as far as I was concerned! I went on to study with this woman as well as many others as I sought to understand the various causes that lead to lack of well-being and disease over the coming years.

Dowsing, as I have said previously, requires that you 'get out of your own way' sufficiently to be neutral about any answers, particularly if you are doing this for yourself. If this is difficult for you then ask another competent dowser to do it instead.

When dowsing for health it helps to have a good understanding of how the body works and a holistic health context to put it within in order to interpret results as well as possible, and if there is some serious imbalance I would always suggest going to a trained practitioner, but for the simpler things in life self-care is always the first step and can often stop things getting any worse.

So there is a lot we can do for ourselves to check things out as a beginning.

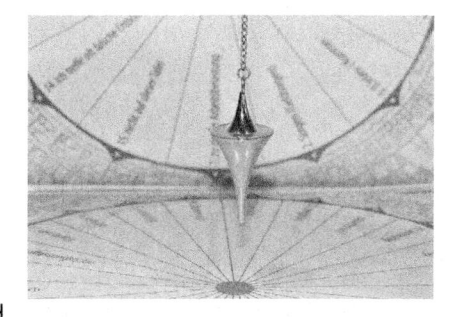

The easiest way is to use a series of charts to track something down, find out which chakra is out of balance, tell which vitamins/minerals/ flower essences etc might be most beneficial for you at any given time. You can even use it to inform you which therapy would be most beneficial for you.

Remember the body is an energetic organism and its needs fluctuate according to a variety of factors so what holds true one day may shift. Your health is never a stationary thing, and your body is always giving you messages regarding this, whether you recognise it or not.

I give you a few simple charts to get started but there are plenty of people who make more available online, or you can make your own – you are limited only by your imagination. The causes of dis-ease and lack of wellness are myriad and often over-looked by taking a conventional approach.

Another simple way of dowsing for health is to using the pendulum to determine both the vitality of food and what we might need or benefit from at any given time. Simply hold your pendulum over the food and ask if this food is beneficial to your body. You can also ask such questions are 'Am I getting all the protein I need?' If the answer is no you can ask what might be the best thing to do so – red meat, chicken eggs, milk etc – and then how often a week.

You are really only limited by the extent of your understanding and imagination in how you can use dowsing to benefit your health. It allows your body to speak directly to you, without your mind getting in on the act and possibly muddying things up.

Many people who have a passion for holistic health make a career out of helping people with health issues via dowsing. Of course, you need qualifications to do this, but you can study to get nutritional knowhow etc and introduce dowsing alongside this, or there are various practitioners who will train you. Your country's dowsing organisation can help put you in touch with them.

A few Dowsing Charts to Get You Started......

Chakras

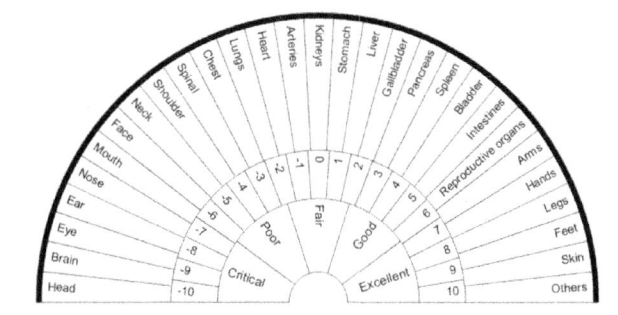

Areas of the Body

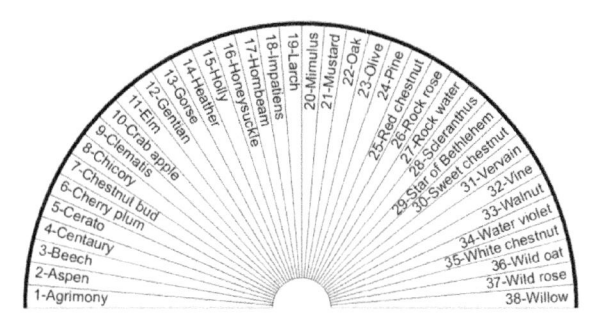

Bach Flower Essences

Different Healing Therapies:

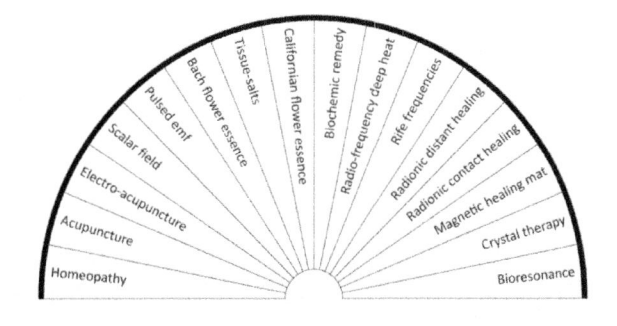

Severity Scale

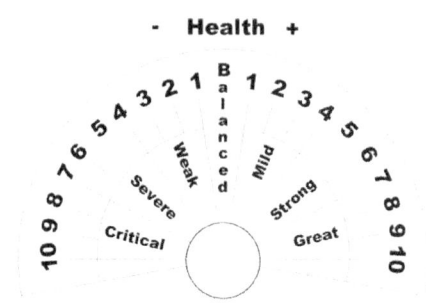

Things you might
need to do

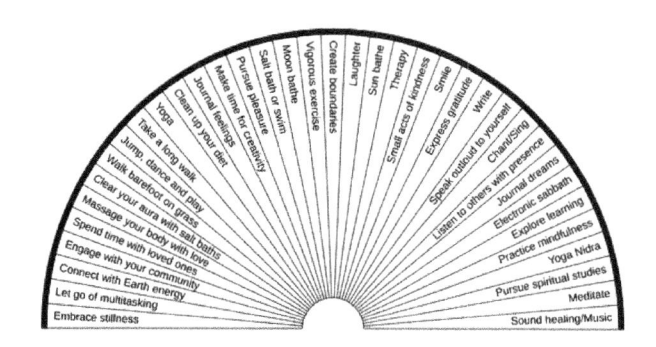

Have some fun playing with these and practising your pendulum dowsing!

The Holistic Model of Health

Any successful healthcare approach has at its heart a philosophy and a model that is easily presented. In the next few pages I shall outline some basic concepts for you to grasp, as this is a different approach to that we are schooled in by Big Pharma and allopathic or evidence-based medicine[16].

In the West we have primarily two very different approaches, and there is a story behind how they developed.

Pasteur v. Beauchamp & Terrain Theory

The current healthcare approach – called the 'medical model' or allopathic approach – all stemmed from one man's view back in the 19th century.

Louis Pasteur came up with a theory of disease called 'germ theory', which basically held that we are surrounded by bugs and bacteria and germs in various guises, and it is these that are responsible for disease. In fairness, this wasn't necessarily a new theory, others had posited it before, but Pasteur put his name to it claiming to have 'discovered' germs.

At the same time a Frenchman Antoine Béchamp, a member of the French Academy of Sciences and one of France's most prominent researchers and biologists was developing another theory, called 'biological terrain', which held that the real cause of disease was the state of the body.

---

[16] You may be surprised to know that much of it isn't, in fact, evidence-based, and that many of the studies that are cited are often considered fraudulent, badly done or inaccurate when examined by independent researchers, Even 'peer-reviewed' is now often seen as subject to corporate or political bias. Many Big Pharma companies have criminal convictions for this fraud and corruption.

Béchamp was able to scientifically prove that germs are the chemical by-products and constituents of microorganisms adapting to environmental conditions ie. Unbalanced, malfunctioning cells and dead tissue. He found that if the body terrain or tissue condition was a diseased, acidic, low-oxygen environment, created by a toxic/nutrient deficient diet, poor lifestyle, toxic emotions and thoughts disease ensued. It was the body terrain, not the germ, that underpinned the disease.

His findings demonstrate how cancer develops with morbid changes of germs to bacteria to viruses to fungal forms to cancer cells, due to the increasingly more toxic state of body tissue. Mere exposure to a germ is not enough for us to get sick.

> 'The primary cause of disease is in us, always in us'
> Antoine Béchamp, 1883

Despite this Pasteur's theory won the day. Why? Pasteur is charged with having distorted and plagiarized Béchamp's findings, but on top of this his theory was more popular because this way no-one had to take any responsibility for their health. It wasn't their fault! It was the germ that dun it m'lord!!!

Pasteur's theory not only allowed people off the hook for all their bad habits and choices, but also enabled the rise of the pharmaceutical industry[17] and for it to profit hugely from the patented drugs and treatments for 'fighting' germs. As a result, despite having seemingly vanquished the major infectious diseases which were mankind's killers for millennia, as a population we have never been so sick with an ever-expanding list of chronic diseases (now numbering over 10,000....and counting).

---

[17] See Appendix 5

The irony is, that on his death bed Pasteur is reported as having admitted that Béchamp's theory was right, and that all disease does, in fact, start with the condition of the body.
If Béchamp's discoveries had been incorporated into the medical curriculum and everyone understood the issues underpinning disease, it is likely that we would now be facing a virtual elimination of disease, and no pharmaceutical industry.

Some might think that a much-to-be desired outcome. Others, whose livelihood and wealth depend upon the illness industry wouldn't agree!

The Disease Tree

Béchamp's theory is easily illustrated by something called The Disease Tree.

The Disease Tree illustrates how if the soil (body terrain) is nutritionally deficient, toxic, inflamed, suffering from free radical damage and in a negative environment, the ensuing tree that grows from this soil will affect all of the branches of the tree (the body systems), with every leaf produced by that tree being one of the plethora of named diseases that result from this.

Every gardener knows you cannot grow a healthy plant in unhealthy soil. If the plant is unhealthy, look to the soil

The same is true of the human being.

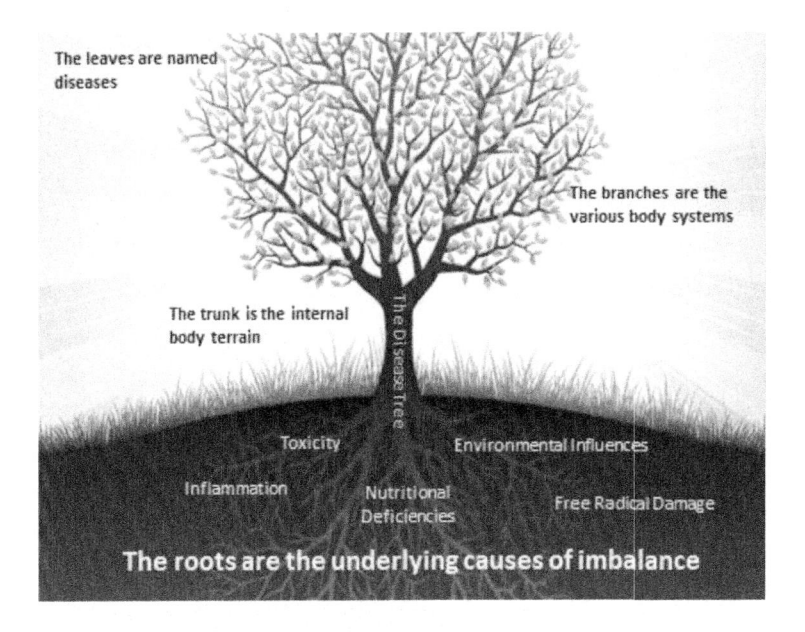

The Iceberg

Another easy to grasp allusion I used with client's to help them make the paradigm shift that is required to approach their health from a very different angle is that of the iceberg.

The top of the iceberg, showing above the water line, is the condition, or symptom, they are struggling with. Underneath this is the vast bulk of the iceberg. This is made up of the same causes that toxify the soil for the disease tree.

Toxins

Environmental influences

Inflammation

Free radical damage

Nutritional deficiencies

Symptom

Underlying Cause of Disease

Nutritional Deficiencies - processed food, over-farmed, depleted soil and even our highly stressed lifestyles all lead to what nutritional scientists called Type B malnutrition – and it is at epidemic proportions within the Western World.

Free Radical Damage – lack of antioxidant nutrients will lead to an excess of free radical damage within the body, leading to damaged cells, damaged DNA, ageing and chronic disease.

Inflammation – often, but not always, a result of free radical damage, chronic inflammation underpins most degenerative disease pictures

Toxins – these come in many shapes and forms, and we are subjected to a massive exposure to these today in a way our forebears never had to contend with, including chemicals in food, toiletries and household cleaners, pharmaceutical drugs, moulds, heavy metals, pesticides, over-the-counter medications and, of course, environmental pollution.

Environmental Influences – pollution, electro-magnetic frequencies, radio micro-waves, lack of earthing, radiation; it also includes negative mental beliefs and thoughts, as well as stressful emotional situations. These are just a few of the potentially damaging effects to our health in our modern environment.

Healthy Helpers

I am going to share with you a few of the modalities which I have found to extremely helpful and effective in helping many of my clients in the past (and myself!) back into a state of balance and health.

I want to make the point here that health is never a done deal. Like a surfer on a surf board, having to constantly shift to remain standing as wind and waves affect his stability, we have to do the same. Our environment is constantly changing, our emotional and mental self has all sorts of ups and down, sometimes we eat well, sometimes we eat poor quality foods, or make bad choices around alcohol or drugs, or …..

Do you start to see what I mean? So much is constantly affecting us and we need to be awake and aware to this, and respond accordingly.

You have a great helper here – your body. It is sending you signals and messages every second of every day – a twinge here, an ache there, a dip in energy, a feeling of resistance towards something or an outright sense of No! It shows up in so many ways, and we have to attune ourselves to these instincts – because that is what they are, our body is a finely honed instrument and knows what it wants or needs, what is not good for it etc.

Unfortunately, all-to-often we are taught not to listen to it and to give our power over to someone else in this respect – do as the doctor tells you syndrome!

We are trained into it from an early age by our parents who themselves have been trained into it by their parents who..... you get the picture!

I well remember crying from a badly scraped knee which smarted and hurt being told 'There, there that doesn't hurt'. Well, yes it did actually! Quite badly in fact! But I soon learnt not to take my hurts and fears to someone else, as it made them uncomfortable and what I was feeling wasn't validated and just left me confused.

Listening to, respecting and trusting your body and its spot-on instincts is a skill we have to re-learn. And it usually requires that we pick apart the overlays of compulsive, addictive or otherwise unhealthy behaviours we have picked up along the way.

Herbs

One of the greatest helpers I use day-to-day to keep things balanced is herbs. Herbs are Nature's pharmacy. Nature has given us what we need to be well. By exploring and embracing the medicine cabinet that very often lies just outside our front door, in our gardens, we are not only helping ourselves, but also contributing to a more balanced way of living.

Herbs have been used by mankind for millennia, and closely studied for their benefits. As science has slowly turned its attention to the miracle that sits under our noses, it has discovered what native peoples knew – the herbal pharmacopeia has much to offer us. And it has tried to isolate 'active' ingredients to use as medicines. These often come with nasty side effects though as this approach overlooks the obvious point that Nature mixes together a broad range of compounds in each plant in a synergistic mix designed to give benefits, not side effects.

I consider herbs to be a first line of defense when it comes to health, and have my go-to herbs for various common conditions which I use as either tinctures or teas usually. Studying herbalism is a life-long voyage of discovery – and then, of course, there is the delight of growing as many fresh herbs as possible in your garden!

There are many wonderful books available – see Further Reading – and courses you can easily find. Don't be intimidated by using herbs. You do not need to be a trained herbalist to know and use a few basics. Often combining a few herbs improves outcomes so find out what works for you.

It is simple to take herbs in the form of infusions, or teas. Indeed, any good health food shop has a good selection of herbal teas ready made for you, some combination mixes being targeted as specific aids, maybe to detox, or help better sleep etc. But don't forget you can walk outside into your garden and pick dandelion leaves, fennel, mint etc, and just pour boiling water over them and leave to infuse.

I could write a book on herbs and their uses and properties, and there is plenty of information around at this level, so it is not difficult to quickly gain a basic understanding.

Nutritional Supplements

It should be as easy as eating a good, fresh, well-balanced diet to achieve the necessary supply of nutrients our body needs in order to keep all of its systems in good working order.

Unfortunately it isn't that simple any longer. Our soils are severely depleted of vital nutrients so food grown in that soil is equally depleted. And that is just the beginning processing, cooking, storage etc all go on to affect nutritional quality.

Here in the West, we are also often preoccupied with how a food looks, rather than how nutritionally dense it is, which is really missing the point as to why we are eating it.

This is a huge topic and I could go on for ages about it. Indeed I used to give long lectures on this back in the days when I was teaching holistic health – it is both a fascinating and shocking topic when you dive deeper into it. But, long story short, the upshot is that in order to ensure you body's nutritional store cupboard has all that it needs day-to-day some form of supplementation is necessary.

And not just any supplements – did you know that a vast array of those you can buy are synthetic vitamins and minerals? Does that matter I hear you say … yes it does, although a food chemist would tell you otherwise.

Did you know that synthetic Vitamin C does not cure scurvy, whereas food-based, organic vitamin C does? Just one example of how choosing the right source of your vitamins can make a difference.

This is a huge topic, and I have a lot of information on this and other similar issues held in The Lost Wisdom Library, available through my website[18], but there are also many good writers on this topic and books you can read to better educate yourself in the choices you make.

Essential Oils

Plants are chemical factories and Nature's bounty continues to be showered on us in the form of essential oils.

These are complex and powerful substances derived from plants. Not only are they usually highly aromatic, but they have amazing healing properties to bestow.

Essential oils are not really oils in the true meaning of the word, but are created from a highly concentrated liquid which comes from the plant, the distilled essence of the plant and its distinctive properties.

They are a great gift both due to their beautiful scents, and their medicinal and healing properties – in fact our forebears valued them more for the latter than the former. They have been in use for many centuries, and modern day research is confirming the properties our ancestors treasured them for.

They work their healing magic without leaving any toxins behind them and are most effective when used by either external application or inhalation, rather than taken orally (although some can be taken this way).

Application methods included massage oil, sitz baths, compresses, body oils and lotions, body and foot baths, steam inhalations, room sprays, room diffusers and perfumes. It is this wide range of potential applications that also make them particularly useful to someone who has digestive impairment of any kind.

These oils are extracted from the plants by various means, depending upon the species and the part of the plant used –

---

[18] www.sairasalmon.com

stems, roots, flowers, bark, leaves, seeds, sap, peel, bean, needles etc.

Some oils are abundant in the plant – lavender for example – whilst others take a great deal of work to produce a tiny amount of oil. Rose oil requires 60,000 rose blossoms to produce a single ounce, and the price obviously reflects this.

The oils come from all over the world, and represent the distilled essence of the plant. Each oil contains an average of 100 components and it is the blending of these compounds which gives the oils their potency – and even today we are still investigating and discovering more and more compounds.

It is important to note *synthetic or reconstituted oils DO NOT have the therapeutic qualities of 'real' essential oils.* So it important if you want to use essential oils for any of their beneficial qualities, be it physically, mentally, emotionally or spiritually that you use a good therapeutic grade oil. Some 'oils' are sold only for their aroma and their fragrance is often made up of artificial compounds to replicate the smell. Others are poor quality and do not express the fullness of the plants potential, so ensure your source of supply is excellent and of therapeutic grade.

Another interesting and important aspect of essential oils to note is they are non-invasive in that they do not interfere with the body's electromagnetic fields, which as we have seen are important to balanced health. Oils have both clockwise and an anti-clockwise characteristics, and combined with the electromagnetic fields of the body this is thought to be one aspect contributing to their ability to stimulate the body's healing mechanisms.

The power of essential oils is often trivialised and under-rated. Due to their beautiful scent this is often their sole use, but they are powerful and complex substances – the essential oil of oregano, for instance, is 26 times more powerful than the antiseptic phenol which is used in many commercial cleaning products.

You don't need an extensive collection of oils to have a basic kit for home use, but they are rather addictive to collect! Each one will fill your home with wonderful scents and uplifting properties, so have fun and enjoy experimenting with these wonderful gifts from Nature!

Flower Essences

Plants and flowers have been part of Nature's Pharmacy, appreciated and used by Mankind for millennia. The history of flower essences can be traced back many thousands of years, to Ancient Egypt and China, with many cultures using flower essences to treat emotional health and wellbeing. Even today aboriginal peoples worldwide still use them in their rituals and ceremonies, and are fully aware of the subtle healing properties of flowers.

Emotional wellbeing is a major component of health in the whole person, and imbalances in this area can have a big impact on our ability to heal quickly, and generally engage with life as we would wish to. Nature's gift to us includes the therapeutic qualities of plants which are not only medicinal, but work gently to bring about emotional wellbeing, which helps to re-balance the body.

Everything in existence has a unique vibrational rate. Flower essences are described as a vibrational or energy therapy, and by tapping into the unique vibrational field of different flowers we have a gentle and safe way of working to right imbalances at this level which impacts so deeply on the quality of our lives.

I very quickly added training in various flower essence ranges into my well-being practice when I saw how many of the issues clients were facing had a big emotional element. They both enabled and supported clients through some of the profound changes needed to bring about wellbeing.

Flower essence therapy is recognized and used worldwide. There are many different ranges available, and all offering something unique.

How Do Flower Essences Work?
Flower essences come under the umbrella of vibrational or energy medicine, which is a holistic approach targeting the 'whole 'person – physical, mental, emotional and spiritual.

The vibrational model focuses on the

animating vital forces that breathe life into the bio-machinery of living systems, treating with pure energy in a range of frequencies designed to bring about harmony within these energy fields – and therefore healing. Fundamental to this approach is the understanding that consciousness is integral to the cellular expression of the body and contributes to both health and illness.

The unseen, energetic makeup of the human being makes a big contribution to the overall wellness – or otherwise – of the human body, and our emotional system is one of the primary ways we interact with this.

Emotions are simply energy-in-motion (e-motion) and are inextricably linked with health or disease. In many modalities including Traditional Chinese Medicine emotions are seen as being the biggest single causative factor in disease.

The process is straightforward:

> Attitudes drive the emotions
> Emotional energy determines the state of the physical body

This is not to preclude the part played by agents of disease such as pathogens, chemical toxicity or trauma but set the scene for the energetic environment in which these things will either thrive or die.

Flower Essences become part of a holistic healing approach that takes into account both physical and energetic aspects to clearing disease and wellbeing issues.

And above all they are totally safe and non-toxic. Whilst using the right remedy will bring great benefit, using the wrong one will not have any ill effects. According to homeopathic principles, less is often more, but even taking a full bottle of an essence in one go will bring no ill effects – it will just leave you needing to buy more!

Phytobiophysics

Phytobiophysics is a range of flower essences produced in a homeopathic format and are the brainchild of Dr Diana Mossop, founder of the Institute of Phytobiophysics.

The formulas are made from the essence of thousands of plants and flowers gathered from all over the world and combined together to produce a resonating frequency of a very precise specification. Each formula has a specific vibration which resonates on a particular colour frequency.

The remedies are held in sugar tablets, not liquid as individual flower essences are. The formulas are so highly energised that they provide maximum healing in the minimum time possible. They restore balance to all levels of consciousness and their effect is profound and far-reaching.

The sugar pill dissolves quickly allowing its potency to be assimilated into the circulatory system very quickly. This is then picked up by the meridians, which connect into the nervous system, and within seconds they begin to regulate the energy system of the body.

Simple, yet extremely effective they are non-toxic and extremely safe to use.

Find out more: www.phytob.com

Homeopathy

Homeopathy is another form of vibrational medicine and uses the ability to imprint water with the essence of a cure and then dilutes it down many times until there is no perceivable molecule of the cure left in the mixture.

What has been discovered is that the more dilute the substance, the more potent the cure!

Homeopathy deeply engages the principles of quantum physics and the discoveries of Dr Emoto on water holding a message. It is truly an energy modality and works to release stagnation and blockage at the energetic level, within the subtle bodies, thereby bringing about change on the material plane.

It also works to clear generational patterns of trauma that we may carry as part of our lineage.

It is a truly holistic form of medicine in that the unique emotional and physical traits of the individual are taken into account. No two people are the same, nor is the root cause for any dis-ease or imbalance the same in any two instances – no matter that the label might be the similar. Much of the art of homeopathy is learning to discern the unique traits of individuals and their circumstances and match them with the right remedies.

Homeopathy as we know it today was formulated into a coherent philosophy by a German physician called Samuel Hahnemann in the late 18th century. It works on the basis of 'like cures like' or the Law of Similars, which was first put forward by the Greek Hippocrates, otherwise known as the Father of Modern Medicine.

Hahnemann was the first in modern times to work with this principle, a process of matching the symptom manifestation of the patient with the symptom manifestation of the remedy. The results were astounding, and despite much pooh-poohing by modern naysayers, homeopathy continues to enjoy excellent results with patients – probably the reason why mainstream medicine is gunning for it!

Like other modalities of energy medicine it is non-toxic and safe to use at home.

One of the principles of modern homeopathy is that a homeopath will look to see what 'constitutional' type you might be, a grouping which looks for physical and emotional characteristics as the starting point for matching remedies.

We have looked at the Placebo effect earlier in this section, and one of the frequent judgements made from ignorance against homeopathy is that it is just placebo effect. Unfortunately this argument crumbles in the face of not only the thousands of studies which attest to its efficacy, but also the fact that it is a very successful remedy when used on animals, who have no concept of 'placebo'.

So whether it is for you or your animals, you might want to consider getting a homeopathy kit as part of your regular first aid kit!

This is just a few of the many holistic options you have available to you to help balance and re-establish your health at home. Just a few of the others worth looking at – acupuncture, iridology, kinesiology, acupressure, chiropractic, Chinese medicine, Ayurveda…..There are so many to choose from. Find what works best for you, and use it!

The more you can learn about your body and how it works, what it needs to keep healthy and strong and the many ways you can help to improve things yourself, the more empowered you will be. The state of your body is your responsibility to a large degree – it is the choices you make (barring accidents of course) which tend to dictate the outcomes you have.

This is really basic knowledge and should be taught to us from the cradle. Unfortunately for us, powerful vested interests have seized control of healthcare[19] and now the majority of people in the Western world are anything but healthy.

---

[19] See Appendix 5

Shamanic Healing

Shamanic healing is where things really start to get interesting.

Shamanism is both a spiritual and a healing practise and is found in cultures around the world. They are the 'medicine doctors' of indigenous tribes, but shamanic tradition does not have a formalised system of beliefs or ideology. Rather it is an understanding of the interconnectedness of all things and the divine in all things.

It is deeply rooted in an understanding and relationship with 'Otherworld' and the practitioner seeks to be in relationship with the spirit of all things. They also seek relationship with invisible guides and helpers and universal energies in order to find and rebalance the underlying issues which underpin illness or disease.

According to Christina Pratt in *The Encyclopedia of Shamanism*, a shaman is a practitioner who has gained mastery of:

- **Altered states of consciousness**, possessing the ability to enter alternate states at will, and controlling themselves while moving in and out of those states.
- **Mediating between the needs of the spirit world and those of the physical world** in a way that can be understood and used by the community.
- **Serving the needs of the community** that cannot be met by practitioners of other disciplines, such as physicians, psychiatrists, priests, and leaders.

Shamanic tradition has it that there are three worlds the shaman can journey to:

The Lower World – this is the world of the ancestors and where spirit animals reside. It is deeply connected to Nature. Entry to this world is through some aspect of nature, maybe entering a hole in a tree or going underground, or into a pond. This world is often equated to the 'collective unconscious'.

The Middle World – a world of many layers this may be difficult to navigate and is multi-dimensional. It is filled with thought forms, extra-sensory perceptions and hidden energies and is seen as being very similar to our earth plane.

The Upper World – this is the world of cosmic beings, angels and spirit guides. Guides from the lower realms are seen as being more practical, whereas these guides generally have a more 'philosophical' form of guidance.

Shamanic Journey

This is a process whereby the shaman leaves the body to travel throughout the created planes, the three worlds, in order to seek the cure or find the answers to the problems of his client.

The shaman will first enter a powerful trance-like state that is often induced through the frequencies achieved by rhythmic drumming. With a clear intention the shaman will call on helper spirits - spirit guides and animals - to accompany him, protect him and help him on his journey as he goes to find answers, retrieve soul fragments, battle unkind spirits or do whatever is needed.

The shamans aim is to return the client to a balanced and harmonious state. It is not a passive treatment, requiring the client to play an active role and can be deeply healing.

Spirit Animals

Also called power or totem animals, shamanism believes that every person has at least one spirit animal by their side. This animal(s) protects them and guides them as well as lending aspects of the unique skills and characteristics of that animal.

It is believed that a human who has no animal spirit or ally is at risk of both falling prey to illness and all sorts of bad luck.

There are many stories that can attest to the efficacy of Shamanic Healing but let me give you just one, which relates to the use I made of it with one of my dogs.

I am not a trained shaman, but have used shamanic techniques frequently in some of the work I do, and find the process a very easy one to slip into so it was particularly fitting it worked here.

My dog, Treacle, was just 13 years old, and one day his back legs collapsed on him. After rushing him to the vets an x-ray revealed a 'shadow' against his spine. They proceeded to an operation to explore further and rang me during the operation to say there was a huge tumour in his hip joint and what did I want to do? They were not recommending further treatment.

Grief-stricken I told them to sew him up and I would come and take him home for the time we had left.

Once home I contacted a Celtic shaman friend and asked for advice, and then proceeded to pick up my drum as I sat by Treacle. I connected into the tumour easily to find the root cause, and had various animal helpers that came in as I addressed the over-riding emotions that fed it.

In total I went through this process 3 times in the next few days, and on the final journey great beings of light joined me and worked on Treacle. At the end, as I put down my drum Treacle got up and walked and then ran, and continued to do so for several more happy years.

Miraculous? Yes! It is easier to achieve these results with animals as they do not have all of the strong negative belief systems that this type of healing is not possible we have been taught that impedes us humans.

I categorically believe that if I can do this, so can you. It is all a question of how you chose to see and understand the world within which we live.

I live in a world where miracles are possible – do you?

Pottenger's Cats

I want to end this section with a story about Pottenger's cats. It is a salutary tale, a story about our genetic wealth, and how easy it is to squander it.

In the 1930s a scientist named Pottenger undertook a series of experiments over several generations of cats.

He took two groups of feral cats. One group was fed a natural, fresh diet, whilst the other was fed a processed de-natured diet (think modern pet foods!)

As the generations unfolded there was a remarkable difference between the groups. From only the second generation on, the processed diet cats started to show ever-increasing levels of structural deformities, birth defects, stress-driven behaviours, susceptibility to illness and allergies, learning difficulties and increasing levels of infertility. By the third generation not only were illnesses and infertility very common but lifespan was decreasing.

The cats on the natural, wild diet on the other hand, thrived!

If you look around you, we are beginning to see this play out in the human population – there are those who are very switched on around good food, food quality and health and are making excellent choices. They stand out, blooming with health and vitality.

But so many people are just hanging in there. By their 30s they are tired, stressed and beginning the long road into ill health – blood pressure, fatigue, bloating, digestive upsets, sleep issues. And currently 1 in 7 couples are infertile, with that predicted to be 1 in 3 within the next 10 years.

Only a few generations of poor quality, nutritionally-depleted diet is enough to see infertility, degenerative disease, birth defects and a whole host of other nasties begin to creep in, and the longer this goes on the worse things get.

It takes quite a few generations to turn things around even when you do revert to an excellent diet, and it is a salutary reminder to us that several generations into convenience foods, and with a preponderance of processed foods in our diet, we are beginning to go the same way as Pottenger's cats. Look around you at the ever increasing incidence of disease, infertility, cancer, weight issues, mental issues and birth problems and you can begin to understand what is unfolding before our eyes.

Our genetic wealth – the good genes and heritage we pass on to our children – is determined by the choices we make every day, particularly our choices around the quality of food we choose to ingest. And it is not just us who pay the price, but our children, and our children's children.

Quite a sobering thought isn't it!!

Part 5
The Grail Essence

The Grail Essence

Now we come to the heart of the matter, the Grail Essence, that spark of the Divine, your Christos consciousness which has chosen to take on material form.

There is one phrase which sums this part up –Know Thyself! The core of Life Alchemy.

We have, in fact, been addressing aspects of this little by little as we have worked our way to this point. We need to know and understand the world around as it really is, a world based on energetic patterns and flows which inform matter, in order to fully understand ourselves – a Divine being descended into the matter fields to take on form for a particular purpose.

Who you really are is a long way from what you have been taught about yourself.

Materialist, reductionist science was the final nail in the coffin for us here in the West. The Roman Church had already eviscerated any sense we had of ourselves as divine beings, having focused for centuries of brainwashing us that we are 'fallen' wicked, sinful creatures. The advent of science finished us off, as we were told we were the result of random and meaningless 'happened by accident' evolution.

Two amoebas crashing together, life coming from sludge, some lucky ape genetics somewhere along the line and – hey presto! – modern life and humanity in all of its complexity has arrived.

Please! It stretches credulity to the breaking point.

Yet say it often enough, with enough conviction to the young, and you soon have a population swallowing this whole. Such is brainwashing and imprinting.

The Wasteland had fully arrived. Disconnected from our roots, from Nature and from our origins, our purpose, with no place for Spirit, or the feminine 'the split' as modern commentators call it, now shows up in so many ways:

Spirit/matter
Inner/outer
Mind/body
Man/nature
Mind/brain
Culture/nature
Fiction/reality
Empirical/archetypal

This 'split' lies at the heart of the untold suffering that now characterises so much of our modern civilisation – a civilisation which is in its death throes. The despair, the hopelessness, the bleakness and lack of purpose felt by so many, the epidemic levels of chronic illness, the widespread depression and ever-climbing rate of suicides all speaks to this.

And everyone is in agreement – what is needed is to heal 'the split'. And yet….our civilisation is a great behemoth, rolling inexorably forward, focused in our brains, our cleverness, our technology, our sense of being at the top of the food chain and answerable to no-one, apart from, not part of the world which birthed us and sustained us for millennia.

As the scholar and mystic Peter Kingsley says *'the apparent ordinariness of people (as they) go about their disconnectedly meaningless lives is the most extraordinary violation of what we humans are meant to be'*.

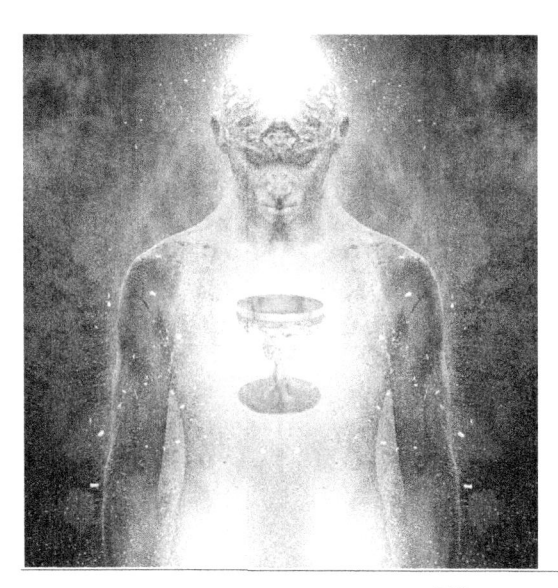

And this has been done to us deliberately. I touched on the true origins of humanity at the start of this book and will one day get round to writing it all down when the time is right. Currently, many would have difficulty taking this history on board, so we begin by taking the first steps, which are awakening the first understandings you have of the Grail that is within.

Suffice it to say things have gone badly wrong for us – and not because we are sinful and fallen. The process of putting it right is up to each one of us.

- ➢ It is You, and many others like you that will rescue the heart of humanity from the damage that has been done.
- ➢ It is You, having the courage to heal 'the split' within yourself, and encouraging others to do the same, who will help birth something new and better than we currently inhabit.
- ➢ It is You, being prepared to seek the answers within, not without, who will bring back what is needed.

How is this to be done?

We begin by being prepared to understand the divine potential that sits within all of us, and having the courage to claim it – not from a place of ego or lack, by with humility and courage and steadfastness (you will need all those) as well as with a will to be of service and a deep and heart-opening love for the Creation which birthed us.

And in order to do this you *must* know who you are warts and all. The magnificent, the humdrum, the ordinary, the extraordinary, the petty and the grandeur of who you are, as well as celebrating your own uniqueness and understanding of the individual gifts you have to bring in service to the collective.

To be sure, the full potential of who we can be – as individuals and as a race – was never part of the everyday awareness of all, that was reserved for the initiates, those who chose to tread the more difficult path into self-awareness and service, but everyone lived from a place of intrinsic connection to all aspects of the world around them, with awareness of Spirit infusing matter at every level, and of there being meaning and purpose to even the most quiet or difficult of lives.

Now, we all need to find a way back to that place and it is people like you and me who are the way-showers, those forging the path that others might follow.

And in order to do this we need to understand what it means to be human, the latent potential of that statement, who we each are individually as a consciousness, what it means to be here in incarnation on this earth, who each of us are at the level of both the personality and as an immortal soul, and then finally as part of a galactic family.

It is not a small thing.

It is huge, it is life-altering, it is stunning!

And you have already been introduced to some of the many ways you can step into this as we have spiralled into your essence, here at the centre of the Grail containers of the Earth, the Home and the Body.

Now we are going to look at some of the many ways available to help you to understand yourself at a deeper level, the personality you have taken on in this incarnation, as well as the immortal soul, birthed from the Divine, that you are, and always will be.

I have always viewed this process as something of an archeological dig – the real Saira was lost beneath layers of misunderstanding, conditioning, limited and wrongful teaching and beliefs and fear. My task has been digging down deep to face each of the demons, look them in the eye and integrate them, to unpick all the wrong beliefs and replace with something that resonated at the deepest level of my being, to rediscover the Truths of my human heritage and to understand why I chose to be here.

It has been hot, dusty, difficult work, and it is by no means over.

But what an adventure!

Becoming You – The Importance of Authenticity

The dictionary describes authenticity as:
> "representing one's true nature or beliefs; true to oneself or to the person identified."

Or

> 'the quality of being real or true'

Why do I mention this?

Because this is where you are hopefully headed – into becoming fully and completely the authentic you, the full honest-to-goodness, no-holds-barred, nothing-to- be-ashamed-of you.

And that not only means you have to know who you are as a personality in the body you currently inhabit, but who you are at a soul level – what are your soul origins, innate gifts and talents, why did you chose to come here, what is your real purpose for being here – it isn't to pay taxes I can promise you that!

Finally claiming your birthright, your uniqueness and the inherent gifts you bring with you, aligning with your True Self, no masks, no pretences, and no fear that you will be punished for being what you were designed to be.

And I do mean designed – as you come to know and understand your true origins you will see how laughable the story of humanity finally emerging from the accidental bumping together of amoebic cells in some primal sludge a long time ago is!

You are far, far more magnificent than this – and the Grail essence is the bright shining Truth of who you are.

Your light has been dimmed by the fall we all make into dense matter, by becoming ensnared in the consciousness nets that have been intrinsic to showing up here, our struggle to understand and master what it means to be part of the 3D world, to understand the emotional tides which pummel us and overcome the conditioning and beliefs and false values we are indoctrinated into by the world around us.

Becoming authentic asks several things of us, amongst them brutal self-honesty, integrity, knowing and standing by our values, being unapologetically true to ourselves and what we believe is right amongst them.

As one of those who are here to help change the paradigm into something new it is never going to be entirely comfortable, you are here to help bring change and that means you may often be out of step with aspects of the collective around you who are still somewhat stuck and resistant to change. But being authentic means you don't compromise yourself to 'fit in'.

You don't serve anyone this way, least of all yourself.

This is not about being perfect – none of us are that, we are all just doing the best we can. There will be things which still trigger you, aspects you know you need to work on, but you are aware of it and dealing with it. You know yourself, warts and all.

Yes, there will be bits of you that you are not proud of, that you might wish were different – but so what! We all have those, and you are everything you were designed to be, in this moment, being perfectly imperfect as we all are!

The more you can do this the more the light shines through you. It is not snagged and blocked on those hidden, unacknowledged bits.

Vulnerability is also essential to being authentic – we need to break through and clear the outer shell we have grown, the carapace which we believe keeps us safe, but which prevents us from showing the world who we are, who we truly are, and then owning it and loving it and celebrating it. It took me many years to understand that only the strong can be truly vulnerable. Vulnerability is not weakness, far from it.

And knowing yourself means that you know your strengths and weaknesses, you know where you can manage and you know where you need to ask for help. Asking for help when you know you are out of your depth, when you know you can't cope, the burden is too heavy, is not weakness it is just good, old fashioned common sense.

It is also self-care and self-love.

And that is what sits at the heart of being authentic – you accept and love yourself, who you really and truly are, as unconditionally as you do a child or your beloved.

You are not perfect – you are not meant to be perfect. You are human, and that can be chaotic and messy and difficult as well as being wonderful and amazing and joyful. But you are perfect, as you are, right now, in all your imperfections.

You are exactly who you are meant to be as you strive to step more fully into all that you have the potential to be.

Celebrate it! Love it!

And appreciate your uniqueness, in all its glory!

Befriending the Shadow

'One does not become enlightened by imagining figures of light, but by making the darkness conscious.'
Carl Yung

One of the most crucial aspects of Know Thyself, is the work of befriending your shadow.

The shadow is that aspect of ourselves which we don't wish to own or acknowledge even to ourselves, let alone the world at large.

We all have this. Certain characteristics, judgments, beliefs, behaviours, desires etc which we feel ashamed of, or judged over, or know are not acceptable in normal society. It is that part of ourselves which we don't want to know, and certainly don't want to introduce anyone else to! Our dark side, our alter ego, the lower self, the 'other', our dark twin, our demon.

And yet…..

As hard as we try to keep our shadow in check, to keep it behind locked doors, stashed away in the dark it has a nasty habit of continuously leaking out.

You may say – and in your conscious mind really mean – that you want to be a good person and yet certain things you do, actions you take, things you say, or the way you say them gives away the fact that there is an angry/nasty/judgemental/hateful/bullying/superior/hypocritical/spiteful/vindictive or anything else you can name person inside you. And that is not to say you are not lovely, and fun, and bright and caring and positive, and lovable and genuine and a beautiful soul also…..you are!

But we are all multifaceted, and some of those facets are a little grubby!

And oftentimes, we don't see this clearly ourselves – others often identify our shadow aspects long before we do. That is how good we are at hiding it from ourselves and kidding ourselves.

That is why one of the most important things you need to cultivate on this path is self- honesty – no matter how brutal it can seem at times. Shining a bright light into your psyche can be as illuminating for us as it is for others, and usually not in a good way.

Most of us set out on the path of illuminating the shadow because of our pain – all our suffering comes from these unacknowledged aspects of who we are, and bringing them into the light, along with the emotions embedded in them, can bring a sense of freedom and be very energising.

It was the psychotherapist Carl Jung who coined the terms 'shadow' and 'shadow work', and he is the person who, more than any other, has attempted to map our unconscious which is where the shadow resides…….it is not work for the faint of heart. His work was difficult and clearly at one point brought him to his knees, but he survived his journey down into the depths of who he was, into the underworld, and came back stronger, more empowered and compassionate a soul as a result.

If it is so difficult why might you want to do this work then?

It is simple - because it is our shadow, those denied parts of ourselves which keeps us from fulfilling our dreams, which wrecks our relationships, which keeps us unhappy and unfulfilled, leading lives of quiet desperation.

Our shadow tells us we are not ok, we do not deserve, we are not worthy….

And it is our shadow which holds great riches within it if we have the courage to penetrate it and claim them.

Jung saw the integrating of the shadow into our understanding of who we are as being an essential part of the road to self-realisation, and becoming Whole. He called the mystery of individuation, of becoming whole, the secret of the Grail. And the only way to discover the Grail vessel was to become it!

This is part of the work we have to do to heal the 'Split', as this shows up in the modern world around us in many forms, and the integrating of our conscious self with that which is unconscious within us gives us a unifying

Your perception of me is a reflection of you.

My reaction to you is my response to looking at myself.

awareness which then allows us to exert some control and element of choice – if you see you are being hypocritical in a behaviour or belief you hold, for example, you can then chose to make a more congruent pattern of behaviour or change your belief consciously to something more aligned with who you really are……or you can chose not to, of course!

Whatever you do, it is the fact it is conscious that is important. If you are bitching about a friend and are fully cognisant of the fact you are doing so and behaving in a very unfriendly manner, you can catch yourself and change what you are saying – and if you don't want to do this, then you can acknowledge to yourself what you are doing and then ask yourself the big question – why? Why am I being nasty about someone I call a friend? Why do I feel the need to do this? What does this say about me? What in me takes pleasure in hurting someone else? Why might this make me feel better/more superior etc?

One of the classic aspects of shadow work we have to look at is projection – where we project unacknowledged and denied parts of ourselves onto others, whom we then castigate or have an issue with, because they show us too clearly who we *really* are as opposed to whom we would like to be!

If we don't like what we see 'out there' we have to start 'in here'. There's nothing new in this, spiritual masters have been teaching it for centuries. It's a fairly simple concept but as a species we find it very hard to work with, because it means digging around in those bits of us we have disowned, and looking at those parts of us we don't want to see.

What few people realise though, is that there is gold in this work. Yes, it's messy, and difficult and will have you on your knees at times. You will feel shame and horror and disbelief at some of what you uncover – is that *really* me! But if you keep your head and don't run screaming for the hills, all these unwanted, unloved, dispossessed parts of yourself are the riches you seek in the process of becoming whole and authentic as you gently bring them into the light.

This is the real alchemy – turning the lead of your lower self into gold. This is life alchemy, an essential part of the transformative work.

Jung asked *'Would you rather be whole or good?'* We are all part angel and part demon. And we are all trying to lighten the load of our lower self, that part of ourselves we don't like and don't want to own, by shining our light as brightly as we can. But the brighter the light, the darker the shadow if you haven't dealt with it – and you will come unstuck. Your demons will come out and dance on the table in front of you when you least expect it, and not dealing with them will be your undoing, time and again.

If you are on the road to self-realisation this is not work you can avoid, and there is no denying it can be tough, but as we have been shown time and again in the various myths of the hero (and heroine's) journey, empowerment and rewards lie at the other end of the journey. Not least the release of trapped life force energy which we have tied up in 'managing' our shadow aspects.

It is also work which reaches far beyond the level of just the personal, because what you do for yourself benefits the Collective also....

And allow me to let you in on a little secret – many of those aspects of yourself you perceive to be your greatest faults, the things you like least about yourself, hide your greatest gifts.

Your weaknesses are your strengths – just badly managed. Once you gain control of them – rather than letting them control *you* – they will work for you, not against you.

As the author Debbie Ford says *'Our shadows hold the essence of who we are. They hold our most treasured gifts. By facing these aspects of ourselves, we become free to experience our glorious totality: the good and the bad, the dark and the light.'*

Most of us have to look to our past to find what we have buried there, what unique gifts and talents lie buried under our mistaken beliefs about ourselves and the world around us. Where we have been shamed or ridiculed for being who we are, and then internalised it to our detriment. Thinking back to what happened in the moment we shut down can lead us to great riches, as we uncover those denied parts of ourselves.

But if we are fully going to do the job we also need to bear in mind both our ancestors – what do we hold of them, good and bad – as well as the karma accrued from previous incarnations which we carry forward into this lifetime, and our full history as part of angelic humanity.

It is another potentially rich seam of becoming fully whole we can mine.

**It is only when we have the courage
to face things exactly as they are,
without any self-deception or illusion,
that a light will develop out of events,
by which the path to success
may be recognised.**
I Ching.

Your Soul Blueprint

There are various things you can do which will be a great help in developing further your understanding of who you are, and opening a doorway of understanding to a whole new level of Being.

I class understanding your Soul Blueprint in this category. You are an immortal soul, a small fragment of the divine which seeks to know itself in every possible way through the experiences of many souls in many different lifeforms, all having their own unique experiences.

It can be quite difficult to get our heads around this idea and what it really means. When we look at the first of the great cosmic laws, the Law of Mentalism, and it talks of what some call Unity Consciousness or Source, the All – whatever you choose to call it - this law tells us there is a single universal consciousness, the 'Universal Mind', the 'All That Is', and that all things flow and manifest from this.

All ancient wisdom traditions also teach the same principle. Often there is a network of gods, but if you follow it back they all flow from one Source.

Your consciousness is part of the Universal consciousness and you are a manifestation of this consciousness.

The 'Universal Consciousness' is now being recognised within the discipline of Quantum Science, with the naming of something called 'The Field' or the 'Zero Point Field'. This is a field of energy which connects all parts of the Universe, and to which all parts of the Universe are connected. It interweaves the fabric of this Universe at every level, connecting everything, near and far and would once have been called Spirit, or Source energy, although these words are anathema to the scientist!

> You don't have a soul.
> You ARE a soul.
> You HAVE a body.
> ~C.S. Lewis

Birthed from this Universal Consciousness, your immortal soul is born in on a predominant frequency or energy. There are 8 major energy or frequency centres and each one has certain characteristics and gifts which define it.

The energy centres or frequencies are
    Energy Centre One – Divine Compassion
    Energy Centre Two - Divine Manifestation
    Energy Centre Three – Divine Order
    Energy Centre Four – Divine Love
    Energy Centre Five – Divine Communication
    Energy Centre Six – Divine Truth
    Energy Centre Seven – Divine Power
    Energy Centre Eight- Divine Wisdom

Not only has your Soul been birthed on a certain frequency but it also comes into its first manifestation somewhere within Creation. Many souls here on Earth at this time are truly Old Souls, having spent many incarnations in other areas of the galaxy. They were birthed in other star systems or even galaxies before choosing incarnations here on Earth for a very specific purpose.

Every star system has individual characteristics which define the beings birthed there – they give 'colour and flavour' if you will to the Soul.

Souls birthed in other areas of the Universe, who have come to Earth are often referred to as Star Seeds ie. their point of origin was elsewhere. Maybe it was Orion, or Sirius, or Arcturus or the Pleidies or one of many others.

There are other aspects of your Soul Blueprint you can discover also – your Soul's current vibrationary rate for example, how congruent we are being in the way we choose to live and the choices we make to our divine blueprint, and how well we are working with the power of free will and intention – the Creator energy we have access to and must learn to use responsibly.

We all have a connection back to Divine Source via something called a Godspark and we can look at whether that is damaged or not, and also if we have been gifted with a secondary Godspark. These are not usual but some souls may require access to extra energetic resources in addition to those they already have in order to fulfil purpose. A secondary Godspark will feed additional life force energy to a specific chakra in order to enable this.

How do you find all this out?

This information is held in the Akashic Records, which is an all-encompassing energetic database held in the higher dimensions. It is beyond space-time, a sort of higher dimensional internet holding information about all souls, and the created universe. Here you can access your soul information across many incarnations and find out more about any karmic patterns and blocks and restrictions you are dealing with in this incarnation.

Someone who is trained to access the Records can gather and give you this information. I call these Soul Blueprint readings[20], but they will go under other names. I made this part of my healing 'toolkit' when I began to understand that so much of the illness, the lack of wellbeing I was seeing before me ultimately came from a lack of understanding of who we are at the great cosmic soul level.

It can be a seminal moment when our perspective of who we are as human beings shifts and we see ourselves as the immortal mortals that we are, and begin to find out more about, and possibly begin to reconnect to memories of, our galactic soul families.

It was this that began my own journey into the galactic histories and great cosmic families of consciousness that are part of the multidimensional, immortal, divine beings we are.

It is a journey that has not been without difficulties, as it has called on resources I didn't even know I possessed, but it is one I wouldn't have missed for the world!

---

[20] For more information see my website or my book 'The Divine Human'

Astrology

You will see astrology described as a 'pseudo-science' by the mainstream, negating the thousands of years of study and understanding which astrology can bring to the table – let alone the accuracy of much of what it depicts.

In a nutshell it is the study of the influence of distant cosmic objects in our solar system on human lives.

The position of all these planets, sun, moon, asteroids etc in relation to the earth and exactly where an individual is on the earth at the time they are born plays a part in shaping their personality and 'fixing' certain characteristics in place.

Many people look upon it as a form of fortune telling or divination, but this is to downplay it real use, and to overlook that it was used at the highest levels of government and rulership for many centuries. By dint of careful study of the heavens it became possible to recognise the cycles and rhythms of the cosmic bodies and predict where they would be on any given date, either moving forwards on the timeline or backwards.

The influence exerted by the patterns formed in the heavens can then clearly be seen in the events playing out on Earth.

In the hands of a good astrologer your unique template at the moment of your birth can give you guidance and insight into who you are and what you are here to do, just as it can give you understanding and insight into the patterns playing out in the world around us.

If you judge astrology from the simple and generalised astrological predictions published in papers and magazines (which are seen by most serious astrologers as being an irrelevance) you are really missing the point of what astrology has to offer us. There is over 6,000 years of study which have gone into this field and astrologers today build on the work achieved by our ancient forebears with only the most primitive of tools.

For many centuries it was seen as being a highly esoteric field of study, the province of scholars, philosophers and priests, or advisers to the ruling classes. It is a profound mathematical and symbolic language which takes years of deep study to master and in the words of one astrologer *'It is the hidden language which shows us how divine intelligence operates in the world'.*

Since the earliest times astrology was seen as not just a means of looking at what might happen, but also a way of coming into harmony with the Universe. It was used in governance, in medicine and many other aspects of life and was seen as higher knowledge, reserved for those who were the elite. It was also taught in monasteries and religious institutions right up until the 17th century, when the so-called Age of Enlightenment began introducing the idea that the Universe (and us) were mechanistic in our nature, and Spirit became divorced from matter.

As astrology did not fit this mechanistic model it fell from grace, and whilst today there are many excellent and learned astrologers doing amazing work, most people only know it in terms of the trivial sun sign predictions.

I am not going to give you an outline of astrology here – most people are aware of at least the basics, and it is a huge field of study. But if you are interested in learning more about your own astrology chart I give you a couple of websites in the Resources section for astrologers whose work I rate highly.

Getting at least a basic birth chart reading can be very helpful and illuminating as you start down the path of self-knowledge.

Human Design

I was first introduced to Human Design around 12 years ago – and I so wished I'd had access to this information earlier in my life. It would have saved me a lot of angst and uncertainty, and helped me realise early on that aspects of myself that were 'different' to the norm, were fully a part of who I was meant to be, and actually very helpful to the purpose I came here to undertake, rather being defective as many tried to make me believe.

Human Design gives deep insight into the *personality* you have taken on in this incarnation. It describes who you are and how you 'operate' at both a level you are conscious of and also one you are unconscious of.

It is therefore extremely illuminating in many ways.

As a system it was brought through in 1987, by a Canadian on the island of Ibiza, where he had a mystic experience with something he called 'the Voice', a superior intelligence which over a period of eight days and nights downloaded into him a transmission of information which became the Human Design system.

His name was Alan (Robert) Krakower, but he came to be known as Ra Uru Hu, and spent the rest of his life establishing the Human Design System.

It is incredibly detailed and many layered, and it is not built on belief or faith but is a logical, empirical system that offers you the opportunity to experiment with its mechanics and find out for yourself how it works for you.

Human Design is a synthesis of both ancient wisdom teachings and the modern science of reading the genetic code. The traditional sciences are astrology, both eastern and western, the Hindu-Brahmin Chakra system, the Zohar or Kabbalah, and most importantly of all, the I Ching, the Book of Changes.

This synthesis points us clearly towards our true nature and helps us identify how deep the conditioning we are exposed to goes.

It is not something you can make sense of by just reading a book. It takes some years of study to become a Human Design reader and many more to become an excellent one. Ra trained many people around the world in this modality, and they have gone on to train others. In a relatively short space of time it has become globally well-established.

Human Design uses your birth data to calculate your design chart, called a Bodygraph, which outlines your type and definition, the foundation of the system. From here you can delve ever deeper into the many layers of who you were designed to be.

Fundamental to this is learning how to operate in alignment with who we really are, and inevitably this begins to bring immediate benefits as your world around you starts to shift to something more authentic for you.

Although the readings can be quite expensive, I found it liberating as a complete stranger described the inner me, one I resonated deeply with, and years of criticism from family and others for aspects of who I was that they disapproved of fell away as I clearly saw this was ME, and trying to be what they wanted was dishonouring myself.

A Human Design reading is so detailed you will find yourself coming back to it over many years, as you become ready to work on another layer of what it has to tell you.

It will enable you to make choices which are in alignment with your authentic nature in this lifetime. Align that with knowledge of your Soul Blueprint and you are well on the way to understanding yourself as the many-layered multi-dimensional being that you are.

The Gene Keys

The Gene Keys are really an extension or evolution of Human Design and is based in a deeper reading of DNA.

There are 64 permutations or combination in which the four letter code of DNA can be translated. These 64 codons relate to the 64 hexagrams of the I Ching and also to the 64 Gene Keys and represent an energetic living field which exists within you at all times.

The 64 Gene Keys are based on a fundamental code found throughout nature and help us to understand what our highest evolutionary potential is. Together with the personalised Hologenetic Profile which forms the blueprint of your Gene Keys you can begin to explore what they have to teach you.

Discovering and understanding this has been the life work of Richard Rudd, a man who initially trained in Human Design under Ra Uru Hu and was a senior teacher of this. Richard acknowledges the debt and the many ways in which they interface, but working with the Gene Keys takes you in a different direction.

As Richard describes it
'Your DNA is a wormhole. It contains a code that, when activated, opens up to the core of the holographic universe. As such, the DNA molecule is really a transducer of light. The more open the wormhole is, the more light pours through it. Like a torus, it both draws light towards itself and emanates it outward. Eventually, so much light will radiate through you that the wormhole itself collapses. The resulting supernova reveals to you your true universal nature as one with all creation.'

This is very much in alignment with what we have been looking at here, the multi-dimensional reality of who you really are.

The purpose of the Gene Keys is to enable each of us to find and ignite the 'eternal spark of genius', the individual and unique beauty which lies within each of us, just waiting for us to bring it forth.

I myself am just beginning to explore the Gene Keys in any depth. I know I could not have engaged with what it has to offer without first exploring the paths I already have. It requires a certain level of insight and metaphysical understanding and is really a self-study path with a clearly laid out way through it.

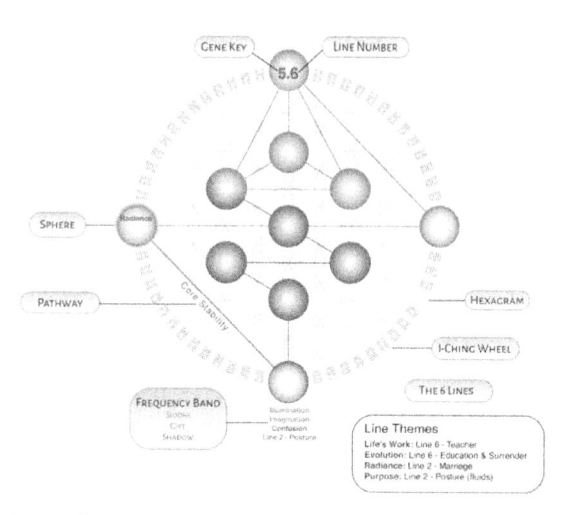

Like Human Design and astrology it uses your birth data to give you your profile, and from there you can begin to explore the deeper levels of your being. Each of the Gene Keys which makes up your individual profile has three levels to them – the Shadow or Challenge aspect, the Gift or Potential and the Siddhi or higher essence. With each Gene Key we work from the lower or shadow to the higher essence, step-by-step opening up to the gifts of each key and letting the light shine through.

> *This is your higher purpose – to be radiant for no other purpose than being alive.*
> **Richard Rudd**

Archetypes

Another big area of study is that of archetypes.

Archetypes are psychological patterns which are immediately recognizable to all – we may give them labels pertinent to our time and place, but their energies cross the cultural divide. For example, the archetype of the Mother is understood everywhere, as is that of the Clown, or the Bully etc.

Archetypal patterns display characteristics, traits and behaviours which are consistent across the board. No matter what culture we are in we understand what constitutes a good mother, compared to a bad one. The one is showing us the positive expression of this archetype, the latter the negative – whether we call it the Smother Mother, the Abusive Mother or the Neglectful Mother - and it becomes an instant shorthand for what we are describing.

It was Carl Jung who, in the early 20th century, suggested the experience of universal forms which channel and capture the emotions and experiences which make up each archetype, resulting in recognizable and typical patterns of behaviour. They are instinctual behaviour patterns that are contained in the collective unconscious, and therefore they are able to be accessed by anyone who has the right frequency.

Mankind has been using the language of archetypes for most of its history, even if it has only become a field of study fairly recently. The ancient Greek philosopher Plato spoke of 'forms', ancient myths embody archetypal energies and this hidden language flows through all legends and fairy stories.

This language can be seen in both ancient mythologies and modern literature. When we learn to recognize the different archetypes and recognize those behaviour patterns in both ourselves and others it can give us great insight and understanding into what is happening in all our lives today.

Each archetype has its positive qualities and its negative, or shadow, side. Should we choose to recognize this darker side of an energy within our nature, it becomes an opportunity for us to work with it and develop its more positive aspects.

It is an aspect of normal human behaviour that in our less developed state, we continually project our shadow self onto others – for example, what most annoys or angers us in others is often an un-owned aspect of our own behaviour.

Part of the process of self-development is to integrate and acknowledge these aspects and work to use them in a more positive form. There are valuable life lessons and opportunities to be found within each archetype, there is no 'good' or 'bad', just what is, and the opportunity to perform some alchemy within ourselves by turning the base to gold.

Archetypes are more than powerful cultural stereotypes, they are potent inner patterns which speak to both our similarities and our differences.

We are all a complex blend of a variety of archetypes. Some are more dominant in us than others, some are currently dormant, only to be awakened by a certain situation or crisis. All have something to teach us, to help us understand who we are and why we think and behave the way we do.

Much as our energy bodies interact with each other, so do our archetypes. Put two King archetypes together and you will feel the field of benign protection and authority if they are working from the positive aspects of this archetype. If from the negative it is more likely their egos will square up and a serious game of one-upmanship will ensue as each tries to dominate the other!

How many Knights are looking for a Lady or Damsel in Distress they can rescue? Or Lovers looking for a Beloved? Or Masters looking for a Slave? Once you grasp archetypes you can have some fun with this as you sit people-watching and see things playing out before you.

Some archetypes complement each other and form a wonderful duo, others clash and bring out the worst in each other. For example, if you have the Servant archetype which at its best is about true service, when it is paired with a negative Bully unless you are really in conscious understanding of what is going on you are likely to find yourself becoming subservient to the more dominant archetype.

Or take a Damsel who is wanting a Knight to ride up and 'rescue' her from day-to-day responsibilities. She won't be best pleased if she becomes attached to an Adventurer who wants to go adventuring all the time, leaving her at home to cope!

So you can begin to see how a deeper understanding of our archetypes can be a useful tool not just in understanding ourselves, but also ourselves in relationship to others and how we interact.

The person who has probably done most to develop this field in modern times is the author and mystic Caroline Myss. Her Sacred Contracts programmes have developed a coherent way of identifying and working with your own personal archetypes.

Many Jungian analysts also incorporate archetypes in their work, and a rich seam to draw on are the mythologies of many cultures that are redolent with archetypal guides and patterns to help us understand not only ourselves, but also life situations and life stages as they develop.

'Archetypes are the psychic lenses through which we view ourselves and the world around us.'
Caroline Myss

Part 6
Becoming the Guardian

The Alchemy of Becoming a Grail Bearer

What we have been exploring in the pages of this book is to a large extent summed up by one word – energy!

Specifically, the many different ways in which energy shows up and is defined in our world. How we interact with it, how being aware of it can make a difference not to just our experience of it, but also to the quality of our lives, how expanding our awareness of it can bring many benefits and is an integral part to our ability to expand and grow our consciousness, and move along the whole path of what is called Ascension mechanics.

And, of course, coming to understand ourselves as conscious, energetic beings.

The process of Ascension is a physical science which was once known to mankind, and practised to a greater or lesser degree by all. It governs the movement of energy and consciousness through a time-space field matrix.

We have lost access to the teachings concerning this, we have lost access to even an understanding of the structure of the Time matrix we are navigating, we have lost access to our own histories and origins and we have lost access to who we truly are and our inherent birthright.

But all that is changing. Humankind has been through a long Dark Age, but it is a testament to both our strength and the Divine spark we hold within that we are still here, and beginning to fight back with a vengeance to reclaim all that has been taken from us.

There are many, many layers to this and part of the deeper work into the Grail Wisdom will give you access once more to much of the lost wisdom teachings and knowledge – and you will inevitably go on to discover more yourself, particularly your own stories within the different timelines.

None of this is a passive process, you are being asked to change and update your understanding of the world in which you live to integrate the subtle layers of energy which surround and interpenetrate us, and begin to expand your consciousness into an understanding of the multidimensional being that you are and how you can reach through these levels.

This is true life alchemy, a process of transformation of not just how you interact with the outer world around you but, more importantly, a process of inner transformation, as you begin to align more and more fully with the True Self, the magnificent, immortal and divine being that you are, that has taken on the mission of coming down into the densest layers of the Universe for a purpose, a reason. Or more likely various reasons – few of us are one-trick ponies with only one task to do whilst we are here!

The process of life alchemy is working as consciously as we can through this transformative process, coming to understand what is being required of each of us as we return, step-by-step to our True Self.

The path is not exactly the same for each one of us, we are all unique and have our own special part to play in the unfolding dramas and new beginnings around us.

But we are here to help each other, to come together and work to restore our world, restore humanity and step once more into the role which is our birthright – that of the Guardians of this beautiful planet and creation, at all levels and in every respect, from her fertile lands and oceans to her intricate and complex Templar architectures of stargates, portals, ley lines and so much more.

And as we do this, we also work with ourselves, evolving our own energetic templating and consciousness.

It's a wonderful win-win, isn't it!

This is what I call Becoming the Guardian, and is the real work that lies ahead of us as we navigate the changing currents and energies of this amazing and turbulent time.

It is an exciting and challenging time to be here on Planet Earth, and there is so much to be done, so much to be restored and so many wonderful things to be explored and re-discovered.

I can speak of what Grail wisdom means until I am blue in the face, but it is you who has to go out and make it happen – connect to the earth and her denizens, befriend your environment, tune into and feel the way energy flows through your home, your body, your landscape. Speak to your soul and acknowledge what makes it sing!

Once you make a commitment to learning more, discovering more, being open to things that, quite frankly, may seem somewhat 'out there' you will start to discover so much that has not made sense in the past begins to fall into place. And that your life starts to change in ways which are quite magical and unexpected.

We are all part of a great web, the Web of Life. Find and know and understand your link within this web. You might think of it like the neural system of the brain, or like a spider's web, or a great grid spread across the universe. However you visualise it know that none of us, seen or unseen, are outside it.

There are many words for this – the Divine Matrix, the Field, Universal Consciousness, Divine Mind. Everything we need is here, all that is, was or shall be is part of this. Time, we are often told, is an illusion – and we can see this clearly when we learn to step outside it (here in the 3D world however, it holds sway….).

As part of this Divine Matrix, the connectedness of all things becomes apparent, all the possibilities and potentials of what you could be await you.

Learning to live from and understand ourselves at this level is part of what we have to re-discover, and there are many techniques and practises that can help.

This is the Quest, to both awaken and embody your innate Grail Wisdom.

And once you embark on the quest as the Grail Seeker the universe will begin to unfold its secrets to you. As a Grail Seeker, one who is pursuing the quest for the Grail, and holding its light within, you stand between worlds of the visible and the invisible, a channel between these realms, a champion to both.

As such you will be subjected to challenges and tests along the way to see if you are worthy, if you can learn and grow from each lesson, if you can become Sovereign unto yourself, without falling into the trap of ego, if you can develop the qualities needed to take on the responsibility of the role, as well as looking after and nurturing a part of the land on which we all live and depend – whether it is just your garden, or local park, or even an area near you that will benefit from conscious connection?

Maybe you undertake to feed the birds when food is scarce or to help out at an animal sanctuary….or maybe you train to be a geomancer and heal the earth wherever you find imbalance. Or maybe you just hold, and wherever possible, expand the Light in your area, your community. Caring for and nurturing the world around you comes in many shapes and sizes.

There are other themes which are part of this Quest: the reintegration of the lost feminine and connection back into the Web of Life, our understanding of sovereignty, igniting and activating the Imaginal World once more within us…..

I see there are two paths I am here to help others follow – one is that of the Grail Wisdom and all that means in our connection to the land, reclaiming our lost knowledge of who we are and our divine origins, understanding the complex Templar energetics and mechanics.

The second is that of Life Alchemy, the deeply transformative work of taking this knowledge and working with it to become a true Grail Bearer, a true Guardian, uncovering once more what we are re-discovering of Ascension mechanics.

When the Land of the inner and outer Self becomes healed and starts to green the possibilities begin to open up. Synchronicities abound and become the sign posts you must follow (no matter how counter-intuitive it sometimes seems!).

The role of the Grail Bearer is to shine a Light in the world, to help awaken others to some of the wonder and magic we are all surrounded by, the abundance that is Creation. And it has never been more important than it is at this time of Shift and great energetic changes when different time-lines of potential are available to achieve.

It goes without saying that we are striving for the timeline that takes in the highest good of all, and the more of us who choose to step up to this challenge and begin this journey the more our beautiful Mother Earth and collective angelic humanity will thrive.

Qualities of the Grail Initiate

There are certain qualities we need to cultivate as we move forwards. Some may come naturally to you, others you may have to work at.

I give you some below, but don't take this list as exhaustive. You may want to sit and think yourself of what it means to be a Grail Bearer and what *you* see as being the qualities required……………..

Courageous – it take courage to leave well-worn pathways, even if they no longer serve, to see and understand the world in a different way to many of those around you, and to be able to honour that understanding.

Resolute and determined – there is a need to be able to pick yourself up after any reversal or wrong turn, dust yourself down and carry on, one step at a time towards your goal.

Compassion – this is truly a Grail quality, which sits without judgment as another tries, and maybe fails, to move forwards. You think 'There but for the grace of God go I' and reach out your hand and smile in encouragement rather than condemnation. You understand that we are all flawed, but we are all perfect in our imperfections.

Open and flexible – you need to be able to change your mind in the light of new information, not be wedded to an idea or belief to such an extent that there is no room for debate or new energy to flow in.

Self-love – how can we love others, really love others, when we cannot love ourselves? And that means we have to drop all judgment of ourselves and understand that whatever and wherever we are it is perfect in this moment. We cannot compare ourselves to others, nor are we wanting in any way, we are all trying our best and that needs to be acknowledged and honoured.

Curiosity – taken to excess this becomes plain nosey or intrusive, but curiosity brings a quality of wonder to life, of endless possibilities and adventures. Think of a child learning to know its world, or a puppy playfully exploring the world around it. They are full of wonder and excitement and…..curiosity.

Patience – patience is a necessary quality for any initiate. We all need to move at the pace that is right for us, which may not necessarily be the pace our ego desires. And things unfold in their own time and to their own rhythm. Rushing things can spoil them, ensure the outcome is not to its highest potential, and be to the detriment of all; Being patient, feeling into the currents, knowing when to sit back and let things bubble under until they are ready is an art. Patience is an art. Cultivate it.

Humility – being humble is not about being subservient or unworthy, more about having the ego firmly in its place – as a good servant and not our master. The ego can give structure to our personality and is not necessarily a bad thing, until it claims the driver's seat. Humility walks a fine line between pride and self-deprecation and says I know and accept my strengths and limitations, I neither defend, extol nor judge myself. This kind of self-acceptance opens the path to compassion.

Responsibility – this means we acknowledge and accept our mistakes, we own those parts of us we have been at pains not to acknowledge, we embrace the fact our choices/beliefs/behaviours create our reality and that if we wish to change something it is our work to do so.

Receptivity – receptivity is both a feminine and a grail power. You need to be receptive and welcome in whatever comes, both the pain and the pleasure of it, be receptive to the changing flows of energy, and be able to dance with that.

Intention – we all need to hone our will, and utilise the power of intention consciously and in service to others. It is our will, harnessed to our increasing frequency which will bring about change for the better. What you put out you attract, and the more consciously you use your will with intention the more accurately things manifest. Be aware, be focused and above all, be conscious to ensure they are what you really want!

Emotionally intelligent – if you want to achieve emotional mastery – and you need to if you are to become master of yourself - you need to develop emotional intelligence. Our emotions are one of the things which define us as humans. Make sure you are in control of them – not the other way around!

Mental control/discipline – thoughts create things through the frequency they generate. What level is your frequency running at? You need to be aware and have sufficient detachment from what is running through your mind that you can jump on unwanted/negative thoughts quickly and change them to what is more aligned with where you want to be.

As a Grail Bearer you are a Seed of Light. Having worked to see the world around you as it is rather than the limited perception you have been taught, now you need to grow that Light and let it shine for others to guide and help them.

The Role of Faithkeeper

In many Native American traditions, one member of the tribe will assume the role of "Faithkeeper".

The role of the Faithkeeper is to remain peaceful and calm, while maintaining spiritual enlightenment and understanding, no matter what the tribe may endure.

Under extreme conditions, if every single tribe member stumbles into fear, doubt, anxiety, worry and pain - the Faithkeeper maintains peace, spirituality and understanding.

Therefore, the Faithkeeper is a mainstay to the "I AM" presence of God, Great Spirit or Creator. They are the lodestone for the community, who serves to keep the faith, remember the bigger picture and hold fast to the eternal truths.

Becoming the Grail Bearer or Guardian is a similar role. The Grail Bearer stands as a way-shower, a beacon of light and hope to others, a guide to fellow seekers, a lighthouse standing firm in even the worst storm, beaming out light to cut through the darkness.

It is not a showy role, or one that necessarily attracts much attention, but if each community had a Grail Bearer at its heart, energetically anchoring and maintaining the Grail light within the community, stable, grounded, aware and ensuring a high vibrational field was maintained then not only would the community thrive but this is work of great service to the collective.

We are living at an amazing time, a time when a great shift of consciousness can and is happening, but before we see the outcome of this, much has to be cleared and dismantled of an old paradigm which no longer serves us (if it ever did!).

This is a time of change, a time of instability, a time of structures and organisations and beliefs and 'truths'

being dismantled, before something new and better can be built in its place.

It is important that the Grail Bearer can stand firm during this time, not become part of the field of fear and confusion, and point the way to a better future, with a message of hope and a vision for what can be.

You have to have done your own inner work, found your own centre, planted your own feet firmly on the ground in order to hold this space for others. And the more you do this with an open heart, with compassion and without judgment of where others are, the bigger the field you can embrace.

Like the Faithkeeper you can remain calm and help others to understand and find a way through the chaos of the outer world. You can help in little ways which add up – maybe start a meditation group, a support group, a community garden….

And because you understand that all is energy, and the ways in which energy moves and flows and manifests you can ensure that negative, denser vibrations and emotions are cleared and cleansed and transmuted for the higher good of all.

It is not a little thing.

RISE UP, SPIRITUAL WARRIOR!

I tripped across this somewhere online. I forget where, and it had no attribution, (if anyone recognises it please let me know!) but I thought you might find it inspiring......

Now more than ever you need to ask yourself:
What is your intention in life, your purpose, your aim?
WHO ARE YOU?
WHY are you here?
Know Thyself.
Forget about the fleeting desires of your ego.
What is your soul yearning for and why did you choose to incarnate right here, right now during these times?

Deep down inside you know.
It is the true Self that KNOWS, not the personality you tend to identify with.
There is a choice to be made and there is no middle ground.
It is not possible to sit on the sidelines anymore in some sort of intellectualized "neutrality".
Are you ready to answer the call, the battle cry?

Did you seriously think "awakening" is going to be a walk in the park where all of a sudden you are in love and light and bliss with angels playing harps around you?
Well, maybe if you took the New Age Pill at some point, engaged in spiritual bypassing, and mistook your DMT or mushroom trips for "awakening".
But those childish immature days are over.
We are not girls and boys anymore building sandcastles.

Nor is the process of awakening going according to how "you" think or want it to be with all your expectations and entitlement.
It's beyond your little ego's control.

We are called to be spiritual warriors in service to the Divine, taking on the dark forces within and without – with courage, determination, humility, love, knowledge, faith, and trust.

There is work to be done and as with anything in life, you only get as much as you are willing to put the effort in and pay WITH YOURSELF. Nothing is "FREE" in the entire universe, not even freedom. There is a price to be paid for everything – a sacrifice, to give yourself completely to the Divine without bargaining.

How sincere are you with yourself?
How much are you willing to give and pay with yourself?
How much do you lie to yourself?
Deep down inside you know that you have been waiting for this moment your entire life but not fully realized yet.
So, join the pilgrimage with 100% commitment, without complaining, and without looking back.

Burn in the fire of transmutation.
Die to your old self;
descend into the darkness within and without;
join the inevitable battle with the Forces of Darkness and illuminate it all with the eternal light of the Divine shining through YOU.
Godspeed

Part 7 - Appendices

Appendix 1 - Ritual to Open Sacred Space

The first thing to understand about this is that it is an *energetic* space you are creating, from within which you can work safely.

It is up to you whether you create *physical* boundaries to this space by laying out a circle and marking the directions or whether you just stand within the space you are working and visualise the boundaries of a circle you will be working within.

Before you begin this ritual bring yourself into coherence. It is the energy and intent you bring to what you do that defines how effective it is.

Below are two different methods of doing this. Neither is right or wrong. What I am hoping you will see from this is the mechanism of creating a sacred space, and you create what works for you. There is a pattern to what you are doing which is basically:

> Calling on elemental forces in each of the four directions
> Calling on elemental forces in each of the quarter points
> Calling on elemental forces above and below

You have thus created a 3-D circle, which you might see as a bubble of energy to work within.

There are all sorts of variations you can bring to this, but the above is the basic pattern.

You can stand in one direction as you go through the ritual, or you can move to each direction as you announce it.

You can use tools – the Western Magical tradition for example uses swords, athames (small daggers), cups, wands and so on – or you can simply find something that represents the elements of each direction to you.

For example, in the North (earth) you might put a plant in a pot, or a heap of soil (in a dish if you are inside!) or a statue of a gnome or something else that represents earth (I was given a small garden statue of a mole I often use....).

In the East (air) you might place a feather, or something light and airy you possess, or a statue of a bird or butterfly or even something blue.

In the South you might place a candle (lighted) or something of a fiery colour or that suggests fire to you.

In the West (water) you might place a bowl of water, or a statue of a fish, or mermaid or something similar that suggests water to you.

Once you have marked the four cardinal points you can mark the quarter points if you wish. I usually use tea lights if I do, whichis rare as I tend to just acknowledge and visualise them in the ritual and this is sufficient.

Then either stand in your chosen position (I usually choose North) or if you wish to move between the directions, stand in the East to begin.

Say in a clear strong voice, with focused intent:

Angelic Ritual:

> I call upon the great Angels of Light, the Angels of Love and Mercy to come today and protect this space for me.
>
> In the East come Raphael, Light of the East, Star of Dawn...Come!
>
> In the South come Michael, Light of the South, Star of Day...Come!
>
> In the West come Gabriel, Light of the West, Star of Eve......Come!
>
> In the North come Uriel, Light of the North, Star of Night...Come!
>
> And in the Heavens come Raguel, Fire of Love
>
> And in the Earth come Remiel, Waters of Love to receive the Fire
>
> In the four quarters stand guard ye Fellowship of Light.
>
> Come forth, protect this space and all who work within it.
>
> Thank you. Thank you. Thank you.

Amen

Elementals Ritual:

I call upon the creatures of the earth, the elements of Nature to come today and protect this space.

In the East, all creatures of air, the great sylphs, the birds, the insects, the butterflies and all who make the air their element.

In the South, all creatures of fire, the great salamanders, the fiery beings of the great lava flows and licking flames and all who make fire their element.

In the West, all creatures of water, the great undines, the mermaids, the fish and the dolphins and whales and all who make water their element.

In the North, all creatures of earth, the great gnomes, the animals and creatures who are in and of the earth, and all who make earth their element.

At the four quarters stand guard all beings of good intent

Come you all!

Protect and energise this space. Keep all within free from harm.

For this we thank you.

So be it.

You can see that although the words are different the pattern is the same.

When you have finished close this down in reverse order. You can either go through it fully in reverse ie.
In the four quarters we thank the Fellowship of Light,
In the Earth   we thank Remiel, Waters   of Love,
In the Heavens we thank Raguel, Fire of Love,
In the North Uriel   etc....

Or you can do a shorthand version:

> In the four quarters we thank you
> In the Heavens and Earth we thank you
> In the North, in the West, in the South, in the East we thank you
> Amen

Closing down the space is important and only polite to the beings you have called in to help you. Never forget to do this.

You can write out and memorise a ritual you wish to use every time you open sacred space, or you can work with the principles I have outlined and use words which come to you in the moment which are appropriate.

As I said, neither is right or wrong. What is important is that what you do is meaningful to you and that you work with focused intent as you go through the ritual. The power to call in great beings to protect you comes from you. Whilst you need to be humble and grateful for their help, you also need to be meeting them as the equal that you are.

Done properly and with intent this opens up a powerful – and safe – sacred space to work within, using the primary energetic archetype of the Wheel of Life, and this basic process is found in many traditions around the globe.

Well used it will never let you down.

Appendix 2 - Solutions for High EMF Readings

Prudent Avoidance

Move bed away from obvious sources ie. fuse box, meter etc

Position electrical appliances at least 4 ft away from bed to avoid their field.

Try not to sleep with your head near a wall socket or have extension cables running under bed.

Do not have electric blankets on whilst in bed.

Do not plug mains adaptors/transformers in next to the bed.

Switch off all appliances at the wall socket and even unplug them at night.

Only use a mobile phone when essential, and then keep the calls short. Do not carry it around next to the heart or other vital organs. Do not place next to the bed at night.

Use a normal phone at home. If using a DECT phone do not station the set near where you sleep or sit.

Use a low radiation monitor on your computer and don't sit nearer than 4 ft behind a monitor.

Manually Switching Off Circuits

This can be done at the fuse box last thing at night. You will need to determine which circuits are causing the problem.

Demand Switches

These automatically switch off the circuits to which they are installed and are the main solution to removing electrical fields from the bedroom. Normally installed for downstairs lights and upstairs socket circuits.

There are two models: NT16-plus recommended for lighting circuits and NT 20-plus recommended for ring mains and other domestic power circuits. Speak to your electrician or look online to find suppliers.

Shielded Cables
You can either buy screened mains cabling or cabling can be shielded behind a metal conduit in the wall. Both need earthing and are best installed when building. Available from good electrical suppliers or look online.

Microshield ™
Radiation protection cases for mobile phones. Contact: www.microshield.co.uk

There are other technologies which claim to protect you from mobile phone radiation. You will have to do your own research to determine whether they are legitimate as I haven't checked any others out.

Paints
There are paints which are of interest for shielding purposes. Although expensive as paints go they are the easiest form of prevention to use and once you have painted the area to be shielded, the paint can be painted over with your colour of choice. The paint needs earthing.
www.electrosmogshield.co.uk, www.emf-protection.co.uk

There are also VOC free paints. Try: www.lakelandpaints.co.uk, www.ecospaints.net

Nickel Mesh
This blocks microwaves and is available as a nickel 'net' curtain. Also available in rolls of material, as a mosquito net, and sheets as well as curtains. Try www.emf-protection.co.uk, www.electrosmogshield.co.uk or search the internet.

There are also non-measurable devices which you can use such as:

Essences which help to rid the body of the radiation. Look for Australian Bush Flower Essences Electro essence.

Crystals placed by a computer etc such as an amethyst cluster. Clean under running water.

RadiTech neutraliser – see www.dulwichhealth.co.uk

Orgonite – contact www.organitesart.com

There are plenty of other things on the market but ensure you go to a reputable supplier who will have checked out its efficacy.

Appendix 3 - A Space Clearing Ceremony

This is a straightforward method you can easily use by yourself.

You need -
A bunch of flowers
Some night lights or candles - enough for every room
Small saucers or containers - enough for every room
Incense sticks – enough for every room (Nag Champa is best for space clearing purposes)
Sage smudge stick or sage in an censor
Bell or chime (if you don't have this you can clap your hands instead)
Sea or rock salt
Spray – I like the Australian Bush Flower Essence Space Clearing spray but use one you like or make your own using pure water and essential oils.
Prayers or statement (see below)

Place a small flower arrangement in each room (except bathrooms) – use saucers with a little water in. Place a few flower heads around a lit night light (or candle), and put three leaves in each saucer also. This represents the 5 elements – fire, metal, earth, wood, water. The more beautiful the arrangements the better as this raises the energy.

Incense is also needed in every room (except bathrooms). Place and light. If you have problems keeping it lit it is usually because there is a spirit in the room and they don't want to be sent to the light.

Set a small table by the front door covered with a clean cloth kept specifically for this purpose.

Put an arrangement on this table and lay out your tools – sage, bell/chime, salt, spray.   Do not put anything on the floor, as the energy at floor level is heavy.

Begin by standing at the front door and announcing your intention.
I'm here to space clear this house and to take away all negative energy and replace it with positive energy so that the house will support ….(names).

Call in your angels and spirit guides to help you, the angels and spirit guides of the people you are helping, the spirit of the house, and the spirit or devas of the area, and thank them for their help.

Sprinkle the salt over the thresholds of all entrances into the house. This is to help absorb any negative energy as it comes into the house. Have in place the intent to cleanse and purify and leave in place for a minimum of 24 hours. Work clockwise around the house from the front door.

If you wish you can start by sensitizing your hands and walking around the house clockwise again sensing the energy so you get a feel for the space. If you do not wish to do this step, don't worry as you will be clearing this energy anyway.

Then light the sage and begin to smudge this around the house, up and down the walls, following the house walls round from the left clockwise, and following the flow of the house. As you go round say a mantra to yourself 'clear negative energies, clear negative energies' and hold this intent firm. If the sage goes out, don't worry just relight and carry on. Clear any big or old pieces of furniture. If you can't reach, let your eyes follow the path, and the smoke goes where your eyes go. Finish back at the front door and end by making an infinity sign (8 on its side) in the doorway.

IMPORTANT: wash your hands after smudging as they have been in negative energy.

Then pick up the bell or chime and ring it once to announce your intention in the doorway. Ring the bell and pull the vibrations along the wall. The sound of the bell should never stop during your circuit of the house. Think 'to purify and harmonise' as you go. Hold this intent firm. Again, don't forget furniture and pay special attention to corners as they can build up stagnant energy. Imagine the sound vibrations carrying out into all the space and clearing any stuck or bad energy. Finish back at the door and complete with an infinity sign. Again: wash your hands.

Then take the spray, and spray around the house in the same manner, once again holding the intent, 'to clear and cleanse'.

Back at the door once more, take the prayer card. You say these out loud, and again mean what you say.

Sealing – now finish by sealing all you have done into the house. Visualise each elevation covered in brilliant white/gold light. Then see a carpet of white light over the ground floor and then over the roof space, all the edges sealing together. Once encased ask for four angels, as tall as the house, to stand in each corner and ask them to love, protect and guide ……. (names), and to keep the space clear.

It is recommended a house is cleared every 6 – 12 months.

Cleanse all tools after use.

Have an Epsom salt bath, drink plenty of water and take some Vitamin C to ensure you are clear of any negative energies that might have stuck, and your immune system is strong.

Space Clearing Prayers

Prayer 1:
May the creator that dwells in all things come forward and fill this home.
I ask that this house be a sanctuary for all who enter.
I ask that good thoughts and actions emanate from this home.
May this home bring comfort and healing for all who live here.
May this home be a healing centre of light and love.
I ask this in the name of the most holy Creator.

Prayer 2:
We ask this land for forgiveness.
We forgive ourselves for any pain, hurt or suffering that we have caused others either knowingly or unknowingly.
Finally, we forgive ourselves and know that we are forgiven by all the forces of light, life and love that flow thought the universe.
We let go of the pain from the past and go forward into the future in Divine love and light.

Prayer 3:
I ask the Highest and Purest energies of Divine love and light to lift and transform:
Any historical negative energy attached to this space.
Any Geopathic stress attached to this space.

Any other negative energy attached to this space.
Any lost souls attached to this space – and we would thank the angels for taking them to the light with love, compassion and forgiveness.

Thank you. Thank you. Thank you. Amen

Then finish with **The Great Invocation:**

From the point of light within the mind of God
Let light stream forth into human minds.
Let light descend on earth.

From the point of love within the heart of God
Let love stream forth into human hearts.
May the Light return to earth.

From the centre where the will of God is known
Let purpose guide the little will of humans –
The purpose which the Masters know and serve.

From the centre which we call the human race
Let the plan of love and light work out
And may it seal the door where evil dwells.

Let light and love and power restore the plan on earth.

Appendix 4 - Closing Down A Portal

If you think you may have a portal you need to check it out. The easiest way to do this is to use a dowsing pendulum.

There are three main portal ways in a property:

>Mirrors (or reflective surfaces)
>Fireplaces
>Toilets

Also be aware the TVs and computers can potentially be problematic as well, as occasionally can pictures.

Mirrors are a time-honoured way of scrying and opening up a channel to Otherworld. Be aware that if a mirror has been in place for a very long time an energetic imprint is left behind on a wall even after you may have moved it. Also, if you track a portal to a mirror check that it is the mirror and not the wall behind it which is the portal, so you know what you are working with.

If you bring an old mirror into your home always check before you hang it if it carries a portal in it.

Tip: NEVER have a mirror at the end of a bed.

If you have an open portalway it gives access to beings from the lower astral as well as attracting lost souls etc. Otherworld is much like this world – there are beings who are benign to our race and those who wish us ill. You do not want to unknowingly connect to the lower astral and bring trouble through so you need to work within a protected space and to ensure you have your spirit team as backup.

Portals can be one way, or they can be two way. If you discover you have an open portal in your home you need to check out (through dowsing) if it is one or two way, and also ask if anything has come through and is in your home as you need to send them back BEFORE closing the portal.

Always begin by opening up sacred space in the form of protection around you. (See Ritual to Open Sacred Space Appendix 1).

NEXT...ask if you have permission to do this work. If it is a no it is a NO! Do not go against this as you will not have your spirit team backing you up and it leaves you open to being unsafe.

Assuming you have permission to go ahead ask through the means of your pendulum:

- Are there any open portals in this room?

If there are, establish through dowsing, where it/they are. Then establish the flow of energy through the portal – is it one way (and which way) or two way?

If the flow of energy is one way into the astral it is effectively a feeding channel where entities in the astral are sucking energy from this plane to feed themselves. Given an opportunity non-benign astral entities will do this. You also need to check if any lost souls/earthbound spirits etc have been taken through as well as they need to be restored to this plane before being sent on their way back to Light/Source.

- Is there any being/phenomena this side that needs to be returned?
- Is there anything the other side that needs to come back?

There is a guardian energy of everything so any portal will have a guardian. Next acknowledge the guardian and ask if work needs doing and their permission and help to do it.

If it is a two way portal check with the guardian the sequence you should do things in ie. should you send back anything which has come through first or retrieve anything that has gone through from this plane first?

If there is call them back/send them back through a violet light (this is cleansing).

Once you have done this, check that nothing further has to be sent back/retrieved and then connect to your team of guides and the guardian spirit and say

'Grant that this portal is now closed and sealed and that any vortex that is left is filled with _____ (insert whatever is right for the space ie. family, guardian of the home, protective spirit, light being etc).

See this being done.

Check that this has been successful, then thank those who have helped you and dismiss sacred space.

Appendix 5 – Big Pharma – Deliberate Manipulation

The name of the Rockefellers has been linked to a lot of what is wrong with the world, but one area which rarely gets mentioned is that of healthcare, and whilst there is a lot right with modern healthcare, it is far from being an ideal model and leads to a lot of unnecessary suffering through ignorance.

So it is worth knowing how 'modern medicine' in the form of Big Pharma came into being – and it is, unfortunately, all about money. Below is the story as it was given to me some years ago:

John D. Rockefeller realized the opportunity first. He was an oil mogul who was the first person in the USA to become a billionaire. By the start of the 20th century, he had 90% control over oil refineries in the US with his company Standard Oil. In 1900, researchers came across petrochemicals, and they found out that it was possible to make many chemicals out of oil. The first plastic, which was Bakelite, was made in 1907 from oil.

The turning point came when researchers found out that synthetic vitamins could be produced from oil and presumed pharmaceutical drugs. This was a financially rewarding opportunity for Rockefeller as he concluded that he could monopolize not only the oil business but also the chemical and medical industries. Petrochemicals were a new discovery that could be patented and which would bring about maximum revenues. The only thing stopping Rockefeller was the fact that herbal and natural remedies were popular in the USA at that time. About half of the medical professionals in the US were practicing holistic medicine, based on understandings from Europeans and Native Americans.

This meant that Rockefeller had to get rid of what was significant competition. He made use of a strategy that was time-proven, problem-reaction-solution. The concept works by developing an issue or making up a problem that would bring terror to people and then offer them a solution that has been pre-planned – a strategy that is still in use successfully today!

He got the help of Andrew Carnegie, who had made lots of money monopolizing the steel industry. The Carnegie Foundation sent Abraham Flexner on a trip around the nation, and he was given the task of reporting the status of medical facilities along with the medical colleges in the United States. This led to the Flexner Report, and this eventually led to modern medication of today.

The report stated that a revamp was needed along with the centralization of medical institutions. Following the report, half of the medical colleges were closed down. Natural medications and homeopathy were rubbished, and some of the medical professionals who practiced holistic medicine were sent to prison. Rockefeller gave over $100 million to medical facilities and colleges to help with the transition and to try to change the minds of doctors and researchers. The General Education Board was also founded.

Medical colleges became homogenized and structured around a core curriculum which taught only drug cures which had been patented. Even the basics of good nutrition were all but ignored.

Scientists were also given huge grants to study the properties of different plants, and how they were able to cure diseases, and to isolate beneficial compounds so that they could be patented, ignoring the synergy of how most healing plants work, and leading to dangerous side effects in many, many cases.

There have been some amazing discoveries concerning health in the years since medicine was hijacked, which had the potential to revolutionise healthcare for the benefit of the people, but they have all been rubbished, shut down and their 'inventors' imprisoned or died in mysterious circumstances.

So 100 years on from this monstrous plan, medical colleges produce doctors who do not know anything about holistic practices or the many benefits that herbs have to offer, or any of the other healing modalities that bring benefit. The modern health care system focuses on symptoms not underlying causes and keeps most people in a spiral of ill health once they have engaged with it with drugs being given to offset the side effects of drugs. Nuts isn't it!

And despite huge advancements in medicine and aspects of our understanding of health, there is still no mainstream cure for the common chronic diseases such as cancer, diabetes, autism, asthma or even the common cold.

Holistic health practitioners would argue otherwise, with many, many healing stories to back this up, but are given no credence or publicity and run the risk of being imprisoned or worse for going against the medical line.

Cures for the many chronic illnesses which have begun to afflict mankind at epidemic levels since the introduction of this type of medicine would only be bad for business. John D. Rockefeller was even behind the establishment of the American Cancer Society in 1913, a quite cynical move to ensure only one version of the story gets out!

Today we live in a world of social media censorship, and anyone who even dares to question the intentions of any of the big pharmaceutical companies is branded insane and given the label of a crazed conspiracy theorist.

Any information brought forward about beneficial holistic practices and plants that cannot be patented are branded phony news due their threats to the drugs and the financial bottom line of the big pharmaceutical companies.

It is a sorry tale of greed and the use of fear as a weapon to keep a large part of the human race ill and suffering and unable to function at their full potential.

Appendix 6 - The Nine Metaphysical/Occult Laws

These laws have been put together by Murry Hope in her book *'Practical Celtic Magic'*. She was an English writer and occultist, a Wiccan priestess and ritual magician who died in 2012. She also maintained she had been connected to a leonine race from Sirius...a starseed maybe?

I have included the occult laws she recorded here because I think for anyone working in this arena they are both interesting and useful.

The Law of Rebound
A superior force will always rebound a lesser power. Ie. If you come up against another practitioner more adept than you whatever you project in his/her direction will return to you PLUS the force of the rebounder.

The Law of Three Requests
All requests from the subtle dimensions are repeated in triplicate:
> First the conscious mind is alerted.
> The second repetition engages the reasoning faculties.
> The third repetition makes a direct contact with the psyche or soul force.

This is an integral part of many magical systems and is part of the mystery of the sacred 3.

Always challenge any new spirit you encounter three times. If they are of dubious intent or character they may lie twice, but not three times.

The Law of Challenge
All visions, dreams, sources of inspiration, suspicions etc – anything from beyond the bounds of rational, logical thinking should be challenged. There is a subtle line that divides present reality from interpenetrative alien frequencies, mischievous spirits and inspiration from delusion.

Absolute honesty and a highly refined sense of 'knowing' are required.

The Law of Equalities
When two equal forces meet, one will eventually give way to the other, which then rises in stature. This law is seen again in science, particularly in particle physics.

The Law of Balance or Equipoise
Everything should function according to its own frequency or at its correct level. Ie. Don't kinetically move a table requiring hours of building up kinetic power, when a simple physical push will do.

This law is also concerned with the state of equipoise necessary for the satisfactory functioning and correct expression of energy at any levels, which relates it particularly to the field of disease and healing. It denounces excesses of any kind and requires that the physical body be treated with courtesy (it hosts other life forms, including the four elements, as well as your consciousness, without which there would be no structure or ability to live/survive).

The Law of Summons
Designates how things do or do not work for you. Depends upon your degree of adeptship. The right to issue a summons has to be earned, so if you issue one and do not get a result as expected you have not earned that level of right. You can be led a merry dance by elemental beings you are trying to control if you over reach yourself.

The Law of Polarities
Positive and negative, animus and anima, masculine and feminine, are all expression of this law. The initiate must be well polarised within him or herself before he/she can pass a certain point along the path.
The Elemental kingdoms strictly adhere to this law and will not respond to those who do not abide by it. The finer the frequencies the more the polarity distinctions become blurred. The ideal state is both anima and animus in perfect balance within the individual – then cosmic law is neither being broken nor intruded upon

The Law of Cause and Effect
Also called the Law of Karma. Covers the 'as ye sow so shall ye reap' principle. A generally unheeded aspect of this Law involves the exchange of energies, meaning that we should never expect anything for nothing,

although the exchange does not necessarily have to be in 'kind'. The gift should be appropriate to someone's means and talents.

The Law of Abundance (Opulence/Attraction)
The attraction of like for like. One has to be aware of not just the value of something, but also the frequency of it, as well as the intent behind an action.

These laws when broken need to be atoned for and peace made with the necessary persons/power.

Further Reading
Part 1 - Introduction to Grail Cosmology & Mythology

There are a plethora of books on the Grail. Here is a small selection for those wanting some further reading:

Dixon, Jeffrey John	Goddess and Grail
	Gawain and the Grail Quest
Jung, Emma & Franz, Marie-Louise	The Grail Legend
The Mabinogion	A series of Welsh tales, various translations available
Richard Barber	The Arthurian Legends
A E Waite	The Holy Grail
John Matthews	The Grail. A Secret History
Ayn Cates Sullivan	Legends of the Grail

And, of course, you can go back to the original stories of Crétien de Troyes:

David Staines	The Complete Romances of Crétien de Troyes
Crétien de Troyes	Arthurian Romances

Part 2 - The Grail & Earth Wisdom

Andrews, Ted	Enchantment of the Faery Realm
Biltcliffe, Gary & Hoare, Caroline	Spine of Albion The Power of Centre

Black, Jonathan	The Sacred History
Broadhurst, Paul & Hamish Miller	The Sun & the Serpent The Dance of the Dragon In Search of the Southern Serpent
Dawkins, Peter	Core Truths, Living Wisdom for Today The Pattern of Initiation
Devereux, Paul	Secrets of Ancient and Sacred Places Illustrated Encyclopaedia of Ancient Earth Mysteries
Dorling Kindersley	Life Cycles: Everything from Start to Finish
Duff, Rory	A Guide to Leylines, Earth Energies & Nodes Grail Found
Froud, Brian, Lee, Alan	Faeries
Gallagher, Kirsty	Lunar Living
Gardner, Grahame	Dowsing Magic
Gordon, Rolf	Are You Sleeping in a Safe Place?
Hall, Manly P	Freemasonry of the Ancient Egyptians
Heath, Robin	Power points - Secret Rulers and Hidden Forces in the Landscape Temple in the Hills Bluestone Magic
Hitching, Francis	Earth Magic
Knoche, Grace F	The Mystery Schools
Lovelock, James	Gaia. A New Look at Life on Earth
Mistle, William R	Mermaid, Sylphs, Gnomes & Salamanders
Newman, Hugh	Geomancy

O'Gaea, Ashleen	Celebrating the Seasons of Life: Beltane to Mabon
	Celebrating the Seasons of Life: Samhain to Ostara
Paungger, Johanna & Poppe, Thomas	Moontime
Pennick, Nigel	The Ancient Science of Geomancy
Pogacnik, Marco	Nature Spirits & Elemental Beings
Newman, Hugh	Earth Grids, The Secret Patterns of Gaia's Sacred Sites
Raven, Susan	Nature Spirits, The Rememberance
Simpson, Liz	The Healing Energies of Earth
Street, Chris	City of Revelation
Thorley, Anthony (Ed)	Legendary London
Thurnell-Read, Jane	The Guide to Geopathic Stress
Twinn, Nigel	Beyond the Far Horizon, Why Earth Energy Dowsing Works
Van Etten, Jaap	Dragons
	The Gifts of Mother Earth

Part 3 – The Grail & the Home Domain

Alexander, Jane	Spirit of the Home
Brown, Simon	Practical Feng Shui
Chiazzari, Suzy	The Complete Book of Colour
Cowan, David & Girdlestone, Rodney	Safe as Houses? Ill Health & Electro-Stress in the Home

Furlong, David	Ancestral Healing
Gardner Grahame	A Basic Guide to Technopathic Stress
Gordon, Rolf	Are you Sleeping in a Safe Place?
Hale, Gill	Practical Encyclopedia of Feng Shui
Kingston, Karen	Creating Sacred Space with Feng Shui
McKnight, Carol	The Aura Soma Sourcebook
Philips, Alasdair & Jean	Killing Fields in the Home
Proctor, Roy and Ann	Healing Sick Houses
Reynolds, Mary	The Garden Awakening
Somers, Suzanne	Tox-Sick
Wentz, Dr Myron & Dave	The Healthy Home

Part 4 – The Grail of the Physical Body

Becker, Robert O	The Body Electric Cross Currents
Brennan, Barbara Ann	Hands of Light Light Emerging
Carr, Kriss	Crazy Sexy Diet
Chopra, Deepak	Perfect Health
Chown, Vicky & Walker, Kim	The Handmade Apothecary The Herbal Remedy Book
Clayton, Dr Paul	Health Defence
Corby, Rachel	The Medicine Garden
Dale, Cyndi	The Subtle Body

Davidson, Wilma	Dowsing for Cures
Dispenza, Dr Joe	You are the Placebo
Eden, Donna	Energy Medicine
Emoto, Dr Masaru	The Hidden Messages in Water
	The Secret Life of Water
Francis, Paul	The Shamanic Journey
Gardner, Grahame	A Basic Guide to Technopathic Stress
Gedgaudas, Nora T	Primal Body, Primal Mind
Gerber, Richard	Vibrational Medicine for the 21st Century
Gladstar, Rosemary	Medicinal Herbs
Judith, Anodea	Wheels of Life
Harvey, Graham	We want Real Food
Jeffereys, Toni	Your Health at Risk
Lindlahr, Henry	Philosophy of Natural Therapeutics
Lockie, Dr Andrew & Geddes, Dr Nicola	The Complete Guide to Homeopathy
Lorius, Cassandra	Homeopathy for the Soul
Mackinnon, Christa	Shamanism
MacManaway, Dr Patrick	Dowsing for Health
Matthews, John	The Celtic Shaman
McTaggart, Lynn	The Field
Ober, Clint	Earthing
Rooman, Lily	All About Chakras
Rudd, Carol	Flower Essences, An Illustrated Guide

Scheffer, Mechthild	Bach Flower Therapy
Sellar, Wanda	The Directory of Essential Oils
Shanahan, Catherine & Luke	Deep Nutrition
Vithoulkas, George	The Science of Homeopathy
Wilcock, David	The Hidden Science of Lost Civilizations: Source Field Investigations
Wong, James	Grow Your Own Drugs How to Eat Better
Worwood, Valerie Ann	The Fragrant Pharmacy
Wren, Barbara	Cellular Awakening Our Return to the Light

Part 5 – The Grail Essence

Bunnell, Lynda & Ra Uru Hu	The Definitive Book of Human Design
Campion, Nicholas	The Ultimate Astrologer
Dale, Brian	Archetypes, Unmasking Your True Self
Ford, Debbie	The Dark Side of the Light Chasers
Furlong, David	Illuminating the Shadow
Hillman, Laurence	Planets in Play
Jung, C.G.	Archetypes & the Collective Unconscious
Kingsley, Peter	Catafalque Reality
Myss, Caroline	Archetypes The Language of Archetypes (Audio) Sacred Contracts

Parker, Julia & Derek   Parker's Astrology

Rudd, Richard   The Gene Keys

Resources

There are so many people I could point you to who have helped me build up, layer by layer, a working understanding of earth consciousness and earth energies. Below are just a few of the various people you might want to check out further to begin with:

Dowsers/Geomancers

Rory Duff	www.roryduff.com
Van Etten, Jaap	www.lemurantis.com
Biltcliffe, Gary & Hoare, Caroline	www.belinusline.com
Gardner, Grahame	www.westerngeomancy.com
MacManaway, Dr Patrick	www.patrickmacmanaway.com

Some Herb Suppliers:

https://www.baldwins.co.uk

http://www.organicherbtrading.com

https://herbalapothecaryuk.com

https://www.indigo-herbs.co.uk

Some Essential Oils Suppliers:

https://www.shirleyprice.co.uk

https://www.tisserand.com

https://www.baldwins.co.uk

Dowsing Organisations

In Britain: www.britishdowsers.org
In America: www.dowsers.org

Land Pilgrimage

www.gatekeeper.org.uk
Facebook: Dragon Walks

Feng Shui in UK

www.fengshuisociety.org.uk

Biodynamic Gardening Organisations

www.biodynamic.org.uk

www.biodynamics.com

Organites

For beautiful and authentic organites go to www.orgonitesart.com

Human Design:
www.jovianarchive.com
www.human.design

The Gene Keys:
www.genekeys.com

Astrology:
www.thenextstep.uk.com and Pam Gregory – YouTube
www.laurencehillman.com

Archetypes:
www.myss.com

Lost Wisdom Library Video interviews
This is a series of interviews with various wisdomkeepers and initiates around the globe, sharing their understandings and insights with you. Some are available via my Youtube channel Saira Salmon, and all of them are available are part of the Lost Wisdom Library, accessible through my website www.sairasalmon.com

Printed in Great Britain
by Amazon